Encyclopaedic History of India Series

EARLY MEDIEVAL INDIA

Dr. Mahesh Vikram Singh
Professor, Deptt. of History
Mahatma Gandhi Kashi Vidyapeeth
Varanasi (UP)

Dr. Brij Bhushan Shrivastava
Head of Deptt., Ancient History, Archeology & Culture
SMMTPG College, Ballia (UP)

CENTRUM PRESS
NEW DELHI-110002 (INDIA)

CENTRUM PRESS
H.O.: 4360/4, Ansari Road, Daryaganj,
New Delhi-110002 (India)
Tel: 23278000, 23261597, 23255577, 23286875
B.O.: No. 1015, Ist Main Road, BSK IIIrd Stage,
IIIrd Phase, IIIrd Block, Bangalore-560085 (INDIA)
Tel: 080-41723429
Email: centrumpress@gmail.com
Visit us at: www.centrumpress.com

Early Medieval India

First Edition, 2011

ISBN 978-93-80836-68-3

PRINTED IN INDIA

Printed at Mehra Offset Press, Delhi

प्रो. विपिन चंद्रा
अध्यक्ष
Prof. Bipan Chandra
Chairman

नेशनल बुक ट्रस्ट, इंडिया
नेहरू भवन
5 इंस्टीट्यूशनल एरिया, फेज-II, वसंत कुंज, नई दिल्ली-110 070
फोन/ Phone: 011-26121880 फैक्स/ Fax: 011-26121883
NATIONAL BOOK TRUST, INDIA
Nehru Bhawan
5 Institutional Area, Phase II, Vasant Kunj, New Delhi-110 070
ई-मेल / E-mail: chairman@nbtindia.org.in
वेबसाइट / Website: www.nbtindia.org.in

FOREWORD

The term 'history' is derived from the Greek word 'historia' that means knowledge acquired through investigation. Obviously, this knowledge can be correct if the method of investigation is objective and not vitiated by any kind of bias. In other words, if the study of human past is comprehensive and obtained through scientific inquiry, it can provide perspective on the present day problems and help one plan for the future.

A true historian has to identify the sources that can be most useful in a given context. Documents, coins, archaeology, anthropology, geography, travel accounts, oral traditions, mythology and so on can be useful but they can be used only after their veracity is tested and they are critically examined. They should be checked and counter-checked.

Over the centuries, one finds the study and writing of history vitiated by biases. There are numerous instances in which historical data have been distorted to support or oppose certain preconceived ideas and purposes. Strictly speaking such history is just like fiction to accord with preconceived notions and serve some ulterior purposes.

The study of the past has never been static. Conclusions go on changing because of the discovery of new materials and tools of investigation. To give a concrete example, the carbon 14 or radiocarbon dating test has revolutionized the study of civilizations and settlements, especially of prehistoric times, for which written documents, coins, etc. are seldom available. This method has enabled historians to determine more accurately than before the time period of a particular civilization or settlement. This method was discovered only 70 years ago by American scientists.

In our country, excavations brought to light the Indus Valley Civilization and its various features, hitherto unknown. Similarly, no complete text of Kautilya's Arthashastra was available before it was discovered by Shamasastry, the chief of the Mysore Government Oriental Library in the first decade of the last century. Likewise, people's knowledge of the history of the Buddhist period got extended after excavations at Sarnath and the ruins of the Asokan period at Patna. In the future, if the Harappan inscriptions are deciphered, our knowledge of the Indus Valley Civilization will increase enormously. All these instances underline the fact that our knowledge of history is never static and its frontiers go on extending.

In the light of what has been said above the encyclopedic history is going to be of great help to students interested in Indian history. It is comprehensive and as far as possible free from biases. It includes the latest materials, and objective conclusions.

Prof . Bipan Chandra
Professor Emeritus, JNU
Chairman, National Book Trust, India

Contents

Preface

The people of India have had a continuous civilization since 2500 B.C., when the inhabitants of the Indus River valley developed an urban culture based on commerce and sustained by agricultural trade. This civilization declined around 1500 B.C., probably due to ecological changes. During the second millennium B.C., pastoral, Aryan-speaking tribes migrated from the northwest into the subcontinent. As they settled in the middle Ganges River valley, they adapted to antecedent cultures.

The political map of ancient and medieval India was made up of myriad kingdoms with fluctuating boundaries. In the 4th and 5th centuries A.D., northern India was unified under the Gupta Dynasty. During this period, known as India's Golden Age, Hindu culture and political administration reached new heights. Islam spread across the Indian subcontinent over a period of 500 years. In the 10th and 11th centuries, Turks and Afghans invaded India and established sultanates in Delhi. In the early 16th century, descendants of Genghis Khan swept across the Khyber Pass and established the Mughal (Mogul) Dynasty, which lasted for 200 years. From the 11th to the 15th centuries, southern India was dominated by Hindu Chola and Vijayanagar Dynasties. During this time, the two systems—the prevailing Hindu and Muslim—mingled, leaving lasting cultural influences on each other.

The first British outpost in South Asia was established in 1619 at Surat on the northwestern coast. Later in the century, the East India Company opened permanent trading stations at Madras, Bombay, and Calcutta, each under the protection of native rulers. The British expanded their influence from these footholds until, by the 1850s, they controlled most of present-day India, Pakistan, and Bangladesh. In 1857, a rebellion in north India led by mutinous Indian soldiers caused the British Parliament to transfer all political power from the East India Company to the Crown. Great Britain began administering most of India directly while controlling the rest through treaties with local rulers.

In the late 1800s, the first steps were taken toward self-government in British India with the appointment of Indian councillors to advise the British viceroy and the establishment of provincial councils with Indian members; the British subsequently widened participation in legislative councils. Beginning in 1920, Indian leader Mohandas K. Gandhi transformed the Indian National Congress political party into a mass movement to campaign against British colonial rule.

—*Authors*

1

Shankaracharya

Shankaracharya is a commonly used title of heads of maþhas (monasteries) in the Advaita tradition. The title derives from Adi Shankara, a theologian of Hinduism, who is one of the best representative of the true tradition of Hinduism.

He is honoured as *Jagadguru,* a title that was used earlier only to Lord Krishna. established mainly four maþhas in four regions of India.

The Shankaracharya tradition is described in Maharishi Mahesh Yogi's commentary on Verse 2, Chapter 4 of the Bhagavad-Gita. The popular view among historians is that there were four mathas established by Adi Uankara which are:

- the *Uttaramnaya matha,* or northern matha at Joshimath
- the *Purvamnaya matha* or eastern matha, the Govardhana matha, at Puri
- the *Dakshinamnaya matha,* or the Sringeri Sharada Peetham, the southern matha, at Shringeri
- the *Pauchimamnaya matha,* or the Dwaraka Pitha, the western matha, at Dwarka.

Jyotirmath

Demographics

As of 2001 India census, Joshimath had a population of 13,202. Males constitute 61% of the population and females 39%. Joshimath has an average literacy rate of 77%, higher than the national average of 59.5%: male literacy is 83%, and female literacy is 67%. In Joshimath, 12% of the population is under 6 years of age.

The Matha

Jyotirmath is the *Uttaramnaya matha* or northern monastery, one of the four cardinal institutions established by Adi Shankara, the others being those at Sringeri, Puri and Dwaraka. Their heads are titled "Shankaracharya". According to the tradition initiated by Adi Shankara, this matha is in charge of the Atharva Veda.

Jyotirmath, which is close to the pilgrimage town of Badrinath, has not always been an active matha. It is sometimes said incorrectly that the original northern matha was established at Badrinath. This place can be a base station for travellers going to Guru Gobind Ghat or the Valley of Flowers National Park.

In its most recent history, the Jyotirmath became inactive in the early 19th century. The formal occupation of the matha was restarted with the aid of the heads of some of the other mathas from about 1940 onward. However, there is an unresolved controversy over the succession to the headship of Jyotirmath. The best known of the claimants to be the current head or Shankaracharya is Svarupananda Sarasvatî who is also head of the Dwaraka matha. The other two claimants are Vasudevananda Sarasvatî and Madhavaurama.

Dwaraka Pipha

The Dwaraka Pipha or *Dwaraka maþha* is situated in the coastal city of Dwaraka, Gujarat – which itself is a popular destination of pilgrimage for the Hindus, dedicated to Krishna. It is one of the four cardinal maþhas said to have been founded by Adi Sankaracarya, and is the *pascimamnaya matha,* or western matha. It is also known as the Kalika Matha, and, as per the tradition initiated by Adi Shankara, is in charge of the Sama Veda.

The current head or Shankaracharya of this order is Swami Svarûpânanda Sarasvatî, who is also the head of the corresponding northern matha at Jyotirmath.

It is also not surprising that there are a number of other mathas, which also claim to have been directly established by Adi Shankaracharya himself. One such institution which is very popular today is Kanchi matha.

Like in all other religions and sects, there is a certain amount of rivalry between certain groups who claim to have been initiated into the Shankaracharya Order.

The existence of such multiple mathas need not be surprising since it is very much possible that a Guru/or descendant of the shankaracharya lineage could have had many disciples. This could have resulted in the branching out of the parent institution. It is also possible that a Guru might have died without naming a successor leading to the formation of rival groups.

It is a historically known fact that some of the mathas-such as the Joshimath and Govardhan matha have a broken lineage and were later revived.Shankara travelled across India and other parts of South Asia to propagate his philosophy through discourses and debates with other thinkers. He founded four *mathas* ("monasteries"), which helped in the historical development, revival and spread of Advaita Vedanta. Adi Shankara is believed to be the organizer of the Dashanami monastic order and the founder of the Shanmata tradition of worship.

His works in Sanskrit, all of which are extant today, concern themselves with establishing the doctrine of Advaita (Nondualism). He also established the importance of monastic life as sanctioned in the Upanishads and Brahma Sutra, in a time when the Mimamsa school established strict ritualism and ridiculed monasticism. Shankara relied entirely on the Upanishads for reference concerning Brahman and wrote copious commentaries on the Vedic Canon (Brahma Sutra, Principal Upanishads and Bhagavadgita) in support of his thesis. The main opponent in his work is the Mimamsa school of thought, though he also offers some arguments against the views of some other schools like Samkhya and certain schools of Buddhism that he was familiar with.

Life

Traditional accounts of Adi Shankara's life can be found in the Shankara Vijayams, which are poetic works that contain a mix of biographical and legendary material, written in the epic style. The most important among these biographies are the *Mdhav+ya ZaEkara VijayaC* (of Madhava, c. 14th century), the *Cidvilsiya ZaEkara VijayaC* (of Cidvilasa, c. between 15th century and 17th century), and the *Karaya ZaEkara VijayaC* (of the Kerala region, extant from c. 17th century).

Birth and Childhood

Shankara was born to Kaippilly Sivaguru Namboodiri and

Aryamba Antharjanam in the region of Kalady, in central Kerala. According to lore, it was after his parents, who had been childless for many years, prayed at the Vadakkunnathan temple, Thrissur that Sankara was born under the star Thiruvathira.

His father died while Shankara was very young. Shankara's *upanayanaC*, the initiation into student-life, was performed at the age of five. As a child, Shankara showed remarkable scholarship, mastering the four Vedas by the age of eight

In the Mahabharata

cognition as such. It is held that all knowledge is ipso facto true (*Satahprama Gyavada*). Thus, what is to be proven is not the truth of a cognition, but its falsity. The Mimamsakas advocate the self-validity of knowledge both in respect of its origin (*utpatti*) and ascertainment (*jnapti*). Not only did the Mimamsakas make the very great use of this theory to establish the unchallengeable validity of the Vedas, but later Vedantists also drew freely upon this particular Mimamsa contribution.

Dharma and Atheism

Dharma as understood by Poorva Mimamsa can be loosely translated into English as "virtue", "morality" or "duty". The Poorva Mimâmsâ school traces the source of the knowledge of dharma neither to sense-experience nor inference, but to verbal cognition (i.e. knowledge of words and meanings) according to Vedas. In this respect it is related to the Nyaya school, the latter, however, allows less Pramanas than Poorva Mimâmsâ.

The Poorva Mimâmsâ school held dharma to be equivalent to following the prescriptions of the Samhitas and their Brahmana commentaries relating the correct performance of Vedic rituals. Seen in this light, Poorva Mimamsa is essentially ritualist (orthopraxy), placing great weight on the performance of Karma or action as enjoined by the Vedas.

Emphasis of Yajnic Karmakandas in Poorva Mimâmsâ is erroneously interpreted by some to be an opposition to Jnanakanda of Vedanta and Upanishadas. Poorva Mimâmsâ does not discuss topics related to Jnanakanda, such as moksha or salvation, but it never speaks against moksha. Vedanta quotes Jaimini's belief in Brahman as well as in moksha : In Uttara-Mimamsa or Vedanta (4.4.5-7), Badarayana cites Jaimini as saying *"(The mukta Purusha is united with the Brahman) as if it were like the Brahman, because descriptions (in Shruti etc) prove so".*

In Poorva Mimâmsâ too, Jaimini emphasises the importance of faith in and attachment to the Omnipotent Supreme Being Whom Jaimini calls "The Omnipotent Pradhaana" (The Main) :

The term Upadesha here is means instructions of the Shastras as taught. We should tend towards the Omnipotent Supreme Being. In the context of Poorva Mimâmsâ 6.3.1 shown above, next two sutras becomes significant, in which this Omnipotent Being is termed as "Pradhana", and keeping away from Him is said to be a "Dosha", hence all beings are asked to get related ("abhisambandhat" in tadakarmaGi ca docas tasmat tato viuecah syat pradhanenabhisambandhat ; Jaimini 6,3.3) to the "Omnipotent Main Being" (api vapy ekadeue syat Pradhana hy arthanirvttir gugamatram itarat tadarthatvat ; Jaimini 6,3.2).

Karma-Mimamsa supports the Vedas, and Rgveda says that one Truth is variously named by the sages. It is irrelevant whether we call Him as Pradhana or Brahman or Vaishvanara or Shiva or God. With such explicit ideas in Poorva-Mimamsa, and supportive evidences from Uttara-Mimamsa, it is wrong to say that the concept of Supreme God is absent in Poorva-Mimamsa. Poorva-Mimamsa believes in Vedas and in Yajnas performed for gods (Devatas), hence it is wrong to call it atheist, esp in light of explicit affirmation of its faith in the Omnipotent.

Kumarila Bhatta

Kumrila Bhatta was a Hindu philosopher and Mimamsa scholar from Prayag (Now Allahabad, Uttar Pradesh, India). Little is known about his biography, but he is famous for many of his seminal theses on Mimamsa, such as *Mimamsaslokavarttika*. Bhatta was an staunch believer in the supreme validity of Vedic injunction, a great champion of Purva-Mimamsa and a confirmed ritualist. The varttika is mainly written as a commentary of Jaimini's Mimamsa Sutras.

Scholars differ as regards Kumarila's views on a personal God. For example, Manikka Vachakar believed that Kumarila promoted a personal God (Parabrahman), which conflicts with the Mimamsa school's Aparabrahman. However, in his *varttika* he goes to great lengths to argue against the theory of a creator God.

He is also credited with the logical formulation of the Mimamsic belief that the Vedas are unauthored (apaurusheya). In particular his defence against medieval Buddhist position on Vedic rituals, is noteworthy. (This may have contributed in some part, to the decline of Buddhism in India.) His work strongly influenced other schools of Indian philosophy, most notably Advaita Vedanta.

Linguistics Views

Kumarila Bhatta and his followers in the Mimamsa tradition (known as *Bhmmas*) argued for a strongly Compositional view of semantics (called *abhihitAnvaya*). In this view, the meaning of a sentence was understood only after understanding first the meanings of individual words. Words were independent, complete objects, a view that is close to the Fodorian view of language.

This view was debated over some seven or eight centuries by the followers of Prabhakara school within Mimamsa, who argued that words do not directly designate meaning; any meaning that arises is because it is connected with other words (*anvit AbhidhAna*, anvita = connected; abhidha = denotation). This view was influenced by the holistic arguments of Bhartrihari's sphoma theory.

Essentially the prabhakaras argued that sentence meanings are grasped directly, from perceptual and contextual cues, skipping the stage of grasping singly the individual word meanings, similar to the modern view of linguistic under specification, which relates to the Dynamic Turn in Semantics, that also opposes purely compositional approaches to sentence meaning.

Criticism of Buddhism

With the aim to prove the superiority of Vedic scripture, Kumarila presented several novel arguments:

> *"Buddhist (or Jain) scripture could not be correct because it had several grammatical lapses." He specifically takes the Buddhist verse: ime samkhada dhamma sambhavanti sakarana akarana vinassanti (These fermentations arise when the cause is present and perish when the cause is present). Thus he presents his argument:*

The scriptures of Buddhists and Jains are composed in overwhelmingly incorrect (asadhu) language, words of the Magadha or Dakshinatya languages, or even their dialects (tadopabhramsa). Therefore false compositions (asannibandhana), they cannot possibly be true knowledge (shastra) ... By contrast, the very form itself (the well-assembled language) of the Veda proves its authority to be independent and absolute.

This argument of Bhatta relies heavily on his idea that the meanings of each individual word should be complete for the sentence to have a meaning. It may be noted, that the Pali Canon was intentionally recorded in local dialects and not in languages germane only to the scholarly.

Every extant school held some scripture to be correct. In order to show that the Veda was the only correct scripture, Kumarila ingeniously said that *"the absence of an author would safeguard the Veda against all reproach"* (apaurusheya). There was *"no way to prove any of the contents of Buddhist scriptures directly as wrong in spirit..."*, unless one challenges the legitimacy and eternal nature of the scripture itself. It is well known that the Pali Canon was composed after the Buddha's parinirvana. Further, even if they were the Buddha's words, they were not eternal or unauthored like the Vedas.

The Sautrantika Buddhist school believed that the universe was momentary (kshanika). Kumarila said that this was absurd, given that the universe does not disappear every moment. Further, no matter how small one would define the duration of a moment, one could divide the moment into infinitely further parts. Kumarila argues: *"if the universe is does not exist between moments, then in which of these moments does it exist?"* Further, because a moment could be infinitesimally small, it essentially means that the Buddhist was claiming that the universe was non-existent. This, in a lot of ways was consistent with his literal Sanskrit understanding of the word Shunya (literally 'zero'), found in the Pali Canon and well commented by several later Buddhists. It is noteworthy here, that the Pali Canon says that 'samsara' is characterized as 'anicca' (impermanent, not momentary). Further, the Mimamsic (and Vedantic) understanding of Shunya is inconsistent with the meaning as described in the Pali Canon.

The Determination of perception (pratyaksha pariccheda). Kant's *Critique of Pure Reason* has a lot of similarities with this work, although they are not the same or even on the same subject matter. Kumarila Bhatta's understanding of Buddhist school was far greater than that of any other non-Buddhist philosopher at the time. His junior contemporary Sankara (whom most modern Vedantists consider to be greater) also did not understand Buddhism so well.

Legendary Life

According to legend, Bhatta went to study Buddhism at Nalanda (the largest 4th century university in the world), with the aim of refuting Buddhist doctrine in favour of ritualist Vedic religion. He was expelled from the university when he protested against his teacher (Dharmakirti) ridiculing the Vedic rituals. Legend has it that even though he was thrown off of the university's tower, he survived with an eye injury. (Modern enthusiastic Mimamsa scholars and followers of Vedanta believe that this was because he imposed a condition on the infallibility of the Vedas.)

Kumarila Bhatta left Nalanda after that and settled down in Prayag (modern day Allahabad). Two years later, he challenged his teacher to a debate on grammar and logic. Life was at stake in this debate-the defeated one was to endure a slow death by self-immolation. It is said that overcome with guilt of causing his teacher to die, he too chose to commit suicide in the same manner.

One medieval work on the life of Sankara (considered most accurate) claims that Sankara challenged Bhatta to a debate on his deathbed. The work however does not expressly clarify if the deathbed was this pile of slow burning fire.

Another work on Sankara's life however claims that Sankara implored Bhatta not to commit suicide. Another contradictory legend however says that Bhatta continued to live on with two wives several students, one of whom was Prabhakara. According to this legend, Bhatta died in Varanasi at the age of 80.

In Hindu culture, Kapalika means bearer of the skull-bowl, and has reference to Lord Bhairava's vow to take the *kapala* vow. As penance for cutting off one of the heads of Brahma, Lord Bhairava became an outcast and a beggar. In this guise, Bhairava frequents waste places and cremation grounds, wearing nothing but a garland of skulls and ash from the pyre, and unable to remove the skull of Brahma fastened to his hand.

The skull hence becomes his begging-bowl, and the Kapalikas (as well as the Aghoris of Varanasi) supposedly use skulls as begging bowls and as drinking and eating vessels in imitation of

Bhairava. Although information on the Kapalikas is primarily to be gleaned from classical Sanskrit sources, where Kapalika ascetics are often depicted as depraved villains in drama, it appears that this group worshiped Lord Shiva in his extreme form, *Bhairava*, the ferocious. They are also often accused of having practiced ritual human sacrifices. Ujjain is alleged to have been a prominent center of this sect.

The Kapalikas may also have been related to the Kalamukhas ("black faces") of medieval South India (Lorenzen 1972). Moreover, in modern Tamilnadu, certain Shaivite cults associated with the Goddess Angaalaparameshwari, Irulappasami, and Sudalai Madan, are known to practice or have practiced ritual cannibalism, and to center their secretive rituals around an object known as a kapparai (Tamil "skull-bowl," derived from the Sanskrit kapala), a votive device garlanded with flowers and sometimes adorned with faces, which is understood to represent the begging-bowl of Shiva (Meyer 1986).

Padmapadacharya

Padmapadacharya (fl. 8th century CE) was an Indian philosopher, a follower of Adi Shankara.

Padmapâda's dates are unknown, but modern scholarship places his life around the middle of the 8th century; similarly information about him comes mainly from hagiographies. What is known for certain is that he was a direct disciple of Shankara, of whom he was a younger contemporary. Padmapâda, together with Sureœvara, developed ideas that led to the founding of the Vivarana school of commentators.

The only surviving work of Padmapada known to be authentic is the *Pancapadika*. According to tradition, this was written in response to Shankara's request for a commentary on his own *Brahmasutrabhasya*, and once written was destroyed by a jealous uncle. The surviving text is supposed to be what Shankara could recall of the commentary; certainly, all that survives of the work is an extended gloss on the first four aphorisms.

Pañcapâdikâ

In this work Padmapâda develops a complete theory of knowledge on the basis of Shankara's notion of *adhyasa* ("superimposition" — "the apparent presentation to consciousness of something as something else"). In developing, expanding, analysing, and criticising this notion, Padmapâda paved the way for the epistemology of Advaita Vedanta.

Also important is Padmapadas "critique of difference"; he argued that the relationship between the *Jiva* (the empirical self) and the *atman* (the underlying, spiritual self) was that of reflection to prototype. According to this theory of reflection (*pratimbavada*), the *Jiva* is an appearance of absolute reality (*brahman/atman*) as reflected in ignorance.

This theory has the effect of moving from the view of Padmapâda's predecessors that the self was to be rejected as not *brahman* to the view that enlightenment brings an understanding that everything is *brahman*: "Thus the *Jiva* or 'face in the mirror' is none other than *Atman* or the original face." For Padmapâda, as for Shankara:

"the ascertainment of the essential Self is not so much a matter of a 'mystical' experience occurring in time as a matter of enquiry consisting of the careful and concentrated introspection of and reflection upon one's ordinary experience."

Hastamalakacharya

Hastamalakacharya (IAST *Hastmalakcrya*) (B.C. 5th century CE) was a disciple of Adi Shankara, the Advaita philosopher. He was made the first Jagadguru (*head*) of the Sharada matha, the monastery founded by Adi Shankara in Sringeri or Dwaraka. (Both Sringeri Math and Dwaraka Math bear the name Sharada Math, so Hastamalakacharya belonged to any one of these Maths.

Meeting Adi Shankara

The Madhaviya UaCkaravijayam states that when Adi Shankara was at Kollur, he accepted invitations by brahmaoas to have Bhika (*alms* or food) at their houses. On such an occasion he visited a village called Uri Bali (present day Shivalli), where every house was said to emit the holy smell of the smoke of Agnihotra sacrifice, to accept Bhika. That place was inhabited by about two thousand brahmaoas who were learned in the Vedas and performed the Yajnas prescribed in the Vedas. There was also a temple dedicated to Shiva and Parvati.

In that village there lived a brahmaoa, Prabhakara, who was noted for his learning. He had a son who though appearing quite handsome, behaved rather like an idiot. Though upanayanam was performed for him, he did not take to studying the Vedas, instead preferred to sit around doing nothing. Hearing about Adi Shankara's visit, Prabhakara approached the Acharya (*teacher*) with a load of fruit and prostrated before him. He also made his son prostrate before him. Prabhakara explained to Adi Shankara that his son behaved rather like an idiot and sat idly throughout the day.

Shringeri

Sringeri, also written as Shringeri, Shringeri and Srngagiri is a taluk located in Chikmagalur district in the Indian state of Karnataka, is the site of the first maþha established by Adi Shankaracharya, Hindu theologian and exponent of the Advaita Vedanta philosophy, in the 8th century C.E. It is located on the banks of the river Tunga.

Origin of the Name

The name Sringeri is derived from Rishyashringa-giri, a nearby hill that is believed to have contained the hermitage of Rishi Vibhandaka and his son Rishyashringa. Rishyashringa appears in an episode in the Bala-Kanda of the Ramayana where a story, narrated by Vasishtha, relates how he brought rains to the drought-stricken kingdom of Romapada.

Legend

According to legend, Adi Shankaracharya is said to have selected the site as the place to stay and teach his disciples, because when he was walking by the Tunga river, he saw a cobra with a raised hood, providing shelter from the hot sun, to a frog about to spawn. Impressed with the place where natural enemies had gone beyond their instincts, he stayed here for twelve years. Adi Shankaracharya also established mathas in the northern (at Jyotirmath, near Badrinath), eastern (at Puri) and western (at Dwaraka) quarters of India.

Ramanuja (Vishishtadvaita)

Ramanuja of the Vishishtadvaita school, addresses the problem of evil by attributing all evil things in life to the accumulation of evil karma of jivas (human souls) and maintains that God is amala, or without any stain of evil. In Sri Bhasya, Ramanuja's interpretation of the Brahma sutras from a Vaishnavite theistic view that Brahman, whom he conceives as Vishnu, arranges the diversity of creation in accordance with the different karma of individual souls.

Furthermore Ramanuja believes that Vishnu wishing to do a favour to those who are resolved on acting so as fully to please Him, engenders in their minds a tendency towards highly virtuous actions, such as means to attain to Him; while on the other hand, in order to punish those who are resolved on lines of action altogether displeasing to Him, He engenders in their minds a delight in such actions as have a downward tendency and are obstacles in the way of the attainment of God.

Madhva (Dvaita)

Madhva, the founder of the Dvaita school, on the other hand, believes that there must be a root cause for variations in karma even if karma is accepted as having no beginning and being the cause of the problem of evil. Since jivas have different kinds of karma, from good to bad, all must not have started with same type of karma from the beginning of time. Thus, Madhva concludes that the jivas are not God's creation as in the Christian doctrine, but are rather entities co-existent with Vishnu, although under His absolute control. Souls are thus dependent on Him in their pristine nature and in all transformations that they may undergo.

According to Madhva, God, although He has control, does not interfere with Man's free will; although He is omnipotent, that does not mean that He engages in extraordinary feats. Rather, God enforces a rule of law and, in accordance with the just deserts of jivas, gives them freedom to follow their own nature. Thus, God functions as the sanctioner or as the divine accountant, and accordingly jivas are free to work according to their innate nature and their accumulated karma, good and bad.

Since God acts as the sanctioner, the ultimate power for everything comes from God and the Jiva only utilizes that power, according to his/her innate nature. However, like Shankara's interpretation of the Brahma Sutras as mentioned earlier, Madhva, agrees that the rewards and punishments bestowed by God are regulated by Him in accordance with the good and sinful deeds performed by them, and He does so of out of His own will to keep himself firm in justice and he cannot be controlled in His actions by karma of human beings nor can He be accused of partiality or cruelty to anyone. Swami Tapasyananda further explains the Madhva view by illustrating the doctrine with this analogy: the power in a factory comes from the powerhouse (God), but the various cogs (*jivas*) move in a direction in which they are set. Thus he concludes that no charge of partiality and cruelty can be brought against God. The Jiva is the actor and also the enjoyer of the fruits of his/her own actions.

Madhva differed significantly from traditional Hindu beliefs, owing to his concept of eternal damnation. For example, he divides souls into three classes: one class of souls which qualify for liberation (Mukti-yogyas), another subject to eternal rebirth or eternal transmigration (Nitya-samsarins), and a third class that is eventually condemned to eternal hell or Andhatamas (Tamo-yogyas). No other Hindu philosopher or school of Hinduism holds such beliefs. In contrast, most Hindus believe in universal salvation: that all souls will eventually obtain moksha, even if it is after millions of rebirths.

Nyaya

The Nyaya school, one of six orthodox schools of Hindu philosophy, states that one of the proofs of the existence of God is karma: Adºiºhþât (lit., from the unforeseen): It is seen that some people in this world are happy, some are in misery. Some are rich and some poor. The Naiyanikas explain this by the concept of Karma and reincarnation. The fruit of an individual's actions does not always lie within the reach of the individual who is the agent. There ought to be, therefore, a dispenser of the fruits of actions, and this supreme dispenser is God. This belief of Nyaya, accordingly, is the same as that of Vedanta.

Relation with Caste

As stated earlier, there are cycles of creations in which souls gravitate to specific bodies in accordance with karma, which as an unintelligent object depends on the will of God alone. Thus, many interpret the caste system in accordance with karma, as those with good deeds are born into a spiritual family, which is synonymous with the *brahmana* caste.

However, Krishna said in the Gita that characteristics of a brahmin are determined by behavior, not by birth. A verse from the Gita illustrates this point: "The duties of Brahmins, Kshatriyas,

Vaishyas as also of Sudras, O scorcher of foes, are distributed according to the gunas (behavior) born of their own nature." (Bhagavad Gita 18.41)

Karma in the Dharmauastras

In Hinduism, more particularly the Dharmauastras, Karma is a principle in which "cause and effect are as inseparably linked in the moral sphere as assumed in the physical sphere by science. A good action has its reward and a bad action leads to retribution. If the bad actions do not yield their consequences in this life, the soul begins another existence and in the new environment undergoes suffering for its past deeds". Thus it is important to understand that karma does not go away, one must either reap the benefits or suffer the consequences of his past actions.

The Brahdaranyakopanisad states, "According as a man acts and according as he believes so will he be; a man of meritorious acts will be meritorious, a man of evil deeds sinful. He becomes pure by pure deeds and evil by evil deeds. And here they say that person consists of desires. An as is his desire so is his will; and as is his will, so is his deed; and whatever deeds he does that he will reap". The doctrine of karma dates from ancient times and besides the above author is mentioned in the Gautama dharma-sutra, Satapatha Brahmana, Kathaaka-grhya-sutra, Chandogyopanisad, Markandeya-purana and many others.

The sastras written about karma go into some detail about possible consequences of karma. There is often talk about coming back as a variety of different object when it comes to reincarnation and pasts lives. In this case, it holds true, or at least insofar as the texts state. The Kathaaka-grhya-sutra states, "some human beings enter the womb in order to have an embodied existence; others go into inorganic matter (the stump of a tree and the like) according to their deeds and according to their knowledge".

More extensively discussed is the consequences of karma in relation to sin. "Karmavipaka means the ripening (or fruition) of evil actions or sins. This fruition takes three forms, as stated in the Yogasutra II. viz jati (birth as a worm or animal), ayuh (life i.e. living for a short period such as five or ten years) and bhoga (experiencing the torments of Hell". There are long lists of birth of lower animals and the diseases and deformities from which sinners suffer. Some authors offer specific ramifications for specific sins. For example, in "the Haritasamhita it is said the killer of a brahmana suffers from white leprosy and the killer of a cow from black leprosy." While the list is extensive for ways of reducing sin and therefore reducing bad karma, some authors, such as Mitaksara, a commentator on the Yarjnavalkya, believe karma is, "not to be taken literally, but is meant to induce sinner to undergo such prayaschittas as Prajapatya which entail great worry and trouble and which no one might willingly undertake."

Further the Karmavipaka states, "that no soul need be without hope provided it is prepared to wait and undergo torments for its misdeeds, that it need not be appalled by the numerous existences foreshadowed in those works and that the soul may in its long passage and evolution but ultimately able to discover its true greatness and realize eternal peace and perfection." Thus the sastras turn to means of reducing sin, some of which are hard to reconcile with the doctrines of karma.

For example, one practice, sraddha, or as the Brahmapurana sates, "whatever is given with faith to brahmanas intending it to be for the benefit of pitrs at a proper time, in a proper place, to deserving persons and in accordance with the prescribed procedure" is meant to honour ancestors, however a believer of karma would agree that when the body dies the soul automatically enters into another body.

Therefore, in contrast with karma, Kane states about sraddha, "the doctorine of offering balls of rice to three ancestors requires that the spirits of the three ancestors even after the lapse of 50 or 100 years are still capable of enjoying in an ethereal body the flavour or essence of rice balls wafted by the wind." Of course the two can be reconciled if taking into account the sastras that state that karma is not to be taken literally, but as evidenced by the variety of opinion written on the subject this will not hold true everywhere.

Other uses in Hinduism

Besides narrow meaning of karma as the reaction or suffering being due to karma of their past lives and that one would have to transmigrate to another body in their next life, it is often used in the broader sense as action or reaction.

Thus, karma in Hinduism may mean an activity, an action or a materialistic activity. Often with the specific combination it takes specific meanings, such as *karma-yoga* or *karma-kanda* means "yoga or actions" and "path of materialistic activity" respectively. Yet another example is Nitya karma, which describes rituals which have to be performed daily by Hindus, such as the Sandhyavandanam which involves chanting of the Gayatri Mantra.

Other uses include such expressions such as "ugra-karma", meaning bitter, unwholesome labour.

Jivanmukta

Jivanmukta (from the Sanskrit words *Jiva* and *mukti*) is someone who, in the Advaita philosophy of Hinduism, has attained nirvikalpa samadhi-the realization of the Self, Parasiva-and is liberated from rebirth while living in a human body.

Jivanmukta is a unique concept in Hindu philosophy, particularly in the school of philosophy known as advaita. The ultimate goal of Hinduism is liberation from the cycles of re-birth. This liberation is technically called 'moksha'. In all schools of Hindu philosophy except advaita, liberation is necessarily an event beyond the experience of human being. But the advaita school of Shankara envisages that human is already liberated and the soul is already free-one only has only to realise, and to accept, this freedom. Souls who have had this realisation are called jivanmuktas.

There are three kinds of Prarabdha karma: *Ichha* (personally desired), *Anichha* (without desire) and *Parechha (due* to others' desire). For a self realized person, a Jivan mukta, there is no Ichha-Prarabdha but the two others, Anichha and Parechha, remain, which even a jivan mukta has to undergo.

Mahatma

Mahatma is Sanskrit for "Great Soul" *atman* [soul]); it is similar in usage to the modern Christian term saint. This epithet is commonly applied to prominent people like Mohandas Karamchand Gandhi and Jyotirao Phule. Many sources, such as Dutta and Robinson's *Rabindranath Tagore: An Anthology*, state that Rabindranath Tagore first accorded Gandhi this title. Others state that the title "Mahatma" was first accorded to Gandhi on January 21, 1915 by Nautamlal Bhagavanji Mehta at Kamribai School in Jetpur, India. The term is also used to refer to adepts, liberated souls, or professionals.

Theosophy

The word, used in a technical sense, was popularised in theosophical literature in the late 19th century when Madame Helena P. Blavatsky, one of the founders of the Theosophical Society, claimed that her teachers were adepts or Mahatmas who reside in Tibet.

According to the Theosophical teachings, the Mahatmas are not disembodied beings, but highly evolved people involved in overseeing the spiritual growth of individuals and the development of civilisations. Blavatsky was the first person in modern times to claim contact with these Adepts, especially the "Masters" Koot Hoomi and Morya.

In September and October 1880, Blavatsky visited A. P. Sinnett at Simla in northern India. The serious interest of Sinnett in the Theosophical teachings of Mme. Blavatsky and the work of the Theosophical Society prompted Mme. Blavatsky to establish a contact by correspondence between Sinnett and the two adepts who were sponsoring the society, Koot Hoomi and Morya.

From this correspondence Sinnett wrote *The Occult World* (1881) and *Esoteric Buddhism* (1883), both of which had an enormous influence in generating public interest in theosophy. The replies and explanations given by the Mahatmas to the questions by Sinnett are embodied in their letters from 1880 to 1885, published in London in 1923 as The Mahatma Letters to Sinnett. The Mahatmas also corresponded with a number of other persons during the early years of the Theosophical Society. Many of these letters have been published in two volumes titled *Letters from the Masters of the Wisdom*, Series 1 and Series 2.

There has been a great deal of controversy concerning the existence of these particular adepts. Blavatsky's critics have doubted the existence of her Masters. See, for example, W.E. Coleman's "exposes." More than twenty five individuals testified to having seen and been in contact with these Mahatmas during Blavatsky's lifetime. In recent years, K. Paul Johnson has promoted an interesting but controversial theory about the Masters.

After Blavatsky's death in 1891, numerous individuals have claimed to be in contact with her Adept Teachers and have stated that they were new "messengers" of the Masters conveying various esoteric teachings. Currently various New Age, metaphysical, and religious organizations refer to them as Ascended Masters, although their character and teachings are in several respects different from those described by Theosophical writers.

Divine Light Mission

The Divine Light Mission (DLM) was a Sant Mat-based movement begun in India in the 1930s by Hans Ji Maharaj and formally incorporated in 1960.

The DLM had as many as 2,000 mahatmas, all from India or Tibet, who taught the DLM's secret meditation techniques called "Knowledge". The mahatmas, called 'realised souls', or "apostles", also served as local leaders. After Hans Ji's death in 1966 his youngest son, Prem Rawat (known then as Guru Maharaj Ji or Bagyogeshwar), succeeded him.

The young guru appointed some new mahatmas, including one from the United States. In one notable incident, a prominent Indian mahatma nearly beat a man to death in Detroit for throwing a pie at the guru. In the early 1980s, Prem Rawat replaced the Divine Light Mission organization with the Elan Vital and replaced the mahatmas with initiators. The initiators did not have the revered status of the mahatmas and they were drawn mostly from Western followers. In the 2000s, the initiators were replaced by a video in which Rawat teaches the techniques himself.

Maya (Illusion)

Maya, has multiple meanings, within a Hindu or Sikh context, the word refers to concepts of "illusion". Maya, is the principal concept which manifests, perpetuates and governs the illusion and dream of duality in the phenomenal Universe. For some mystics this manifestation is real, but it is a fleeting reality; it is a mistake, although a natural one, to believe that Maya represents a fundamental reality or Truth.

Each person, each physical object, from the perspective of eternity is like a brief, disturbed drop of water from an unbounded ocean. The goal of enlightenment is to understand this — more precisely, to experience this: to see intuitively that the distinction between the self and the Universe is a false dichotomy. The distinction between consciousness and physical matter, between mind and body (refer bodymind), is the result of an unenlightened perspective.

Maya in Illusional Hinduism

The word origin of maya is derived from the Sanskrit roots ma ("not") and ya, generally translated as an indicative article meaning "that." The mystic teachings in Vedanta are centered on a fundamental truth that cannot be reduced to a concept or word for the ordinary mind to manipulate. Rather, the human experience and mind are themselves a tiny fragment of this truth. In this tradition, no mind-object can be identified as absolute truth, such that one may say "That's it." So, to keep the mind from attaching to incomplete fragments of reality, a speaker could use this term to indicate that truth is "Not that."

In Hinduism, Maya is to be seen through, like an epiphany, in order to achieve moksha (liberation of the soul from the cycle of samsara). Ahamkar (ego-consciousness) and karma are seen as part of the binding forces of Maya. Maya may be understood as the phenomenal Universe of perceived duality, a lesser reality-lens superimposed on the unity of Brahman. It is said to be created by the divine by the application of the Lila (creative energy/material cycle, manifested as a veil-the basis of dualism). The sanskaras of perceived duality perpetuate samsara.

Maya in Hindu Philosophy

In Advaita Vedanta philosophy, Maya is the limited, purely physical and mental reality in which our everyday consciousness has become entangled. Maya is held to be an illusion, a veiling of the true, unitary Self — the Cosmic Spirit also known as Brahman. The concept of Maya was introduced by the great ninth century Hindu philosopher Adi Shankara. Many philosophies or religions seek to "pierce the veil" of Maya in order to glimpse the transcendent truth, from which the illusion of a physical reality springs, drawing from the idea that first came to life in the Hindu stream of Vedanta.

Maya is neither true nor untrue. Since Brahman is the only truth, Maya cannot be true. Since Maya causes the material world to be seen it is true in itself but is untrue in comparison to the Brahman. On the other hand, maya is not false. It is true in itself but untrue in comparison with the absolute truth. In this sense, reality includes maya and the Brahman. The goal of spiritual enlightenment ought to see Brahman and maya and distinguish between them. Hence, Maya is described as indescribable.

Maya has two principal functions – one is to veil Brahman and obscure and conceal it from our consciousness. The other is to present and promulgate the material world and the veil of duality instead of Brahman.

The veil of Maya may be pierced and with diligence and grace, may be permanently rent. Consider an illusion of a rope being mistaken for a snake in the darkness. Just as this illusion gets destroyed when true knowledge of the rope is perceived, similarly, Maya gets destroyed for a person when they perceive Brahman with transcendental knowledge.

A metaphor is also given – when the reflection of Brahman falls on Maya, Brahman appears as God (the Supreme Lord). Pragmatically where the duality of the world is regarded as true, Maya becomes the divine magical power of the Supreme Lord. Maya is the veritable fabric of duality and she performs this role at the behest of the Supreme Lord. God is not bound by Maya, just as magicians do not believe the illusions of their own magic.

By Sri Shankaracharya:

1. The Supreme Self (or Ultimate Reality) who is Pure Consciousness perceived Himself by Selfhood (i.e. Existence with "I"-Consciousness). He became endowed with the name "I". From that arose the basis of difference.
2. He exists verily in two parts, on account of which, the two could become husband and wife. Therefore, this space is ever filled up completely by the woman (or the feminine principle) surely.
3. And He, this Supreme Self thought (or reflected). Thence, human beings were born. Thus say the Upanishads through the statement of sage Yajnavalkya to his wife.
4. From the experience of bliss for a long time, there arose in the Supreme Self a certain state like deep sleep. From that (state) Maya (or the illusive power of the Supreme Self) was born just as a dream arises in sleep.
5. This Maya is without the characteristics of (or different from) Reality or unreality, without beginning and dependent on the Reality that is the Supreme Self. She, who is of the form of the Three Guna (qualities or energies of Nature) brings forth the Universe with movable and immovable (objects).

6. As for Maya, it is invisible (or not experienced by the senses). How can it produce a thing that is visible (or experienced by the senses)? How is a visible piece of cloth produced here by threads of invisible nature?
7. Though the emission of ejaculate onto sleeping garments or bedclothes is yielded by the natural experience of copulation in a wet dream, the stain of the garment is perceived as real upon waking whilst the copulation and lovemaking was not true or real. Both sexual partners in the dream are unreal as they are but dream bodies, and the sexual union and conjugation was illusory, but the emission of the generative fluid was real. This is a metaphor for the resolution of duality into lucid unity.
8. Thus Maya is invisible (or beyond sense-perception). (But) this universe which is its effect, is visible (or perceived by the senses). This would be Maya which, on its part, becomes the producer of joy by its own destruction.
9. Like night (or darkness) Maya is extremely insurmountable (or extremely difficult to be understood). Its nature is not perceived here. Even as it is being observed carefully (or being investigated) by sages, it vanishes like lightning.
10. Maya (the illusive power) is what is obtained in Brahman (or the Ultimate Reality). Avidya (or nescience or spiritual ignorance) is said to be dependent on Jiva (the individual soul or individualised consciousness). Mind is the knot which joins Consciousness and matter.
11. Space enclosed by a pot, or a jar or a hut or a wall has their several appellations (eg.,pot space, jar space etc.). Like that, Consciousness (or the Self) covered here by Avidya (or nescience) is spoken of as Jiva (the individual soul).
12. Objection: How indeed could ignorance become a covering (or an obscure factor) for Brahman (or the Supreme Spirit) who is Pure Consciousness, as if the darkness arising from the night (could become a concealing factor) for the sun which is self-luminous?
13. As the sun is hidden by clouds produced by the solar rays but surely, the character of the day is not hidden by those modified dense collection of clouds, so the Self, though

pure, (or undefiled) is veiled for a long time by ignorance. But its power of Consciousness in living beings, which is established in this world, is not veiled.

Understanding Maya through Bhagavad Gita verses

Spoken by Krisna (also spelled Krishna) to Arjuna on the battlefield of Kurukshetra *Bhagavad Gita, Ch.14, Verse 3*. "My womb is the great Nature (Prakriti or MAYA). In that I place the germ (embryo of life). Thence is the birth of all beings".

Bhagavad Gita, Ch. 14, Verse 4 "Whatever forms are born, O Arjuna, in any womb whatsoever, the great Brahma (Nature) is their womb and I am the seed-giving father."

Explanation: Prakriti (Nature), made up of the three qualities (Sattwa, Rajas and Tamas), is the material cause of all beings.

In the great Prakriti, I place the seed for the birth of Brahma (the creator, also known as Hiranyagarbha, or Ishwar, or the conditioned Brahman); and the seed gives birth to all beings. The birth of Brahma (the creator) gives rise to the birth of beings.

The primordial Nature (prakriti) gives birth to Brahma, who creates all beings.

Bhagavad Gita, Ch.13, verse 26: "Wherever a being is born, whether unmoving or moving, know thou Arjuna, that it is from the union between the field and the knower of the field". (Purusha is the knower of the field; Prakriti is the field; Shiva is another name for the knower of the field and Shakti is the field; Spirit is another name for the knower of the field and Matter (Prakriti) is the field).

Bhagavad Gita, Ch. 7, Verse 5: "I am endowed with two Shaktis, namely the superior and the inferior natures; the field and its knower (spirit is the knower of the field; matter is the field.) I unite these two".

Bhagavad Gita Ch.7, Verse 6: "Know these two-my higher and lower natures-as the womb of all beings. Therefore, I am the source and dissolution of the whole universe".

Bhagavad Gita, Ch.13, Verse 29: "He sees, who sees that all actions are performed by nature alone, and that the Self is action less".

Bhagavad Gita, Ch.9, Verse 17: "I am the father of this world, the mother, the dispenser of the fruits of actions and the grandfather; the one thing to be known, the purifier, the sacred monosyllable (AUM), and also the Rg, the Sama and the Yajur Vedas".

Bhagavad Gita, Ch.18, Verse 61: "The sovereign Lord dwells in the heart space of beings and moves them to act by his divine Maya, as though mounted on a machine".

Maya in Hindu Mythology

Maya may also be visualized as a guise or aspect of the Divine Mother (Devi) or Devi Mahamaya concept of Hinduism.

In Hinduism, Maya is also seen as a form of Laksmi, a Divine Goddess. Her most famous explication is seen in the Devi Mahatmyam, where she is known as Mahamaya. Because of its association with the goddess, Maya is now a commonly used girl's name in India and amongst the Indian diaspora around the world.

Essentially, Mahamaya (great Maya) both blinds us in delusion (moha) and has the power to free us from it. Maya, superimposed on Brahman, the one divine ground and essence of monist Hinduism, is envisioned as one with Laxmi, Durga, etc. A great modern (19th century) Hindu sage who often spoke of Maya as being the same as the Shakti principle of Hinduism was Shri Ramakrishna.

In the Hindu scripture 'Devi Mahatmyam,' Mahamaya (Great Maya) is said to cover Vishnu's eyes in Yoganidra (Divine Sleep) during cycles of existence when all is resolved into one. By exhorting Mahamaya to release Her illusory hold on Vishnu, Brahma is able to bring Vishnu to aid him in killing two demons, Madhu and Kaitabh, who have manifested from Vishnu's sleeping form. Sri Ramakrishna Paramahamsa often spoke of Mother Maya and combined deep Hindu allegory with the idea that Maya is a lesser reality that must be overcome so that one is able to realize his or her true Self.

Maya, in Her form as Mahalaxmi, also known as Durga, was called upon when the gods and goddesses were helpless against the attacks of the demon Mahisasura. The combined material energy of all the gods, including Brahma, Vishnu and Shiva, created Her. She is thus said to possess the combined material power of all the gods and goddesses. The gods gave her ornaments, weapons, and her bearer, the lion. She was unassailable. She fought a fierce battle against the demon Mahisasura and his huge army. She defeated the demon's army, killed the demon, and hence restored peace and order to the world. Thus She is, even now, the protector of the Universe, which is lying in her lap.

Devi Mahamaya is also a Kuldev of the Gowd Saraswat Brahmins of Goa, India.

Maya in Sikhism

In Sikhism, the world is transitory and a passing phase. However, it is viewed as relatively real. God is viewed as the only reality, but within God exist both conscious souls and unconscious objects; these created objects are also real. The events which occurs in nature are real but the effects they generate are unreal.Maya is as the events are real yet Maya is not as the effects are unreal. Consider the following examples. In the moonless night, a rope laying on the ground may be mistaken for a snake. We know that the rope alone is real, not the snake. However, the non apprehension of the rope gives rise to the misapprehension of the snake. Once the darkness is removed, the rope alone remains; the snake disappears. Similarly, in the darkness of the night, a pole may be mistaken for a ghost. As the darkness is removed, the ghost disappears; only the pole remains as reality.

1. Sakti adher jevarhee bhram chookaa nihchal siv ghari vaasaa: In the darkness of Maya, I mistook the rope for the snake, but that is over, and now I dwell in the eternal home of the Lord.
2. Raaj bhuiang prasang jaise hahi ab kashu maram janaaiaa.

Like the story of the rope mistaken for a snake, the mystery has now been explained to me. Like the many bracelets, which I mistakenly thought were gold; now, I do not say what I said then.

Jainism

Jainism is an ancient dharmic religion from India that prescribes a path of non-violence for all forms of living beings in this world. Its philosophy and practice relies mainly on self-effort in progressing the soul on the spiritual ladder to divine consciousness. Any soul which has conquered its own inner enemies and achieved the state of supreme being is called *jina* (Conqueror or Victor). Jainism is often referred to as *Jain Dharma* or *Shraman Dharma* or the religion of Nirgantha by ancient texts.

Jainism was revived by a lineage of 24 enlightened ascetics called tirthankaras culminating with Parshva (9th century BCE) and Mahavira (6th century BCE). In the modern world, it is a small but influential religious minority with as many as 4.9 million followers in India, and successful growing immigrant communities in North America, Western Europe, the Far East, Australia and elsewhere.

Jainism is Divided into Digambaras and Swetambaras

Jains have sustained the ancient *Shraman* or ascetic religion and have significantly influenced other religious, ethical, political and economic spheres in India. Jains have an ancient tradition of scholarship and have the highest degree of literacy in India; Jain libraries are the oldest in the country.

Principles and Beliefs

Jainism regards every living soul as potentially divine. When the soul sheds its karmic bonds completely, it attains divine consciousness. It prescribes a path of non-violence to progress the soul to this ultimate goal.

A *Jain* is a follower of *Jinas* ("conquerors"). Jinas are spiritually advanced human beings who rediscover the *dharma,* become fully liberated and teach the spiritual path to benefit all living beings. Practicing Jains follow the teachings of 24 special jinas who are known as *Tirthankaras* "('ford-makers", or "those who have discovered and shown the way to salvation"). Tradition states that the 24th, and most recent, *Tirthankar* is Shri Mahavir, lived from 599 to 527 BC. The 23rd Tirthankar, Shri Parsva, lived from 872 to 772 BC.

Jainism encourages spiritual development through reliance on and cultivation of one's own personal wisdom and self-control. The goal of Jainism is to realize the soul's true nature. "Samyak darshan gyan charitrani moksha margah", meaning "true/right perception, knowledge and conduct" (known as the triple gems of Jainism) provides the path for attaining liberation (moksha) from samsara (the universal cycle of birth and death). Moksha is attained by liberation from all karma. Those who have attained moksha are called *siddha* (liberated souls), and those who are attached to the world through their karma are called *samsarin* (mundane souls). Every soul has to follow the path, as described by the Jinas (and revived by Tirthankaras), to attain the ultimate liberation.

Jaina tradition identifies Rishabh Bhagwan (also known as Adhinath) as the First Tirthankar of this declining (avasarpini) time cycle (kalachakra). The first Tirthankar, Rushabhdev/ Adhinath, appeared prior to the Indus Valley Civilization. The swastika symbol and naked statues resembling Jain monks, which archaeologists have found among the remains of the Indus Valley Civilization, tend to support this claim.

Jains hold that the Universe and Dharma are eternal, without beginning or end. However, the universe undergoes processes of cyclical change. The universe consists of living beings ("Jiva") and non-living beings ("Ajiva"). The samsarin (worldly) soul incarnates in various life forms during its journey over time. Human, sub-human (animal, insect, plant, etc.), super-human (deity or devas), and hell-being are the four macro forms of the samsari souls. All worldly relations of one's Jiva with other Jiva and Ajiva (non-living beings) are based on the accumulation of karma and its conscious thoughts, speech and actions carried out in its current form.

The main Jain prayer (*Namokar Mantra*) therefore salutes the five special categories of souls that have attained divine consciousness or are on their way to achieving it, to emulate and follow these paths to salvation.

Another major characteristic of Jain belief is the emphasis on the consequences of not only physical but also mental behaviours.

Jain practices are derived from the above fundamentals. For example, the principle of non-violence seeks to minimize karmas which may limit the capabilities of the soul. Jainism views every soul as worthy of respect because it has the potential to become Siddha (Param-atma-"highest soul"). Because all living beings possess a soul, great care and awareness is essential in one's actions in the incarnate world. Jainism emphasizes the equality of all life, advocating harmlessness towards all, whether these be creatures great or small. This policy extends even to microscopic organisms. Jainism acknowledges that every person has different capabilities and capacities and therefore assigns different duties for ascetics and householders. The "great vows" (mahavrata) are prescribed for monks and "limited vows" (anuvrata) are prescribed for householders. There are five basic ethical principles (vows) prescribed. The degree to which these principles must be practiced is different for renunciant and householder. Thus:

- Non-violence (Ahinsa)-to cause no harm to living beings.
- Truth (Satya)-to always speak the truth in a harmless manner.
- Non-stealing (Asteya)-to not take anything that is not willingly given.
- Celibacy (Brahmacarya)-to not indulge in sensual pleasures.
- Non-possession (Aparigraha)-to detach from people, places, and material things.

Ahimsa, "Non-violence", is sometimes interpreted as not killing, but the concept goes far beyond that. It includes not harming or insulting other living beings, either directly, or indirectly through others. There can be even no room for thought to injure others, and no speech that influences others to inflict harm. It also includes respecting the views of others (non-absolutism and acceptance of multiple views). Satya, "truthfulness", is also to be practiced by all people. Given that non-violence has priority, all other principles yield to it, whenever there is a conflict. For example, if speaking truth will lead to violence, it is perfectly ethical to be silent. Thiruvalluvar in his Tamil classic devotes an entire chapter clarifying the definition of 'truthfulness'.

Asteya, "non-stealing", is the strict adherence to one's own possessions, without desire to take another's. One should remain satisfied by whatever is earned through honest labour. Any attempt to squeeze others and/or exploit the weak is considered theft. Some of the guidelines for this principle are:

- Always give people fair value for labour or product.
- Never take things which are not offered.
- Never take things that are placed, dropped or forgotten by others
- Never purchase cheaper things if the price is the result of improper method (e.g. pyramid scheme, illegal business, stolen goods, etc.).

Brahmacarya, "monastic celibacy", is the complete abstinence from sex, which is only incumbent upon monastics. Householders practice monogamy as a way to uphold brahmacarya in spirit. Aparigraha, "non-possession", is the renunciation of property and wealth, before initiation into monkhood, without entertaining thoughts of the things renounced. This is done so one understands how to detach oneself from things and possessions, including home and family, so one may reach *moksa*. For householders, non-possession is owning without attachment, because the notion of possession is illusory. The reality of life is that change is constant; thus, objects owned by someone today will be property of someone else in future days. The householder is encouraged to discharge his or her duties to related people and objects as a trustee, without excessive attachment.

Main points:

- Every living being has a soul.
- Every soul is potentially divine, with innate qualities of infinite knowledge, perception, power, and bliss (masked by its karmas).
- Therefore, regard every living being as yourself, harming no one and be kind to all living beings.
- Every soul is born as a celestial, human, sub-human or hellish being according to its own karmas.
- Every soul is the architect of its own life, here or hereafter.
- When a soul is freed from karmas, it becomes free and attain divine consciousness, experiencing infinite knowledge, perception, power, and bliss.
- Right View, Right Knowledge and Right Conduct (triple gems of Jainism) provide the way to this realization. There is no supreme divine creator, owner, preserver or destroyer. The universe is self-regulated and every soul has the potential to achieve divine consciousness (siddha) through its own efforts.
- Navakar Mantra is the fundamental prayer in Jainism and can be recited at any time of the day. Praying by reciting this mantra, the devotee bows with respect to liberated souls still in human form (Arihantas), fully liberated souls (Siddhas), spiritual leaders (Acharyas), teachers (Upadyayas) and all the monks. By saluting them, Jains receive inspiration from them for the right path of true bliss and total freedom from the karma of their soul. In

this main prayer, Jains do not ask for any favours or material benefits. This mantra serves as a simple gesture of deep respect towards beings who are more spiritually advanced. The mantra also reminds followers of the ultimate goal, nirvana or moksha.

- To be in Soul Consciousness rather than body consciousness is the foundation of right View, the condition of right Knowledge and the kernel of right Conduct.It leads to a state of being unattached to worldy things and therefore being nonjudgemental and Non-violent which includes compassion and forgiveness in thoughts, words and actions toward all living beings and respecting views of others (Non-absolutism).
- Jainism stresses on the importance of controlling the senses, as they can drag you far away true nature of the soul into being increasingly addicted to the material world leading into the tunnel of darkeness,ignorance,love, hate and violence (Led by the fear of losing what we are attached to)
- Limit possessions and lead a pure life that is useful to yourself and others. Owning an object by itself is not possessiveness; however attachment to an object is. Non-possessiveness is the balancing of needs and desires while staying detached from our possessions.
- Enjoy the company of the holy and better qualified, be merciful to those afflicted and tolerate the perversely inclined.
- Four things are difficult for a soul to attain: 1. human birth, 2. knowledge of the law, 3. faith in the law, and 4. practicing the right path.
- It is important not to waste human life in evil ways. Rather, strive to rise on the ladder of spiritual evolution.
- The goal of Jainism is liberation of the soul from the negative effects of unenlightened thoughts, speech and action. This goal is achieved through clearance of karmic obstructions by following the triple gems of Jainism.
- Jains mainly worship idols of Jinas, Arihants and Tirthankars, who have conquered the inner passions and attained divine consciousness. Jainism acknowledges the

existence of powerful heavenly souls (Yaksha and Yakshini) that look after the well beings of Thirthankarars. Usually, they are found in pair around the idols of Jinas as male (yaksha) and female (yakshini) guardian deities. Even though they have supernatural powers, they are also wandering through the cycles of births and deaths just like most other souls. Over time, people started worshiping these deities as well.

Tirthankaras

Jains believe that knowledge of the truth (*dharma*) has declined and revived cyclically throughout history. Those who rediscover dharma are called *Tirthankara*. The literal meaning of *Tirthankar* is 'ford-builder'. Jains, like Buddhists, compare the process of becoming a pure human to crossing a swift river, an endeavour requiring patience and care. A ford-builder has already crossed the river and can therefore guide others. One is called a 'victor' (Skt: *Jina*) because one has achieved liberation by one's own efforts. Like Buddhism, the purpose of Jain dharma is to undo the negative effects of karma through mental and physical purification. This process leads to liberation accompanied by a great natural inner peace.

Having purified one's soul of karmic impurities, a *tirthankar* is considered omniscient, and a role model. Identified as divine, these individuals are called *bhagavan*, lord (e.g., Bhagavan Rushabha, Bhagavan Parshva, etc.). Tirthankar are not regarded as gods in the pantheistic or polytheistic sense, but rather as examplars who have awakened the divine spiritual qualities which lie dormant in each of us. There have been 24 Tirthankaras in what the Jains call the 'present age'. The last two Tirthankaras: Parsva and Mahavira are historical figures whose existence is recorded

Mahavira established the fourfold community (*chaturvidhi sangha*) of monks, nuns, and male and female laypersons.

The 24 Tirthankaras, in chronological order, are Adinath (Rushabhnath), Ajitnath, Sambhavanath, Abhinandan Swami, Sumatinath, Padmaprabhu, Suparshvanath, Chandraprabhu, Pushpadanta (Suvidhinath), Sheetalnath, Shreyansanath, Vasupujya Swami, Vimalnath, Anantnath, Dharmanath, Shantinath, Kunthunath, Aranath, Mallinath, Munisuvrata Swami, Nami Natha, Neminath, Parshvanath and Mahavir (Vardhamana).

According to Jain Scriptures, Bahubali (also known as Gommateshvara) was the second of the one hundred sons of the first Tirthankara, Lord Rishabha and king of Podanpur. A statue of Lord Bahubali is located at Shravanabelagola in the Hassan district of Karnataka State. Shravanabelagola is a sacred place of pilgrimage to Jain with a splendid and lofty statue of stone on top of a hillock there. When standing at the statue's feet looking up, one sees the inspiring vision of the saint against the vastness of the sky. The figure is lofty like the sky, and the serenity of the face is unique and incomparable in its beauty. This statue of Gommateshwara Bahubali is carved from a single stone fifty-seven feet high. The giant image was carved in 981 A.D., by order of Chavundaraya, the minister of the Ganga King Rachamalla. Bahubali is another name for Gommateshwara.

Emphasis on Non-violence in Thought and Practice

Jains believe that every human is responsible for his/her actions and all living beings have an eternal soul, *Jiva*. Jains believe all souls are equal because they all possess the potential of being liberated and attaining moksha. Tirthankaras are role models only because they have attained moksha. Jains insist that we live, think and act respectfully and honor the spiritual nature of all life. Jains view divinity as the unchanging traits of the pure soul of each living being, described as Infinite Knowledge, Perception, Consciousness, and Happiness (*Ananta Jnana, Ananta Darshana, Ananta Caritra* and *Ananta Sukha*). Jains do not believe in an omnipotent supreme being, creator or manager (*karta*), but rather in an eternal universe governed by natural laws.

Jains hold that this temporal world inflicts much misery and sorrow. Thus, to attain lasting bliss, one must transcend the cycle of transmigration, lest one remain eternally trapped in its never-ending repetition. The only way to break out of this cycle is to practice detachment through rational perception, rational knowledge and rational conduct.

Jain scriptures were written over a long period of time, but the most cited is the *Tattvartha Sutra*, or "Book of Reality", written by the monk-scholar, Umasvati (aka Umasvami) almost 1800 years ago. The protagonists of this sutra are Tirthankaras. The two main sects of Jainism are called Digambar and Svetambar. Both sects affirm ahimsa (or *ahinsa*), asceticism, karma, sanskar, and Jiva.

Though practice differs between the two sects, Jain doctrine is uniform, with great emphasis placed on rational perception, rational knowledge and rational conduct. {"samyagdar [anajnnacritr Gimokcamrgah", Tattvarthasutra, 1.1}

Compassion for all life, both human and non-human, is central to Jainism. Human life is valued as a unique, rare opportunity to reach enlightenment. To kill any person, no matter their crime, is considered unimaginably abhorrent.

History suggests that various strains of Hinduism became vegetarian due to strong Jain influences.. Jains run animal shelters all over India. For example, Delhi has a bird hospital run by Jains. Every city and town in Bundelkhand has animal shelters run by Jains where all manner of animals are sheltered, even though the shelter is generally known as a Gaushala ("sacred cow").

Jainism's stance on nonviolence goes far beyond vegetarianism. Jains refuse food obtained with unnecessary cruelty. Many practice a lifestyle similar to veganism, due to the violence of modern dairy farms, and others exclude root vegetables from their diets to preserve the lives of these plants. Potatoes, garlic and onions in particular are avoided by Jains.. Traditionally oriented Jains do not eat, drink, or travel after sunset, and prefer to drink water that is boiled and then cooled to room temperature. Many Jains abstain from eating root vegetables as the plant, which is a living organism, is usually uprooted during the harvest. The purpose of these practices is to minimise the harm that may otherwise be caused to living organisms inadvertently.

Anekantavada, a foundation of Jain philosophy, which literally means search of truth from different points of view, is the application of the principle of equality of souls in the sphere of thought. It is a jain philosophical standpoint just as there is the Advaitic standpoint of Sankara and the standpoint of the Middle Path of the Buddhists. This search leads to understanding and toleration of different and even conflicting views. When this happens prejuidices subside and tendency to accommodate increases. The theory of Anekanta is therefore unique experiment of non-violence at the root..

A derivation of this principle is the doctrine of Syadvada that highlights every view is relative to its view point. It is a matter of our daily experience that the same object which gives pleasure to us under certain circumstances becomes boring under different situations. Nonetheless relative truth is undobutedly useful as it is a stepping stone to the ultimate realisation of reality. The theory of Syadvada is based on the premise that every proposition is only relatively true.

It all depends on the particular aspect from which we approach that proposition. Jains therefore developed logic that encopasses sevenfold predication so as to assist in the construction of proper judgement about any proposition.

Syadvada provides Jainas with a systematic methodology to explore the real nature of reality and consider the problem in a non-violent way from different perspectives. This process ensures that each statement is expressed from seven different conditional and relative viewpoints or propositions, and thus it is known as theory of conditioned predication.

These seven propositions are described as follows:

- Syad-asti — "in some ways it is"
- Syad-nasti — "in some ways it is not"
- Syad-asti-nasti — "in some ways it is and it is not"
- Syad-asti-avaktavyah — "in some ways it is and it is indescribable"
- Syad-nasti-avaktavyah — "in some ways it is not and it is indescribable"
- Syad-asti-nasti-avaktavyah — "in some ways it is, it is not and it is indescribable"
- Syad-avaktavyah — "in some ways it is indescribable".

Jains are usually very welcoming and friendly toward other faiths and often help with interfaith functions. Several non-Jain temples in India are administered by Jains.

A palpable presence in Indian culture, Jains have contributed to Indian philosophy, art, architecture, science, and to Mohandas Gandhi's politics, which led to the mainly non-violent movement for Indian independence.. Though Mohandas Gandhi states clearly in his Autobiography that his mother was a Vaishnava, Jain monks visited his home regularly.

He spent considerable time under the tutelage of Jain monks, learning the philosophies of non-violence and doing good always.

Creation and Cosmology

Bhaktamara Stotra and 10th couplet in Thirukural, a Tamil classic: A *Tirthankara* is a shelter from ocean of rebirths.

According to Jain beliefs, the universe was never created, nor will it ever cease to exist. Therefore, it is *shaswat* (infinite). It has no beginning or end, but time is cyclical with progressive and regressive spirituality phases.

Rishi divide time into *Utsarpinis* (Progressive Time Cycle) and *Avsarpinis* (Regressive Time Cycle). An *Utsarpini* and an *Avsarpini* constitute one Time Cycle (*Kalchakra*). Every *Utsarpini* and *Avsarpini* is divided into six unequal periods known as *Aras*. During the *Utsarpini* half cycle, humanity develops from its worst to its best: ethics, progress, happiness, strength, health, and religion each start the cycle at their worst, before eventually completing the cycle at their best and starting the process again.

During the *Avsarpini* half-cycle, these notions deteriorate from the best to the worst. Jains believe we are currently in the fifth *Ara* of the *Avsarpini* phase, with approximately 19,000 years until the next *Ara*. After this *Ara* we will enter the sixth phase, which will last for approximately 21,000 years. After this, the *Utsarpini* phase will begin, continuing the infinite repetition of the belief that at the upswing of each time cycle, people will lose religion again. All wishes will be granted by wish-granting trees (*Kalpavrksa*), and people will be born in sets of twins (*Yugalika*) with one boy and one girl who stay together all their lives. This symbolizes the fully integrated human with male and female characteristics in balance.

Jain philosophy is based upon eternal, universal truths. During the first and last two *Aras*, these truths lapse among humanity and then reappear through the teachings of enlightened humans, those who have reached moksha or total knowledge (*Kevala Jnana*), during the third and fourth Aras. Traditionally, in our universe and in our time, Lord Rushabha is regarded as the first to realize the truth. Lord Vardhamana (Mahavira) was the last Tirthankara to attain enlightenment (599-527 BCE). He was preceded by 23 others, making a total of 24 Tirthankaras.

It is important to note that the above description stands true "in our universe and in our time", for Jains believe there have been infinite sets of 24 Tirthankaras, one for each half of the time cycle, and this will continue in the future. Hence, Jainism does not trace its origins to Rushabh Deva, the first, or finish with Mahavira, the 24th, Tirthankara.

According to Jainism, the universe consists of infinite amount of *Jiva* (life force or souls), and the design resembles a man standing with his arms bent while resting his hands on his waist. The narrow waist part comprises various *Kshetras*, for *vicharan* (roaming) for humans, animals and plants. Currently we are in the *Bharat Kshetra* of *Jambu Dweep* (*dweep* means island).

The *Deva Loka* (Heavens) are at the symbolic "chest" of Creation, where all *devas* (gods) reside. Similarly, beneath the "waist" are the *Narka Loka* (Hell). There are seven *Narka Lokas*, each for a varying degree suffering a *Jiva* has to go through to face the consequences of its *paap karma* (sins). From the first to the seventh *Narka*, the degree of suffering increases and light reaching it decreases (with no light in the seventh *Narka*).

The *sidhha kshetra* or *moksha* is situated at the symbolic forehead of the creation, where all the *jivas* having attained nirvana reside in a state of complete peace and eternal happiness. Outside the symbolic figure of this creation nothing but *aloka* or *akaasha* (sky) exists.

Historical and Cultural Impact

At the time of Adi Shankara's life, Hinduism was increasing in influence in India at the expense of Buddhism and Jainism. Hinduism was divided into innumerable sects, each quarreling with the others. The followers of Mimamsa and Sankhya philosophy were atheists, insomuch that they did not believe in God as a unified being. Besides these atheists, there were numerous theistic sects. There were also those who rejected the Vedas, like the Charvakas. Adi Shankara held discourses and debates with the leading scholars of all these sects and schools of philosophy to controvert their doctrines. He unified the theistic sects into a common framework of Shanmata system. In his works, Adi Shankara stressed the importance of the Vedas, and his efforts helped Hinduism regain strength and popularity. Many trace the present worldwide domination of Vedanta to his works. He travelled on foot to various parts of India to restore the study of the Vedas.

Even though he lived for only thirty-two years, his impact on India and on Hinduism was striking. He reintroduced a purer form of Vedic thought. His teachings and tradition form the basis of Smartism and have influenced Sant Mat lineages. He is the main figure in the tradition of Advaita Vedanta. He was the founder of the *Da[anmi Sampradya* of Hindu monasticism and *baGmata* of Smarta tradition. He introduced the *Pancyatana* form of worship.

Adi Shankara, along with Madhava and Ramanuja, was instrumental in the revival of Hinduism. These three teachers formed the doctrines that are followed by their respective sects even today. They have been the most important figures in the recent history of Hindu philosophy. In their writings and debates, they provided polemics against the non-Vedantic schools of Sankhya, Vaisheshika etc. Thus they paved the way for Vedanta to be the dominant and most widely followed tradition among the schools of Hindu philosophy.

The Vedanta school stresses most on the Upanishads (which are themselves called Vedanta, *End or culmination of the Vedas*), unlike the other schools that gave importance to the ritualistic Brahmanas, or to texts authored by their founders. The Vedanta schools hold that the Vedas, which include the Upanishads, are unauthored, forming a continuous tradition of wisdom transmitted orally. Thus the concept of *apaurusheyatva* ("being unauthored") came to be the guiding force behind the Vedanta schools. However, along with stressing the importance of Vedic tradition, Adi Shankara gave equal importance to the personal experience of the student. Logic, grammar, Mimamsa and allied subjects form main areas of study in all the Vedanta schools.

Regarding meditation, Shankara refuted the system of Yoga and its disciplines as a direct means to attain moksha, rebutting the argument that it can be obtained through concentration of the mind. His position is that the mental states discovered through the practices of Yoga can be indirect aids to the gain of knowledge, but cannot themselves give rise to it. According to his philosophy, knowledge of brahman springs from inquiry into the words of the Upanishads, and the knowledge of brahman that shruti provides cannot be obtained in any other way.

It has to be noted that it is generally considered that for Shankara the Absolute Reality is attributeless and impersonal, while for Madhava and Ramanuja, the Absolute Truth is Vishnu. This has been a subject of debate, interpretation, and controversy since Shankara himself is attributed to composing the popular 8th century Hindu devotional composition Bhaja Govindam (literal meaning, "Worship Govinda").

This work of Adi Shankara is considered as a good summary of Advaita Vedanta and underscores the view that devotion to God, Govinda, is not only an important part of general spirituality, but the concluding verse drives through the message of Shankara: "Worship Govinda, worship Govinda, worship Govinda, Oh fool! Other than chanting the Lord's names, there is no other way to cross the life's ocean". Bhaja Govindam invokes the almighty in the aspect of Vishnu; it is therefore very popular not only with Sri Adi Shankaracharya's immediate followers, the Smarthas, but also with Vaishnavas and others.

Adi Shankara begins his Gurustotram or Verses to the Guru with the following Sanskrit Sloka, that has become a widely sung Bhajan:

Guru Brahma, Guru Vishnu, Guru Deva Maheshwara. Guru Sakshath Parambrahma, Tasmai Shri Gurave Namaha. (tr: *Guru is the creator Brahma, Guru is the preserver Vishnu, Guru is the destroyer Shiva. Guru is directly the supreme spirit — I offer my salutations to this Guru.*)

Samkhya

Sankhya, also Samkhya, is one of the six schools of classical Indian philosophy. Sage Kapila is traditionally considered to be the founder of the Sankhya school, although no historical verification is possible. It is regarded as one of the oldest philosophical systems in India.

Sankhya was one of the six orthodox systems (*astika,* those systems that recognize vedic authority) of Hindu philosophy. The major text of this Vedic school is the extant *Samkhya Karika,* written by Ishvara Krishna, circa 200 AD. This text (in karika 70) identifies Sankhya as a Tantra and its philosophy was one of the main influences both on the rise of the Tantras as a body of literature, as well as Tantra sadhana. There are no purely Sankhya schools existing today in Hinduism, but its influence is felt in the Yoga and Vedanta schools.

Sankhya is an enumerationist philosophy that is strongly dualist. Sankhya philosophy regards the universe as consisting of two realities: Purusha (consciousness) and Prakriti (phenomenal realm of matter). They are the experiencer and the experienced, not unlike the *res cogens* and *res extensa* of Rene Descartes. Prakriti further bifurcates into animate and inanimate realms. On the other hand, Purusha separates out into countless Jivas or individual units of consciousness as souls which fuse into the mind and body of the animate branch of Prakriti.

There are differences between Sankhya and Western forms of dualism. In the West, the fundamental distinction is between mind and body. In Sankhya, however, it is between the self (as Purusha) and matter (Prakriti).

Literature

Sage Kapila is considered as the founder of the Samkhya school, but there is no evidence to prove that the texts attributed to him, the *Sakhyapravacana Sktra* and the *Tattvasamsa* were actually composed by him. The earliest extant text of this school is *SAkhya Krik* of I[varak[cGa (3rd century). I[varak[cGa in his *Krik* described himself as being in the succession of the disciples from Kapila, through *suri and* Pancaikha.

Gauapda wrote a commentary on this *Krik*. The next important work is Vcaspati's *Sakhyatattvakaumudi* (9th century AD). NryaGa's treatise *SAkhyacandrik* is based on the *Krik*. The *Sakhyapravacana Sktra* is assigned to the 14th century, as GuGaratna (14th century) did not refer to this text but referred to the *Krik*. This text consists of 6 chapters and 526 sktras. The most important commentary on the *Sakhyapravacana Sktra* is Vijnnabhikcu's *Sakhyapravacanabhcya* (16th century). Anirruddha's *Kpilas Akhyapravacanasktrav [tti* (15th century) and Mahdeva's *Sakhyapravacanasktravttisra* (c. 1600) and Nge[a's *LaghusAkhyasktrav[tti* are the other important commentaries on this text.

Epistemology

According to the Sankhya school, all knowledge is possible through three *Pramanas* (means of valid knowledge)-

1. Pratyaksha or Drishtam-direct sense perception,
2. Anumana-logical inference and
3. Sabda or Aptavacana-verbal testimony.

Sankhya cites two kinds of perceptions: Indeterminate (*nirvikalpa*) perceptions and determinate (*savikalpa*) perceptions.

Indeterminate perceptions are merely impressions without understanding or knowledge. They reveal no knowledge of the form or the name of the object. There is only external awareness about an object. There is cognition of the object, but no discriminative recognition. For example, a baby's initial experience is full of impression. There is a lot of data from sensory perception, but there is little or no understanding of the inputs. Hence they can be neither differentiated nor labeled. Most of them are indeterminate perceptions.

Determinate perceptions are the mature state of perceptions which have been processed and differentiated appropriately. Once the sensations have been processed, categorized, and interpreted properly, they become determinate perceptions. They can lead to identification and also generate knowledge.

Metaphysics

Ontology

Broadly, the Samkhya system classifies all objects as falling into one of the two categories: Purusha and Prakriti. Metaphysically, Samkhya maintains an intermingled duality between spirit/ consciousness (*Purusha*) and matter (*Prakrti*).

Purusha

Purusha is the Transcendental Self or Pure Consciousness. It is absolute, independent, free, imperceptible, unknowable, above any experience and beyond any words or explanation. It remains pure, "nonattributive consciousness ". Purusha is neither produced nor does it produce. Unlike Advaita Vedanta and like Purva-Mimamsa, Samkhya believes in plurality of the *Purusha*s.

Prakriti

Prakriti is the first cause of the universe—of everything except the *Purusha,* which is uncaused, and accounts for whatever is physical, both matter and force. Since it is the first principle (*tattva*) of the universe, it is called the *Pradhana,* but, as it is the unconscious and unintelligent principle, it is also called the *Jada.* It is composed of three essential characteristics (*trigunas*).

These are:

- sattva-fineness, lightness, illumination, and joy;

- rajas-activity, excitation, and pain;
- tamas-coarseness, heavyness, obstruction, and sloth.

All physical events are considered to be manifestations of the evolution of *Prakriti,* or primal nature (from which all physical bodies are derived). Each sentient being is a *Purusha,* and is limitless and unrestricted by its physical body. *Samsaara* or bondage arises when the *Purusha* does not have the discriminate knowledge and so is misled as to its own identity, confusing itself with the physical body, which is actually an evolute of *Prakriti.* The spirit is liberated when the discriminate knowledge of the difference between conscious Purusha and unconscious Prakriti is realized.

Ishvara (Creationist God)

The *Sakhyapravacana Sktra* states that there is no philosophical place for a creationist God in this system.

It is also argued in this text that the existence of Ishvara cannot be proved and hence cannot be admitted to exist and an unchanging Ishvara as the cause cannot be the source of a changing world as the effect.

Almost all modern scholars are of view that the concept of Ishvara was incorporated into the *nirishvara* (atheistic) Samkhya viewpoint only after it became associated with the Yoga, the Pasupata and the Bhagavata schools of philosophy. This theistic Samkhya philosophy is described in the Mahabharata, the Puranas and the Bhagavad Gita

Nature of Duality

The Samkhya recognizes only two ultimate entities, *Prakriti* and *Purusha.* While the *Prakriti* is a single entity, the Samkhya admits a plurality of the *Purushas.* Unintelligent, unmanifest, uncaused, ever-active, imperceptible and eternal Prakriti is alone the final source of the world of objects which is implicitly and potentially contained in its bosom.

The *Purusha* is considered as the intelligent principle, a passive enjoyer (*bhokta*) and the *Prakriti* is the enjoyed (*bhogya*). Samkhya believes that the *Purusha* cannot be regarded as the source of inanimate world, because an intelligent principle cannot transform itself into the unintelligent world. It is a pluralistic spiritualism, atheistic realism and uncompromising dualism.

Theory of Existence

The Sankhya system is based on Satkaryavada. According to Satkaryavada, the effect pre-exists in the cause. Cause and effect are seen as different temporal aspects of the same thing-the effect lies latent in the cause which in turn seeds the next effect.

More specifically, Sankhya system follows the *Prakriti-Parinama Vada. Parinama* denotes that the effect is a real transformation of the cause. The cause under consideration here is Prakriti or more precisely Mula-Prakriti (Primordial Matter). The Sankhya system is therefore an exponent of an evolutionary theory of matter beginning with primordial matter. In evolution, Prakriti is transformed and differentiated into multiplicity of objects. Evolution is followed by dissolution. In dissolution the physical existence, all the worldly objects mingle back into Prakriti, which now remains as the undifferentiated, primordial substance. This is how the cycles of evolution and dissolution follow each other.

The Twentyfour Principles

Sankhya theorizes that Prakriti is the source of the world of becoming. It is pure potentiality that evolves itself successively into twenty four tattvas or principles. The evolution itself is possible because *Prakriti* is always in a state of tension among its constituent strands-

- *Sattva*-a template of balance or equilibrium;
- *Rajas*-a template of expansion or activity;
- *Tamas*-a template of inertia or resistance to action.

All macrocosmic and microcosmic creation uses these templates. The twenty four principles that evolve are-

- *Prakriti*-The most subtle potentiality that is behind whatever is created in the physical universe, also called "primordial Matter". It is also a state of equilibrium amongst the Three Gunas.
- *Mahat*-first product of evolution from Prakriti, pure potentiality. *Mahat* is also considered to be the principle responsible for the rise of *buddhi* or intelligence in living beings.
- *Ahamkara* or ego-sense-second product of evolution. It is responsible for the self-sense in living beings. It is also one's identification with the outer world and its content.

- "Panch Tanmatras" are a simultaneous product from Mahat Tattva, along with the Ahamkara. They are the subtle form of Panch Mahabhutas which result from grossification or Panchikaran of the Tanmatras. Each of these Tanmatras are made of all three Gunas.
- *Manas* or "Antahkaran" evolves from the total sum of the *sattva* aspect of *Panch Tanmatras* or the "Ahamkara"
- *Panch jnana indriyas* or five sense organs-also evolves from the *sattva* aspect of *Ahamkara.*
- *Pancha karma indriya* or five organs of action-The organs of action are hands, legs, vocal apparatus, urino-genital organ and anus. They evolve from the *rajas* aspect of *Ahamkara.*
- *Pancha mahabhuta* or five great substances-ether, air, fire, water and earth. They evolve from the "tamas" aspect of the "Ahamkara". This is the revealed aspect of the physical universe.

The evolution of primal nature is also considered to be purposeful-Prakrti evolves *for* the spirit in bondage. The spirit who is always free is only a witness to the evolution, even though due to the absence of discriminate knowledge, he misidentifies himself with it.

The evolution obeys causality relationships, with primal Nature itself being the material cause of all physical creation. The cause and effect theory of Sankhya is called *Satkaarya-vaada* (theory of existent causes), and holds that nothing can really be created from or destroyed into nothingness-all evolution is simply the transformation of primal Nature from one form to another.

The evolution of matter occurs when the relative strengths of the attributes change. The evolution ceases when the spirit realizes that it is distinct from primal Nature and thus cannot evolve. This destroys the purpose of evolution, thus stopping Prakrti from evolving for Purusha.

Sankhyan cosmology describes how life emerges in the universe; the relationship between Purusha and Prakriti is crucial to Patanjali's yoga system. The evolution of forms at the basis of Sankhya is quite remarkable. The strands of Sankhyan thought can be traced back to the Vedic speculation of creation. It is also frequently mentioned in the Mahabharata and Yogavasishta.

Moksha

Like other major systems of Indian philosophy, Sankhya regards ignorance as the root cause of bondage and suffering (*Samsara*). According to Sankhya, the Purusha is eternal, pure consciousness. Due to ignorance, it identifies itself with the physical body and its constituents-Manas, Ahamkara and Mahat, which are products of Prakriti. Once it becomes free of this false identification and the material bonds, Moksha ensues. Other forms of Sankhya teach that Moksha is attained by one's own development of the higher faculties of discrimination achieved by meditation and other yogic practices as prescribed through the Hindu Vedas.

Views of what happens to the soul after liberation vary tremendously, as the Sankhya view is used by many different Hindu sects and is rarely practiced alone.

Carvaka

Crvka is a system of Indian philosophy that assumes various forms of philosophical skepticism and religious indifference. It is also known as Lokyata. It is named after its founder, Crvka, author of the Brhaspatya-sktras.

In overviews of Indian philosophy, Carvaka is classified as a "heterodox" (*nastika*) system, the same classification as is given to Buddhism and Jainism. It is characterized as a materialistic and atheistic school of thought. While this branch of Indian philosophy is not considered to be part of the six orthodox schools of Hindu philosophy, it is noteworthy as evidence of a materialistic movement within Hinduism.

Name and Origins

The name Lokyata can be traced to Kautilya's *Arthashastra*, which refers to three *nvikcikis* (logical philosophies), Yoga, Samkhya and Lokayata. Lokayata here still refers to logical debate (*disputatio*, "criticism") in general and not to a materialist doctrine in particular. Similarly, Saddaniti and Buddhaghosa in the 5th century connect the "Lokayatas" with the Vitandas (sophists).

Only from about the 6th century is the term restricted to the school of the *Lokytikas*. The name *Crvka* is first used in the 7th century by the philosopher Purandara, who refers to his fellow materialists as "the Carvakas", and it is used by the 8th century philosophers Kamalalila and Haribhadra. Shankara, on the other hand, always uses *Lokyata,* not *Crvka.* The etymological meaning of the word *Crvka* is 'a person who is clever in speech and is extremely fond of wrangling (debate)'.

E. W. Hopkins, in his *The Ethics of India* (1924) assumes that Carvaka philosophy is co-eval with Buddhism, mentioning "the old Carvaka or materialist of the 6th century BC"; Rhys Davids assumes that *lokayata* in ca. 500 BC came to mean "scepticism" in general without yet being organized as a philosophical school, and that the name of a villain of the Mahabharata, *Carvaka,* was attached to the position in order to disparage it. The earliest positive statement of skepticism is preserved from the epic period, in the *Ramayana.*

The Carvaka school thus appears to have gradually grown out of generic skepticism in the Mauryan period, but its existence as an organized body cannot be ascertained for times predating the 6th century. The Barhaspatya sutras were likely also composed in Mauryan times, predating 150 BC, based on a reference in the Mahabhasya of Patanjali (7.3.45).

Loss of Original Works

Chatterjee and Datta explain that our understanding of Carvaka philosophy is fragmentary, based largely on criticism of the ideas by other schools, and that it is not a living tradition:

"Though materialism in some form or other has always been present in India, and occasional references are found in the Vedas, the Buddhistic literature, the Epics, as well as in the later philosophical works we do not find any systematic work on materialism, nor any organised school of followers as the other philosophical schools possess. But almost every work of the other schools states, for refutation, the materialistic views. Our knowledge of Indian materialism is chiefly based on these."

Available evidence suggests that Carvaka philosophy was set out in the *Barhaspatya sutras,* probably in Mauryan times. Neither this text nor any other original text of the Carvaka school of philosophy has been preserved. Its principal works are known only from fragments cited by its Hindu and Buddhist opponents. Carvaka philosophy appears to have died out some time in the 15th century.

Countering the argument that the Carvakas opposed all that was good in the Vedic tradition, Dale Riepe says, "It may be said from the available material that Carvakas hold truth, integrity, consistency, and freedom of thought in the highest esteem."

Tattvopaplavasimha of Jayaraasi Bhatta

The *Tattvopaplavasimha* of Jayarashi Bhatta (ca. 8th century) is often cited as the only extant authentic Carvaka text, but which also shows Madhyamaka influence. It is, in any case, among the most important documents for the study of the Carvaka school.

Beliefs

The Carvaka school of philosophy had a variety of atheistic and naturalistic beliefs.

No Life after Death

The Carvaka believed there was no afterlife, no life after death

Springing forth from these elements itself solid knowledge is destroyed when they are destroyed— after death no intelligence remains.

Naturalism

The Carvaka believed in a form of naturalism, that is that all things happen by nature, and come from nature (not from any deity or Supreme Being). Fire is hot, water cold, refreshingly cool is the breeze of morning; By whom came this variety?

They were born of their own nature.

Sensual Indulgence

Unlike many of the Indian philosophies of the time, The Carvaka believed there was nothing wrong with sensual indulgence, and that it was the only enjoyment to be pursued.

That the pleasure arising to man from contact with sensible objects, is to be relinquished because accompanied by pain— such is the reasoning of fools.

The kernels of the paddy, rich with finest white grains, What man, seeking his own true interest, would fling them away because of a covering of husk and dust? While life remains, let a man live happily, let him feed on butter though he runs in debt; When once the body becomes ashes, how can it ever return again?

Religion is Invented by Man

The Carvaka believed that religion was invented and made up by men.

The three authors of the Vedas were buffoons, knaves, and demons.

All the well-known formulae of the pandits, jarphari, turphari, etc. and all the obscene rites for the queen commanded in Aswamedha, these were invented by buffoons, and so all the various kinds of presents to the priests, while the eating of flesh was similarly commanded by night-prowling demons.

Madhavacharya and Carvaka

Madhavacharya, the 13th & 14th-century Vedantic philosopher from South India starts his famous work *The Sarva-darsana-sangraha* with a chapter on the Carvaka system with the intention of refuting it. After invoking, in the Prologue of the book, the Hindu gods Shiva and Vishnu, ("by whom the earth and rest were produced"), Madhavacharya asks, in the first chapter:

But how can we attribute to the Divine Being the giving of supreme felicity, when such a notion has been utterly abolished by Charvaka, the crest-gem of the atheistic school, the follower of the doctrine of Brihaspati? The efforts of Charvaka are indeed hard to be eradicated, for the majority of living beings hold by the current refrain:

While life is yours, live joyously;

None can escape Death's searching eye:

When once this frame of ours they burn,

How shall it e'er again return?

Quotations Attributed to Carvaka from Sarva-Darsana-Sangraha

The Agnihotra, the three Vedas, the ascetic's three staves, and smearing oneself with ashes — Brihaspati says, these are but means of livelihood for those who have no manliness nor sense.

In this school there are four elements, earth, water, fire and air; and from these four elements alone is intelligence produced— just like the intoxicating power from kinwa &c, mixed together; since in "I am fat", "I am lean", these attributes abide in the same subject, and since fatness, &c, reside only in the body, it alone is the soul and no other, and such phrases as "my body" are only significant metaphorically.

If a beast slain in the Jyothishtoma rite will itself go to heaven, why then does not the sacrificer forthwith offer his own father?

If the Sraddha produces gratification to beings who are dead, then why not give food down below to those who are standing on the house-top?

If he who departs from the body goes to another world, how is it that he come not back again, restless for love of his kindred?

Hence it is only as a means of livelihood that Brahmans have established here all these ceremonies for the dead, — there is no other fruit anywhere.

The three authors of the Vedas were buffoons, knaves, and demons.

All the well-known formulae of the pandits, jarphari, turphari, etc. and all the obscene rites for the queen commanded in Aswamedha, these were invented by buffoons, and so all the various kinds of presents to the priests, while the eating of flesh was similarly commanded by night-prowling demons.

Those parts which survive indicate a strong anti-clerical bias, accusing Brahmins of fostering religious beliefs only so they could obtain a livelihood. The proper aim of a Charvakan or Charvaka, according to these sources, was to live a prosperous, happy, and productive life in this world.

Astika Schools, Buddhism, and Jainism Versus Carvaka

Carvakas cultivated a philosophy wherein theology and what they called "speculative metaphysics" were to be avoided. The Carvakas accepted direct perception as the surest method to prove the truth of anything. Though their opponents tried to caricature the Lokayatikas' arguments, the latter did not completely reject the method of inference. Debiprasad Chattopadhyaya quotes S. N. Dasgupta:

"Purandara (a Lokâyata philosopher) [...] admits the usefulness of inference in determining the nature of all worldly things where perceptual experience is available; but inference cannot be employed for establishing any dogma regarding the transcendental world, or life after death or the law of karma which cannot be available to ordinary perceptual experience." While a Carvaka's thought is characterized by an insistence on joyful living on one hand and Jainism is known to emphasize penance on the other, Buddhism is said to stand for a "middle way", avoiding indulgence in sensual pleasures and penance alike. Temperance-the enjoyment of life's pleasures in a moderate manner, rather than total abstinence-was the Carvakas' primary *modus operandi*. In this respect, they much resemble the Epicureans of Greece.

The Carvakas did not deny the difference between the dead and the living and recognized both as realities. A person lives, the same person dies: that is a perceived, and hence the only provable, fact. In this regard, the Carvakas found themselves at odds with all the other religions of the time. Of the five fundamental elements, the *Panchamahaabhutas*, Prithvi (earth or solidity), *jal* (water or liquidity), *agni* (fire or fieriness or brightness), *vaayu* (wind or movement), and *aakaasha* (lit.space-aether or emptiness), the Carvakas recognised the validity of only the first four and thought that a combination of these four elements produced a certain vitality called life.

Rejection of the soul as separate from the body led the Carvakas to confine their thinking to this world only. This does not mean that they denied the cause-effect relationship. They accepted the "like causes like result" (*Karmavipaaka*) rule, restricted it to this life and this world and admitted exceptions to that rule.

Whereas most systems of Astika philosophy advocated a caste system, the Carvakas denounced the caste system, calling it artificial, unreal and hence unacceptable. "What is this senseless humbug about the castes and the high and low among them when the organs like the mouth, etc in the human body are the same?"

2

Taittiriya Upanishad

The *Taittiriya* Upanishad is one of the older, "primary" Upanishads commented upon by Shankara. It is associated with the *Taittiriya* school of the Yajurveda. It figures as number 7 in the Muktika canon of 108 Upanishads. It belongs to the Taittiriya recension of the Yajurveda and is constituted by the eighth and ninth chapters of Taittiriya Aranyaka. The tenth chapter of the same Aranyaka is the Mahanarayana Upanishad.

The Taittiriya Upanishad describes the various degrees of happiness enjoyed by the different beings in creation.

The Taittiriya Upanishad is divided into three sections or *vallis*, the *Siksha Valli*, the *Brahmananda Valli* and the *Bhrigu Valli*. Each Valli further subdivided into *anuvakas* or verses.

Shiksha Valli

The Siksha Valli deals with the discipline of Shiksha (which is the first of the six Vedangas or "limbs" or auxiliaries of the Vedas), that is, the study of phonetics and pronunciation.

1. First Anuvaka of this Valli starts with Shanti Mantra "OM Sham no Mitra..".
2. Second Anuvaka lists the contents of Shiksha discipline.
3. Third Anuvaka tells about the intimate connection between the syllables using five examples and implicitly tells that one should meditate on those examples to realise connections told in them. Each of these examples are called a Maha Samhita. Each Syllable is called a Samhita. There is also a method of reciting Vedic Mantras where each syllable of mantra is recited separately of preceding

and next syllables known as "*Samhita Patha*". This anuvak also declares that one who realises connection between syllables, will get good fruits including heaven. One of the example used under the heading of *Self* or *Adhyaatmaa* tries to make point that the connection between syllables is as intimate and innate as speech and elements producing it. "*Lower jaw is former form (or first syllable), upper jaw is next form (next syllable), speech is union or connection, tongue is connector*"

4. Fourth Anuvaka consists of Mantras and rituals to be done by those who aspire for Divine Knowledge (Medha Kama) and Wealth (Shree Kama). In this anuvak teacher prays that "*As water flows from high land to low land, as months join to become year, let good disciples come to me from everywhere*"
5. Fifth and Sixth Anuvakas try to describe Brahman in the form of Vyahrutis. The words "Bhooh", "Bhuvah", "Suvah", "Mahah", "Janah", "Tapah" and "Satyam" arecalled seven Vyahruti's or Sapta Vyahrutis. These denote different worlds in Puranas. The term "Vyahruti" means pronunciation, since these above mentioned words are pronounced in Vedic rituals like Agnihotra, these are called Vyahruti's. Fifth Anuvaka states that the fourth Vyahruti "Mahah" was discovered by a Rishi called "*Mahachamasya*" and "Mahah" is Brahman all other Vyahrutis are its organs. This Anuvak says that "Bhooh" denotes earth, fire, Richa's and Prana. "Bhuvah" denotes space, air, Sama's and Apana. "Suvah" denotes heaven, sun, Yajus and Vyana. "Mahah" denotes sun, moon, Holy Syllable OM and food. This way, each of first four Vyahrutis become four each and in total they are 16. So all these four Vyahrutis should be meditated as all of their sixteen manifestations, this is known as famous vedic term Shodasha Kala Purusha in vedic literature. Finally this anuvak says that one who knows all sixteen manifestations of Vyahrutis knows Brahman and all gods bring gifts to him.
6. Sixth Anuvaka tells that in the space inside the heart there exists an immortal golden being (Hiranmaya Purusha) and states that there is a subtle route through the middle of the head through which a self realized Yogi travels

when he/she leaves the body and joins the all pervading Brahman.

7. The Seventh Anuvaka describes a meditation called Paanktha Upasana, where Brahman is meditated upon as a Set Of Five called Paanktha. There is also a vedic meter of five lines called Paanktha. Outer world seen is classified into 3 set of five things called "*AdiBootha*" and also inner body world into 3 sets of five things called "*Adhyaathma*". This inner-outer grouping is then meditated upon and meditator realizes both inner and outer paankta are one and the same Brahman and every thing is Paanktha. This Anuvak states that Earth (Prithvi), Space (Antariksha), Heaven (Devloka), Directions (North, South etc), Subdirections (South-East, North-West etc..) (Worldly set of Five or Loka-Paankta) and Fire (Agni), Air (Vayu), Sun (Aditya), Moon (Chandra), Stars (Nakshatra) (Divine-Five or Deva-Paanktha) and Water, Herbs (Oshadhi), Trees, Sky (Akasha), Body of meditator (Elemental Five or Dhaatu-Paanktha) are called Adibhuta or Outer Elements further it states that Prana, Vyana, Apana, Udana, Samana (all these are Five inner pranas of the body) and Eye, Ear, Mind, Speech (Vaak), Outer-Skin (Tvak) (Sensory-Five or Indriya-Paanktha) and Inner-Skin (Charma), Flesh, tendon-Ligaments, bones, Fat or Bone-Marrow (Elemental Five or Dhaatu Paanktha) are called Adhyaatma or Inner Elements. The Rishi who realized oneness among these says "Thus everything is Paankta". It further says that one who realized everything as Paanktha, completes Paanktha with Paanktha itself.
8. Eighth Anuvaka states the greatness of Holy Syllable OM. It says that OM is Brahman and everything.
9. Ninth Anuvaka explains a pious way of life to be lead by persons aspiring realization of Brahman.
10. Tenth Anuvaka is a Mantra for self practice (Swadhyaya) or meditation. It is stated by a Rishi called Trishanku as an exclamation of awe after he realized that he is one with Brahman. It is also called *Mantramnaya* of Trishanku.
11. Eleventh Anuvaka is a set of instructions that teacher (Acharya) gives to his disciple after completion of vedic

education. The ninth and eleventh Anuvaks collectively define a prescription for an ideal life.

12. Twelfth Anuvaka concludes the Shikshavalli with Shanti Mantra *"OM Sham no mitra"* expressing gratitude toward gods who removed obstacles for study of Upanishad as prayed for in first anuvak of this Valli.

Brahmananda Valli

The statement "Brahmavida Apnoti Param" which means "The one who knows Brahman attains supreme state" is the formula (Sutra-Vaakya) to get the high level gist of this Valli. First Anuvak starts with Shanti Mantra "OM sham no mitra" and "Sahana vavatu" pleasing gods and removing obstacles for study of Upanishad being the objective of these Mantras. Second Anuvak starts with formula sentence "Brahmavida Apnoti Param" as stated above and also tries to define Brahman succinctly as "Truth, Omniscient, and Infinite" (Satyam Jnyanam Anantam Brahma).

Anuvaks Second to Fifth describe that Five sheaths subtle bodies or (Five Atmans) reside in one another in human body. Starting with grosser, tangible human body called "Annamaya" or "Formed out of Food" to "Pranamaya" or "formed out of Vital life force" to "Manomaya" or "Formed out of Mind" to "Vijnyanamaya" or "One who is of Knowledge" to Final and subtle most being "Anandamaya" or one who is full of Joy.

In Sixth and Seventh Anuvaks, some of the questions asked by a disciple are answered such as;

"Brahman being equal to both knower and ignorant, who gets the Brahman after death, knower or ignorant and why?"

Eighth Anuvak, compares happiness of various evolved beings starting from Man to that of next higher level till Happiness of Brahman itself.

Ninth Anuvak describes that knower of Brahman doesn't repent for not having done any good because for him/her, the terms good and bad loses their meaning and he/she has equalled them with Brahman since it is the only one which is really existing.

Bhr.gu Valli

This Valli describes how son of Varuna (The Water God) Bhr.gu obtained realization of Brahman through repeated Tapas under his fathers guidance. Rest of the part of Valli describes greatness of donating food, that is feeding the hungry. It also emphasises on greatness of Food. It says that since food is support of all life, food should not be insulted, food should not be declined.

Prescriptions

The ninth and eleventh anuvakas of *Shiksha Valli* prescribe a moral or religious way of life which a person aspiring for self realization or divine knowledge follow. Ninth Anuvak emphaises heavily on learning, studying and teaching (Swadhyaya and Pravachana) and ordains that this should be done althrough the life of an individual. Accoding to this anuvaka, the following are the duties to be performed.

Observing truth always, observing perseverance, controlling indulgence in sensory organs or sensory pleasures (Shama), controlling external flow of mind (Dama), performing mandated vedic rituals like Agnihotra etc, hospitality to guests, facing worldly odds and pleasures with even mind, procreation and begetting children and grand children (family life emphasised). Further this verse says, According to truthful *Raathithara,* he says, truth must be observed as priority. According to great penance performer *Paurushishti,* perseverance/penance (*Tapas*) should be observed. According to *Naka the son of Mudgala,* studying/learning-teaching of Vedas (*Swadhyaya and Pravachana*) should be observed.

So there seems to be three teachers emphasizing on one of the aspects of ideals of pious life. This part of the verse lead some scholars think that there was a difference of opinions on way of life leading to divine knowledge/realization at time of composition of this Upanishad. All through this anuvak, emphasis is laid on continuous study, learning and teaching of Vedas to students. This is termed as Swadhyaya and Pravachana.

Eleventh Anuvak is a set of instructions that teacher (Acharya) gives to his disciple after the completion of vedic education and the disciple is about to start a household life. In this anuvak we find famous saying "*Matrdevo bhava*" which emphasizes on reverence to ones mother, father, teacher and guests. Here teacher ordains disciple as follows.

Tell truth always, observe Dharma or (eternal divine laws), continue progeny, never leave truth, never leave Dharma, never abandon care of your health, never abstain from good rituals ordained in scriptures, never leave study/learning and teaching, never abandon worshipping gods (Deva's) and revering ancestors (Pitru's). Treat mother as a God. Treat father as a God. Treat your teacher as a God. Treat guests as Gods. Those deeds, rituals that are good and lauded by people should be done have reverence for great men, sages and wise ones.

Engage in charity work with diligence, donate according to your wealth, donate with faith, donate with humility. Donate with friendliness (not belittling the receiver) in case of any doubts about performing these duties follow as do the selfless, kindhearted sages do. Finally to emphasize that these duties to be performed with greater importance and due care, this verse says that, *This is divine ordain and divine commandment*. Form the gist of these two Anuvaks, one can guess what kind of life a house holder, aspiring divine knowledge tried to lead at the time of this Upanishad.

Film

In 1983 a film directed by G. V. Iyer named *Adi Shankaracharya* was premiered, the first film ever made entirely in Sanskrit language in which all of Adi Shankaracharya's works were compiled.

Chandrashekarendra Saraswati

Jagadguru Chandrashekarendra Saraswati Swamigal (May 20, 1894–January 8, 1994) or the Sage of Kanchi was the 68th Jagadguru in the Kanchi Kamakoti Peetam. He is usually referred to as Paramacharya or MahaSwami or Maha Periyavaal.

Early Life

Maha Periyavaal was born on 20 May 1894, under Anuradha star according to the Hindu calendar, into a Kannadiga Smartha Hoysala Karnataka Brahmin family in Viluppuram, South Arcot District, Tamil Nadu as Swaminatha. He was the second son of Subramanya Sastri, a District Education Officer. The child was named Swaminatha, after the family deity, Lord Swaminatha of Swamimalai, near Kumbakonam.

Swaminatha began his early education at the Arcot American Mission High School at Tindivanam, where his father was working. He was an exceptional student and excelled in several subjects. He won a prize for his proficiency in the recitation of the "Holy Bible". In 1905, his parents performed his Upanayanam, a Vedic ceremony which qualifies a Brahmin boy to begin his Vedic studies under an accomplished teacher.

Incidents Leading to Sainthood

During the childhood of the Acharya, his father consulted an astrologer who, upon studying the boy's horoscope, is said to have been so stunned that he prostrated himself before the boy exclaiming that *"One day the whole world will fall at his feet."* In 1906, the 66th Acharya of Sri Kanchi Kamakoti Peetham performed the annual *Chaturmasyam* (a forty-day annual ritual performed by Hindu ascetics while remaining in one place), in a village near Tindivanam in Tamil Nadu. This was Swaminathan's first exposure to the Math and its Acharya. Later, Swaminathan accompanied his father whenever he visited the Math where the Acharya was deeply impressed by the young boy.

In the first week of February 1907, the Kanchi Kamakoti Math had informed Subramanya Sastrigal that Swaminathan's first cousin (son of his mother's sister) was to be installed as the 67th Peetathipathi. The presiding Acharya was then suffering from smallpox and had the premonition that he might not live long. He had, therefore, administered *upadesa* to his disciple Lakshminathan before he died. Sastrigal being away in Trichinopoly on duty arranged for the departure of Swaminathan with his mother to Kanchipuram. The boy and his mother started for Kalavai (where Lakshminathan was camping) to console his aunt who, while also being a widow, had just given up her only son to be an ascetic. They travelled by train to Kanchipuram and halted at the Sankara Math. By then, Lakshminathan had fallen ill:

I had a bath at the Kumara Koshta Tirtha. A carriage of the Math had come there from Kalavai with the people to buy articles for the Maha Puja on the tenth day of the passing of the previous 66th Acharya. One of them, a hereditary maistry (mason) of the Math, asked me to accompany him. A separate cart was engaged for the rest of the family to follow me. During the journey the maistry hinted to me that I might not return home and that the rest of my life might be spent in the Math itself. At first I thought that my elder cousin having become the Head of the Math, it was his wish that I should live with him. But the maistry gradually clarified matters as the cart rolled on. The acharya had fever which developed into delirium and that was why I was being separated from the family to be taken to Kalavai... I was stunned by this unexpected turn of events. I lay in a kneeling posture in the cart, shocked as I was, repeating "Rama... Rama," the only prayer I knew. My mother and other children came some time later only to find that instead of her mission of consoling her sister, she herself was placed in the state of having to be consoled—T.M.P. Mahadevan, *The Sage of Kanchi.*

The 67th Acharya also died, after reigning for a brief seven days as the head of the Math. Swaminathan was immediately installed as the 68th head of the Kanchi Kamakoti Peetam on February 13, 1907, the second day of the Tamil month of Masi, Prabhava year. He was given Sanyasa Asramam at the early age of 13 and was named Chandrasekharendra Saraswati. On May 9, 1907 his "Pattabishegam" as the 68th Peetathipathi of Kanchi Kamakoti Peetam was performed at the Kumbakonam Math. Devotees including Shivaji Maharaja of Tanjavur, government officials and pundits participated in the event.

Even though there was not enough property in the mutt to be administered, the court considering the benefit of the mutt, ordered the mutt to be administered under the "Guardian and Wards Act". Sri C.H. Venkataramana Iyer, an illustrious personality from Kolinjivadi (Colinjivadi) village near Coimbatore was appointed as guardian by the court. The administration of the mutt was under guardianship from 1911 to May,1915. On the day of Sankara Jayanthi in the year 1915, Swamigal took over the administration of the mutt on the completion of his 21 st year.

The administration of the mutt was taken over in name, but the actual work was taken care of by an agent, one Sri Pasupathi Iyer. He was an able administrator who volunteered to do the job without compensation and hailed from Thirupathiripuliyur. Sri Swamigal does not sign any document, instead Sri Mukham stamp is placed on documents.

Maha Periyavaal spent several years in the study of the scriptures and dharma Shastras and acquainted himself with his role as the Head of the Math. He soon gained the reverence and respect of the devotees and people around him. To millions of devotees he was simply "Periyava"—the revered one or Maha-Periyava. "Periyava" in Tamil means a great person, and conveys endearment, reverence, and devotion. "Mahaswami" and "Paramacharya" are his other well-known appellations.

Maha Periyavaal was the head of the Mutt for eighty-seven years. During this period, the Sri Kanchi Kamakoti Peetam acquired new strength as an institution that propagated Uankara's teachings. The devotion, fervour, and intensity with which the Paramacharya practiced what Uankara had taught are considered to be unparalleled by his devotees. Throughout his life, the focus of his concern and activities was rejuvenating Veda adhyayana, the Dharma Sasthras, and the age-old tradition, which had suffered decline. "Veda rakshanam" was his very life breath, and he referred to this in most of his talks.

Remaining active throughout his life, the sage of Kanchi twice undertook pilgrimages on foot from Rameshwaram in the far south of the Indian peninsula to Benares in the North.

Providing support through Veda Patashalas (schools teaching Vedic lore) through the Veda Rakshana Nidhi which he founded and honouring Vedic scholars, he reinvigorated Vedic studies in India. He organised regular sadhas ('conferences') which included discussions on arts and culture—these led to a renewed interest in Vedic religion, Dharma sasthras, and the Sanskrit language. His long tenure as Pitadhipathi is considered by many to have been the Golden Era of the Kanchi Kamakoti Peetham. He attained Mukti (died) on January 8, 1994 and was succeeded by Jayendra Saraswati Swamigal.

Spiritual Leadership

Periyava stressed the importance of a Guru in one's life. He repeatedly preached about the importance of following the Dharmic path. His various discourses are available in a volume of books called 'Deivathin Kural' (Voice of the Divine) which have been compiled by R. Ganapathi, a devotee of Periyava. These books are available both in Tamil and English. A condensed form of these books is also available in English. These are available in any branch of the Kanchi math.

Periyava and the Indian Freedom Movement

Though Periyavaa did not get directly into politics, he was interested in the happenings. At Nellichery in Palakkad (Present Day Kerala), Rajaji and Mahatma Gandhi met the Acharya in a cow shed. It was a practice in the mutt to wear silk clothes. But Acharya was the first one to do away with them and shifted to

Khadi robes at Rameshwaram. He requested his devotees to do away with foreign/non natural clothes some time earlier at Trichy. The day India became free, he gave the Maithreem Bhajata song, which was later to be sung at the UN by M S Subbulakshmi. He gave a speech on the significance of the flag and the Dharma chakra in it on that day.

Devotees

Periyava's charm invited the rich and the poor, the old and the young alike to be his devotees. Some of his famous devotees include, their highness the King and Queen of Nepal, the Queen Mother of Greece, the Dalai Lama, M. S. Subbulakshmi, Indira Gandhi, R. Venkatraman and Atal Bihari Vajpayee among others. To the Acharya, the VIPs and the common man were one and the same. There were thousands of personal experiences to lakhs of his devotees, who still revere him, and pray to him as a messenger of the Supreme or an ultimate Guru.

Kanchi Matha

The Kanchi matha is a Hindu monastic institution located in Kanchipuram, Tamil Nadu, one of the five *pancha-bhUta-sthalas* (five "material" sites). It is known formally as *Shri Kanchi* Kamakoti Peetham. *The head of the matha is referred to as a "Shankaracharya", a title* that is also applied to the heads of the four Shankara mathas.

The Kanchi matha has been gaining prominence since the 18th century, when it was at Kumbakonam. Some accounts claim that it was founded there as a branch of the Sringeri matha, and branched out afterwards. Today it is one of the most important religious institutions of South India.

History

The matha's official history states that it was founded by Adi Shankara of Kaladi, and that Jayendra Saraswati is its 69th head in succession, tracing its history back to the fifth century BCE.

Other, historical accounts state that the matha was established more recently (probably in the 18th century) in Kumbakonam, as a branch of the Sringeri-Matha, and that it later declared itself independent. The heads of a matha in Kumbhakonam acquired control of the Kamakshi temple in Kanchipuram and moved their establishment to that city, between the years 1842 and 1863. This marks the origin of the Kanchi matha. The Kanchi Matha claims to have been moved from Kanchipuram to Kumbakonam during the 18th century when Hyder Ali invaded the region. It is also claimed that archeological evidence in the form of stone architecture depicting the Shankaracharya and the epigraphy by the side situated in various temples in Kanchipuram indicate the 2500 year age of the Matha.

The Matha's published materials also claim that the present structure at Sannidhi Koil Street at Kanchipuram has been established there centuries before, which claim is however contradicted.

The Kamokoti Peetam however, traditionally refers to Sri Kamakshi referred popularly as Kamakodi. 'Kamakodi' is of Tamil origin, referring to Goddess Durga. 'Kodi' refers to Durga in the ancient Tamil Sangam literature. Kanchipuram is referred to as Kachi. The Vyakarana Mahabhashya of Patanjali uses the word 'Kanchi' and it can be thus understood that the word Kanchi also has a Sanksrit base. However, KamakOti is a latter Sanksrit form taken from the original Tamil form of Kamakodi. Tamil literature also refers to Kamakodi as Kamakanni.

The Original Kamakoti Peetam, in which Sri Adi Shankara established the Sri Chakra Yantra during the latter period of 8th century and the beginning of the 9th century' is at present known as "Adi Peeteshwari Ambal' and this temple is near the present famous shrine of Kamakshi. The form of the deity here is with *ankusa, pasa, abhaya and a kaphala*respectively in each of the 4 hands. This matches precisely with Girvanendra Saraswath's *Prapancha Sara Sara Sangraha.*

It is noteworthy that the Sri Chakra in the present day Kamakshi Amman temple was installed by one Nrusimha Advari during the 16th century, which is evidenced by a stone inscription in the vicinity. The Present day Kamakshi was originally a Budhist temple, and the present Kamakshi was perhaps Tara Devi. The process of conversion of the present temple from a Budhist temple into the Hindu Pantheology was complete perhaps by the 12th Century AD.

Thiruthondar Puranam of Sekkilar Perumal written during the 12th Century mentions the old & original Kamakoti Peeta as Kamakottam. It also mentions about the new shrine which is the present day kamakoti Peetam. Arunagiri Nadar also refers only to the Original Adi Peeteswari with four hands as described above. He mentions that she is *kumaran's mother* and that she resides very near to *Kumarakottam* It should be noted that the Original Kamakoti temple is just adjacent to Kumarakottam. Arunagirinathar has obviously taken no notice of the present day Kamakshi temple.

In recent years the institution of Shankaracharya at the matha has come under increased stress. In 1983, when Jayendra Saraswati was already junior Acharya, the widely revered and popular Chandrasekharendra Saraswati appointed 13-year-old Vijayendra Saraswati as Shankaracharya as well, possibly owing to his differences with Jayendra. "Three Shankaracharyas for a single math was unprecedented", and Jayendra Saraswati abandoned the math and disappeared, and the Paramacharya anointed Vijayendra Saraswati as the math head. After about two weeks, Jayendra Saraswati returned, and a compromise was reached.

Murder and Turmoil

Sankararaman, son of an ex-employee of the Kanchi matha, Managing Trustee of the Lord Varadaraja Perumal temple at Kancheepuram, was murdered on September 3, 2004, allegedly at the behest of the Shankaracharya, police charged the Shankaracharya and several of his close associates with the murder. The murdered person, Sankararaman, had pointed out issues such as the Shankaracharya's trip to China crossing the seas by air, which according to him Hindus were forbidden to make.

Investigators alleged that calls to the assailants had been made from the matha mobile phone, and charges have been filed against Jayendra Saraswati as well as the junior acharya Vijayendra Saraswati. On November 11, 2004, Jayendra Saraswati was arrested from Mehboobnagar, Andhra Pradesh. The arrest initially caused a tremendous uproar among the Hindu laity across the nation, and Bharatiya Janata Party and other Hindu groups started canvassing widely for his release. During the bail hearings, Justice R. Balasubramanian of the Madras High Court observed, without prejudicing the final verdict:

> *"materials relied upon by the prosecution... would prima facie constitute reasonable grounds to believe' that the petitioner is shown to be guilty of an offence punishable with death or imprisonment for life."*

However, in a subsequent appeal to the Supreme Court, bail was granted, with the court observing that:

No worthwhile prima facie evidence apart from the alleged confessions have been brought to our notice to show that the petitioner along with other accused was party to a conspiracy

The Supreme Court also agreed to shift the trial to Pondicherry, after the defence argued that the media attention and other factors in Tamil Nadu made a fair trial impossible there.

In March 2006, both Jayendra as well as Vijayendra Saraswati, as well as a number of others, were charged on 14 counts, including murder and conspiracy. The police have not yet provided substantial evidences against the Shankarcharyas involvement in the case. It has been believed that the cases were slapped due to vindicative actions by the former Chief Minister of Tamilnadu J.Jayalalitha. The validity of the case, and the truth behind still remains a mystery.

List of Kamakoti Matha Heads

Chronological list of heads of the matha, according to the official account:

1. Sri Suresvaracharya
2. Sri Sarvajnatman
3. Sri Sathyabodhendra Saraswati
4. Sri Jnanandendra Saraswati
5. Sri Suddhanandendra Saraswati
6. Sri Aanandaghanendra Saraswati
7. Sri Kaivalyanandayogendra Saraswati
8. Sri Krpa Sankarendra Saraswati
9. Sri Sureswara
10. Sri Sivananda Chidghanendra Saraswati
11. Sri Chandrasekharendra Saraswati
12. Sri Satchidghanendra Saraswati
13. Sri Vidyaghanendra Saraswati
14. Sri Gangadharendra Saraswati
15. Sri Ujjvala Sankarendra Saraswati
16. Sri Sadasivendra Saraswati
17. Sri Shankarananda Saraswati

18. Sri Martanda Vidyaghanendra Saraswati
19. Sri Muka Sankarendra Saraswati
20. Sri Chandrasekharendra Saraswati II
21. Sri Bodhendra Saraswati
22. Sri Satchisukhendra Saraswati
23. Sri Chitsukhendra Saraswati
24. Sri Satchidanandaghanendra Saraswati
25. Sri Prajnaghanendra Saraswati
26. Sri Chidvilasendra Saraswati
27. Sri Mahadevendra Saraswati I
28. Sri Purnabhodhendra Saraswati
29. Sri Bhodhendra Saraswati II
30. Sri Brahmanandaghanendra Saraswati
31. Sri Chidanandaghanendra Saraswati
32. Sri Satchidananda Saraswati
33. Sri Chandrasekharendra Saraswati III
34. Sri Chitsukhendra Saraswati
35. Sri Chitsukhanandendra Saraswati
36. Sri Vidyaghanendra Saraswati III
37. Sri Abhinava Sankarendra Saraswati
38. Sri Satchidvilaasendra Saraswati
39. Sri Mahadevendra Saraswati II
40. Sri Gangadharendra Saraswati II
41. Sri Brahmanandaghanendra Saraswati
42. Sri Anandaghanendra Saraswati
43. Sri Purnabhodhendra Saraswati II
44. Sri Paramasivendra Saraswati I
45. Sri Sandranandabhodhendra Saraswati
46. Sri Chandrasekharendra Saraswati IV
47. Sri Advaitanandabodhendra Saraswati
48. Sri Mahadevendra Saraswati III
49. Sri Chandrachudendra Saraswati I
50. Sri Kamachandrendra Saraswati
51. Sri Vidyateerthendra Saraswati (1297-1370)

52. Sri Sankaranandendra Saraswati (1370-1417)
53. Sri Purnananda Sadasivendra Saraswati (1417-1498)
54. Sri Vyasachala Mahadevendra Saraswati (1498-1507)
55. Sri Chandrachudhendra Saraswati II (1507-1524)
56. Sri Sarvajna Sadasiva Bhodhendra Saraswati (1524-1539)
57. Sri Paramasivendra Saraswati II (1539-1586)
58. Sri Atma Bodhendra Saraswati (1586-1638)
59. Sri Bhagavannama Bodhendra Saraswati (1638-1692)
60. Sri Advaitatma Prakasendra Saraswati (1692-1704)
61. Sri Mahadevendra Saraswati IV (1704-1746)
62. Sri ChandrasekharendraSaraswati V (1746-1783)
63. Sri Mahadevendra Saraswati V (1783-1813)
64. Sri Chandrasekharendra Saraswati VI (1813-1851)
65. Sri Sudarsana Mahadevendra Saraswati (1851-1891)
66. Sri Sri Chandrasekharendra Saraswati VII (1891-February 7, 1907)
67. Sri Sri Mahadevendra Saraswathi VI (February 7, 1907-February 13, 1907)
68. Sri Chandrasekharendra Saraswati Swamigal(February 13, 1907-January 3, 1994)
69. Sri Jayendra Saraswati Swamigal
70. Sri Sankara Vijayendra Saraswati Swamigal.

Govardhana Matha

The Govardhana maþha is located in the city of Puri in Orissa state (India), and is associated with the Jagannath temple. It is one of those four cardinal mathas said to have been founded by Adi Shankara, and is the eastern matha. As per the tradition initiated by Adi Shankara, it is in charge of the Rig Veda.

Its current head or Shankaracharya is Nishcalananda Sarasvati. He was appointed by his predecessor Niranjandev Tirth in the early 1990s.

Adhokshajanand

A person named Swami Adhokshajanand (or Swami Adhokshanand) has occasionally claimed to be the Sankaracharaya of Puri. He was arrested in July 2000 under Section 173, 188, 186 and 204 of the CrPC. He has been debarred from using the title of Jagadguru Shankracharaya of Goverdhan Peeth, and has been pro.ıibitingfrom going within the radius of 1,000 meters of the temple by the court.presently nischalananda saraswati is the revered shankarachrya of the math.

Adhokshajanand is known for using harsh words unusual for a Hindu monk. He has visited homes of Kashmiri terrorists killed by Indian security forces. In an article in Paigam-Rahbar, he called Palestinians freedom fighters and Israel a "terrorist state".

He spent a chaturmas in Gujarat at the invitation of Shankersinh Vaghela, although later Vaghela claimed that Adhokshajanand arrived there on his own.

Shankaracharya Temple

The Shankaracharya Temple, also known as the Jyesteshwara temple is located in Srinagar, India.

It is dedicated to Lord Shiva. The temple is located on the summit of the Takt-e-suleiman hill overlooking Srinagar town.The temple dates back to 200 B.C.E although the present structure probably dates back to the 9th century C.E. The temple was supposedly visited by the Adishankaracharya and has ever since been associated with it.

Sri Bharati Tirtha

Shri Bharati Theertha Swaminah (born, 11 April 1951 as Sitarama Anjaneyulu) is the Jagadguru and Shankaracharya of the Advaitic Sringeri Sharada Peetham. Born in Narasaraopet in Guntur District of Andhra Pradesh to a pious Telugu Brahmin couple, Shri Venkateshwara Avadhani and Smt. Ananthalakshamma, he became a disciple of Shri Abhinava Vidya Theertha Swaminah. He attended a local school here. He excelled in his studies. Highly proficient in English and mathematics, he performed the duties of a brahmacharin meticulously.

When he was 9 years old he got a chance to speak in Sanskrit in front of Sri Abhinava Vidyatheertha Mahaswamigal. When he received his blessings, he felt a change in himself. This was a turning point in his life. In 1966 Sri Mahasannidhanam was observing *chathurmasya* in Ujjain. The thought of acharya attracted Sri Anjaneyalu. He left home, reached Ujjain and prostrated before

Mahasannidhanam. From that day he learned Shastras from him. The Seer then appointed the boy as his successor on 11 November 1974. After initiation into Sanyasa, the young man meticulously followed the instructions of his Guru and impressed everyone with his knowledge and understanding of philosophy. Mahaswami spent huge amount time on meditation and was called as Tapas Chakravarty.

Mahaswami became the Jagadguru on 19 October 1989 following the mahasamadhi of the erstwhile Jagadguru Abhinava Vidya Tirtha on 21 September 1989.

Sringeri Sharada Peetham

Sringeri Sharada Peetham is the southern Advaita maþha. It is located in Sringeri. It is claimed that it is the first of the four original maþhas said to have been established by Adi Shankara.

Location

The maþha is in the temple town of Sringeri (also spelled *Shringeri*), on the banks of river Tunga, in the Chikmagalur district of the Karnataka state, India. It is about 105 kilometres from Mangalore.

History

The origin of the maþha is described in various traditional sources, including the *Eankara Vijaya* of Madhava. Úankara is said to have lived here for twelve out of his short life-span of thirty-two years.

According to legends, Eankara and his four disciples, accompanied by Bharati, an incarnation of Goddess Sarasvati reached Sringeri on an exceptionally hot noon, and as they proceeded to the river Tunga for their ablutions, they saw a frog struggling in the blazing sun to be delivered of its spawn. A cobra, a natural enemy of frogs, had raised its hood to provide the frog with shelter and protection from the ravages of the tropical sun. Uankara was greatly moved by the sight. If there was paradise on earth, here it was, where the lion and the lamb, the tiger and the cow, the cobra and the frog lived in mutual amity and peace. He turned round when, as she had already stipulated, Bharati, known also as Sharada, decided to stay for good at Sringeri on the banks of the sacred river Tunga.

Vishwarupa, assuming the name of Suresvaracharya, was installed here as the successor of Uankaracarya before the latter resumed his tour to found his three pithas at Puri, Dwaraka and Badrinath. Thus the maþha traces its lineage from Suresvaracharya.

The Sringeri maþha records its tradition from the 8th century onwards. The history of the Sringeri Maþha since the period of Sri Bharathi Tirtha (I) and Sri Vidyaranya (14th century) onwards has been extensively documented. Most of the names from the Sringeri lineage up to Vidyaranya are also found in the *Sri Guru Charitra*, a 15th-century Marathi work by Gangadhara Saraswathi. Sringeri maþha sources report that Uankara was born in the fourteenth year of the reign of Vikramaditya. Some believe this Vikramaditya to be the Vikramaditya II of the Western Chalukya Dynasty, which ruled from Badami in Karnataka. Others believe him to the Vikramaditya of the 1st century BCE.

The maþha continues to flourish to this day, and governs many institutions.

Philosophy and Traditions of the Maþha

The maþha gurus follow the philosophy of Advaita Vedanta. Following the tradition initiated by Uankara, the maþha is in charge of the Yajur Veda (the Krishna (Black) Yajurveda is more prevalent in South India, over which the maþha has authority in the Smarta tradition). The gurus of the maþha teach that all the demigods (devas), described in the Vedas and the Puranas, are mundane manifestations of the same one cosmic spirit, called Brahman. Moreover, the innermost self of the human being is also not different from Brahman.

They subscribe to the Vedic phrase "Aham Brahma Asmi", which means: "I am the Universal spirit". The gurus wear ochre robes, smear their forehead with sacred ashes or *vibhuti*, and worship God for many hours every day. They practice intense penance and meditation, which they believe helps in the control of the mind. They sustain themselves on an optimum diet and minimal sleep. They meditate/chant on the Rudraksha and Tulasi beads and worship both the Linga (Shiva) and Saligrama (Lord Vishnu) every day. To an Advaitin, the heart of Shiva is Vishnu and the heart of Vishnu is Shiva. Both are one and the same. The Sringeri gurus advocate that an individual must not merely revere a guru and listen to his teachings, but imbibe the good habits of the guru in their own life. Some of the things advocated by the gurus are:

1. Satvic habits which include vegetarianism, cleanliness, discipline, etc.
2. Regular worship of God and development of *bhakti.*
3. Giving importance to learning and knowledge.
4. Good conduct, honesty, generosity, and adherence to scriptures.
5. Austerity and simplicity.
6. Love, respect, and responsibility towards one's family or community.
7. Destruction of pride and ego.

The material world is considered as *maya,* or temporary, like a dream, so they believe that one should be involved in the material world only in order to fulfill one's responsibility. Although they adhere to the teachings of Uankara, they read other secular and religious works. Within the recorded history of the last two centuries, every one of the gurus at Sringeri has been a polyglot and a scholar with knowledge of a wide range of subjects. They do not advocate religious conversion, and believe that individuals must follow the religion of their own birth properly and correctly.

Shringeri Sharada Suprabhatha

The Shringeri Sharada Suprabhatha was adopted by the Shringeri matha in the late 1970's by his holiness Jagadguru Sri Abhinava Vidyatirtha swamiji. The very famous *Sree Sharada Suprabhata Stotram* was composed by Veda Brahma. Turuvekere Subrahmanya Vishweshwara Dikshith also known as Sri. T. S. Vishweshwara Dikshith for the divine *Shringeri Sharada maata* (God Mother). Veda. Brahma. T. S. Vishweshwara Dikshith was born in Turuvekere, a small town in Tumkur district and was the Sanskrit professor in Maharaja College in the Royal Kingdom of Mysore and resided at Mysore. He was also the *Aasthana Vidwan* of Alankaara Shasthra of King Jayachamaraja Wodeyar Bahadur. Sri. T. S. Vishweshwara Dikshith was a learned Sanskrit scholar in several Vedas (Yajur Veda in particular) and specialised in *Ghana Krama*-which is the essense of the Vedas.

He also composed the *Sree Srikanteshwara Suprabhata* and *Sree Chandramoulishwara Suprabhata* of Lord. Srikanteshwara of

Nanjangud, and Sri Chandramoulishwara temple in V. V. Mohalla, Mysore respectively. He was a *Ghana Pati* and had mastered several Shastras such as *Alankara Shastra*, *Jyothishya Shastra* (Astrology), *Tarka*, and *Vyakarana* (Literature) to name a few. He received several awards and accolodates from the Maharaja of Mysore, and their holiness the pointiffs' of Sringeri Sharada Peetham and Kanchi Kamakoti Peetam respectively for his contributions made to Sanskrit Literature.

Followers of the Maþha

The maþha has a huge following, especially among the Vedic community. People of all castes from all over India visit the Uankaracharya at the maþha, but the majority of followers are Smartha Brahmins of South India and Maharashtra. Succession to the Uankaracharya title is through disciplic selection by the existing Uankaracharya. The successor to the maþha is usually named at a young age, from among the Vedic Brahmana community.

Activities of the Maþha

A number of Vedic schools and temples are maintained by the maþha. Besides this, the maþha also runs a hospital and a few colleges. It has established branches in many parts of India. The Sharada Temple at Sringeri is managed by the Sringeri maþha. There is also a library in Sringeri, with rare Sanskrit volumes, which is managed by the maþha. The maþha has also played an important role in preserving the natural beauty of Sringeri.

Relationships with other Maþhas and Institutions

The maþha has enjoyed patronage from many kings and rulers. Its sage Vidyatheertha was contemporary with the founders of Vijayanagar Empire, and the maþha was given lavish grants of land by the Vijayanagar Kings. Vidyaranya another maþha head, was the founder of Vijananager empire and also served as advisor to the Vijayangar King. Tipu Sultan, the famous Muslim ruler of Mysore, also respected the Sringeri Acharyas, and helped it to sustain itself.

Even in modern times the maþha has had good relations with the State and Central Governments, as it has always been politically neutral and non-controversial. In Independent India, however, with the coming of land reforms, the Sringeri maþha lost much of its traditional land and sources of income, and at one time was struggling to maintain itself. With the increase in donations by NRIs, however, things have turned for the better.

The maþha maintains good relationships with the three other maþhas believed to have been founded by Uankara, located in Puri, Dwaraka, and Jyotirmath (near Badrinath). In addition, over the centuries, the successive heads of the Sringeri maþha had established branch institutions, many of which continue to function, with their own collateral lineages. In the interests of preserving all the traditions derived from the Vedas, the Sringeri maþha also maintains cordial working relationships with institutions belonging to other Vedanta schools, such as the Sri Vaishnava and Madhva institutions.

Guru Parampara

Head of the Maþha

The head of the maþha is usually chosen as a Brahmachari, educated in the Vedas. The existing head of the maþha decides upon a worthy disciple, initiates him as a sannyasin, and appoints him as the head. The present head of the maþha is Sri Bharati Tirtha Swaminah.

Ramachandrapura Math

"Sri Jagadguru Shankaracharya Mahasamstanam Sri Samstana Gokarna Shree Ramachandrapura Matha" is a Hindu religious establishment that was established in Gokarna by Shree Shankaracharya for the propagation of Sanathana Dharma. Initially, the Math was called as Shree Raghotham Peeta, and subsequently came known to be the "Shree Ramachandrapura Math".

History

Shree Math has an illustrious history of more than 1300 Years and was established by deciple of Shree Adi Shankaracharya. It is the only Math with an unbroken lineage (Avichchinna Parampara) of Peethadhishas. The first Peethadhisha Shree Vidyananda Acharya was the disciple of Adi Shankara. Shree Shankaracharya bestowed a rare Chandramouleeshwara Lingam and Idols of Shree Rama, Seetha, Lakshmana and other deities to the Math. These were worshiped with great devotion and reverence by the subsequent Swamijis and to this day the worship continues. The twelfth pontiff Shree Ramachandra Bharathi Swamiji built a new Math on the banks of River Sharavathi in Hosanagara, Shimoga District, Karnataka, in the 15th century and since then the Math at Hosanagara has gained prominence as the main one as there was nobody in the lineage at ragoottam muutt at kekkar. Historical documents state that the Math was revered and held in great esteem by the Emperors of Vijayanagara, Keladi and Mysore. Even the Nawabs of Hyderabad and rulers of Mysore like Hyder Ali and Tippu Sultan acknowledged both the temporal and spiritual sway of the Shree Math which is symbolised by the Throne and Crown of the Peeta.

Crown

The Ramachandrapura Math is a Raja Peeta/Jagadguru Peeta, (a blending of both Adhyatmika/Sanyasa and Royal patronage). The Gold Crown was honoured at the time of Vijayanagar Dynasty, with few of royal patronage as Adda Pallaki (Palkin), Hagalu Deevatike, Boparak (Praise of Honour), etc. It is the peeta which conducts, Addapallaki & Keeritotsava on special occasions, since ages. It is the peeta which has seen many Dynasties, Rulers, its rise & fall, had been considered a moral guideline by many in past & even present.

Throne

The Shree Math has a stunningly beautiful ivory throne. This invaluable piece of art was carved during the period of Shree Ramachandra Bharathi Swamiji (the 34th pontiff), out of the tusks of Ramabhadra, the elephant whose love and devotion to Shree Raghaveshwara Bharathi Swamiji (33rd pontiff) is legendary. This manually carved throne with its intricate designs, which depict scenes from the Ramayana, Mahabharatha and Bhagavatha, is studded with precious stones and gold inlay work. It was carved by the well known Mudugodu Manja Aachari, in Soraba town.

Prospects

Shree Shree Raghaveshwara Bharathi Swamiji is the 36th Jagadguru and he is greatly revered by some as the an illustrious and illuminating personality in the field of Sanskrit, Vedanta and social welfare. Shree Math under the holy and able guidance of its current pontiff Shree Shree Raghaveshwara Bharathi Swamiji is helping people to live in a better world not only by preserving and propagating the Sanathana Dharma but also by taking-up social welfare programmes. The present pontiff, greatly revered by all as the incarnation of Adi Shankara. Shree Raghaveshwara Bharathi Swamiji believes that the Math has to help the people live in a better world not only by preserving and propagating the Sanathana Dharma but also by taking-up social welfare programmes. Relentlessly working on his dream, Shree Swamiji has embarked on massive social welfare programmes such as Value Based Education System, Hospitals and Health Care for Rural Poor, Food distribution for poor, Cancer Research, protecting and preserving native Indian breed Cows, Propagation of organic farming, etc. to name a few. Some of these projects are unique and are being widely appreciated in India and Abroad. The success of these projects are already visible and people from all walks of life are involving themselves in realizing Swamiji's dream of gifting ourselves a better tomorrow.

The Mutt has majority in recent years concentrated on Indian breed cattle preservation (Cows). In fact, the census by Animal Husbandry shows decline in Cattle over years, and most of Indian breed are in verge of extinction (e.g. Vachuru breed of Kerala is expected around 100 Nos. in all and after the initiation to protect Indian breed by math, the Keral Govt.very recently has taken steps to protect the same). Of 36 Indian cattle breeds now known in India, all are found in Math, which are preserved for future generation.

It is the only institution in India with single largest collection of Indian Cow breed (Bos Indicos), and the present pontiff, have declared his future work to concentrate only around the protection of the Indian cow breed (Bharathiya Go Samrakshane). Future concentration is on research, on them to give more to society of the benefits of these breeds, and also it 'Gavyautpanna' or products from Cow, as, Gavya Arka, Doopa, Danthamanjana, Medicines, etc. In fact, the State Governments have noted the importance from here, and have announced projects based on the work developments here.

In April 2006, the Math organized the mega festival of the epic Ramayana-the Ramayana Mahasatra-at its premises at Hosanagar in Karnataka. It attracted 15 lakhs of devotees from all walks of life. The event was a whole bunch Ramayana Festival. All the cultural, deity forms of Ramayana as worshiped in different parts of India, was brought under the event, so that people can have the glimpse of the entire cultural events of Ramayana in India. Many of dignitaries attended the event with praise, and food was served to all with name of Maha Annasantharpana (i.e. megha food charity/ offerings).

In April 2007, a megha International event 'Vishwa Go-Sammelan' a big convocation as to protect the endangered Indian breed catte, was held at math. Many resourceful persons had appeared from different parts of world. This sammelan was a bunch of events like Kamadhenu Maha Yaga, many semminars, religious meet of different sanyasis & various organisations, & many educative & entertainment events, of course all related to Indian breed cattle.

The August 2008, was a historical period in the math history, with receiving back the full administration, of Sri Samstan Gokarna Mahabaleshwar Temple in Gokarna. The Temple was under full control of math for over 1,200 years, with just missing administration for a short period. The temple was officially passed to the math by the Government of Karnataka, as there were sufficient documents and scriptures of the past administration by the math.

Sri Mahadevendra Saraswathi V

Sri Mahadevendra Saraswathi V was the 67th Shankaracharya of the Kanchi matha. He was born Lakshmi Narasimha to Narasimha Sastri and Lakshmi. He was given the title Mahadevendra Saraswathi and made the Shankaracharya in 1907. He occupied the post for a brief period of seven days and died in 1907. He was succeeded by his nephew, Swaminathan, a boy of thirteen, who became the sixty-eighth Shankaracharya with the title Chandrasekarendra Saraswathi VIII.

Mahadevendra saraswathis Samadhi is located in Kalavai, next to his Gurus samadhi. Mahadevendra was also stuck by the same disease that caused the Siddhi of his Guru. He died within seven days of ascending the throne of the mutt. But before he died, he had sent word for Swaminathan to be his successor.

Jagadguru Swami Sri Bharati Krishna Tirthaji Maharaja

Jagadguru Swami Sri Bharati Krishna Tirthaji Maharaja was the Jagadguru (literally, *teacher of the world*; assigned to heads of

Hindu mathas) of the Govardhana matha of Puri during 1925–1960. He was one of the most significant spiritual figures in Hinduism during the 20th century. He is particularly known for his work on Vedic mathematics.

Early Life

Venkatraman Shastri was born in March, 1884 to P. Narasimha Shastri, originally a *tehsildar* at Tirunelveli in Madras Presidency. Narasimha Shastri later became the Deputy Collector of the Presidency. Venkatraman was born in a highly illustrious family. His uncle, Chandrasekhara Shastri was the Principal of the Maharaja's College in Vizianagaram, while his great-grandfather, Justice C. Ranganath Shastri was a judge in the Madras High Court.

Educational Career

Venkatraman Shastri started his educational career as a student of the National College in Trichanapalli. After that he moved to the Church Missionary Society College and eventually the Hindu College, both in Tirunelveli. He was consistently first place in all subjects in all of his classes. Shastri passed his matriculation examination from the Madras University in January, 1899, where he also finished at the head of the class.

As a student Venkatraman was marked for his splendid brilliance, superb retentive memory and an insatiable curiosity. By deluging his teachers with piercing questions, making them uneasy, and frequently forcing them to admit ignorance he was considered a terribly mischievous student.

Although Venkatraman always scored high in subjects like mathematics, sciences and humanities, he was also proficient in languages and particularly adept in Sanskrit. According to his own testimonials, Sanskrit and oratory were his favourite subjects. Such was his mastery over the language, that he was awarded the title "*Saraswati*" by the Madras Sanskrit Association in July, 1899 at the age of 16. At about that time, Venkatraman was profoundly influenced by his Sanskrit guru Sri Vedam Venkatrai Shastri whom he remembered with deepest love, reverence and gratitude, with tears in his eyes.

Venkatraman won the highest place in the graduation B.A. examination in 1902. He then appeared for the M.A. Examination for the American College of Sciences, in Rochester, New York from the Bombay centre in 1903. He passed the M.A. examination in seven subjects that he had chosen-Sanskrit, philosophy, English, mathematics, history, science and another-simultaneously scoring the highest honours in all, which was perhaps an all-time world record at the time.

Venkatraman Saraswati, as he was called after receiving the title, also contributed to W. T. Stead's *Review of Reviews* on topics as diverse as religion and science. During his college days, he also wrote extensively on history, sociology, philosophy, politics and literature. Reading of the latest scientific research and discoveries was his hobby throughout his life.

Early Public Life

Venkatraman Saraswati worked under Gopal Krishna Gokhale in 1905 for the National Education Movement and the South African Indian problems. However, his inclination towards science and Indic studies led him to study the ancient Indian holy scriptures, Adhyatma-Vidya. In 1908 he joined the Sringeri Matha in Mysore to study under the Sringeri Shankaracharya Sri Satchidananda Sivabhinava Nrisimha Bharati Swami.

However, his spiritual practise was interrupted when he was pressurized by nationalist leaders to head the newly started National College at Rajmahendri. Prof. Venkatraman Saraswati taught at the college for three years. But in 1911, he suddenly left the college to go back to Sri Satchidananda Sivabhinava Nrisimha Bharati Swami at the Sringeri Math in his quest for spiritual knowledge.

Spiritual Path

Returning to Sringeri, Venkatraman spent his next eight years studying advanced Vedanta philosophy at the feet of Shri Nrisimha Bharati Swami. This cannot be true. The then Sringeri Jagadguru until April 1912 was Sri Sachidananda Shivabhinava Nrusimha Bharathi Swamigal. The Swamigal attained Mahasamadhi during April 1912 and was immediately succeeded to the Peeta, by his Disciple Jagadguru Sri Chandrashekhara Bharathi Swamigal. Jagadguru Sri Chandrashekara Bharathi was in the Peeta until 1954. Venkaraman Saraswathi could not have hence learnt for 8 years with Sri Nrusimha Bharathi Mahaswamigal from 1911 at

Sringeri. Also, When Jagadguru Sri Chandrashekara Bharathi Swamigal was in the Peeta, there was no one else nominated as the Successor, until much later when Jagadguru Srimad Abhinava Vidya Theerta Swamigal was nominated as the Successor.

He also practised vigorous meditation, *Brahma-sadhana* and *Yoga-Sadhana* during those years in the nearby forests. It is believed that he attained spiritual self-realization during his years in the Sringeri Math. He would leave the material world and practise Yoga meditation in seclusion for many days. During those eight years, he also taught Sanskrit and Philosophy to local schools and *ashrams*. He delivered a series of sixteen lectures on Shankaracharya's philosophy at Shankar Institute of Philosophy, Amalner [Khandesh]. During that time, he also lectured as a guest professor at various institutions in Mumbai, Pune and Khandesh.

Initiation into Sanyasa *Order*

After Venkatraman's eight-year period of spiritual practice and study of the Vedanta and Vedic philosophy, he was initiated into the holy order of *Samnyasa* at Benaras by Jagadguru Shankaracharya Sri Trivikram Tirthaji Maharaj of Sharadapeeth on July 4, 1919 and on this occasion he was given the title of *Swami* and the new name, "Swami Bharati Tirtha".

Shankaracharya of Sharada Peetha

Swami Bharati Tirtha was installed as Shankaracharya of Sharada Peetha in 1921 after just two years of *Sanyasa*. After assuming the pontificate Shri Jagadguruji, he was given another title, *Jagadguru*, as is the tradition. The Swami then toured India from corner to corner giving lectures on *Sanatana Dharma*, Vedic philosophy and Vedanta. By his scintillating intellectual brilliance, powerful oratory, magnetic personality, sincerity of purpose, indomitable will, purity of thought, and loftiness of character he took the entire intellectual and religious class by storm.

Shankaracharya of Govardhan Math

Around the time the Swami became Shankaracharya of Sharada Peetha, the Shankaracharya of Govardhan Math Puri, Jagadguru Uankaracarya Sri Madhusudhan Tirtha, was in failing health and was greatly impressed by Bharati Krishna Tirtha. Madhusudan Tirtha requested Bharati to succeed him at the Govardhan Math, however the Swami respectfully declined the offer. However, in

1925, Uankaracarya Sri Madhusudhan Tirtha's health took a serious turn and Swami Bharati Tirtha had to accept the Govardhan Math's *Gadi*. In 1925, Swami Bharati Tirtha assumed the pontificate of Shankaracharya of Govardhan Math, Puri and relinquished the pontificate of Sharadapeeth Gadi of Sringeri. He installed Sri Swarupanandji as the new Shankaracharya of Sharada Peetha.

Jagadguru

After becoming the Shankaracharya of Govardhan Math, Swami Bharati toured all over the world for 35 years to spread the values of peace, harmony and brotherhood and to spread the message of the Sanatana Dharma. He took upon himself the colossal task of the renaissance of Indian culture.

While being a pontiff, he wrote a large number of treatises and books on religion, sciences, mathematics, world peace and social issues. In 1953, at Nagpur, he founded an organization called "*Sri Vishwa Punarnirmana Sangha*" (World Reconstruction Association). Initially, the administrative board consisted of Jagadguruji's disciples, devotees and admirers of his spiritual ideals for humanitarian service, but later many distinguished people started to contribute to the mission. The Chief Justice of India, Justice B.P. Sinha served as its President. Dr. C. D. Deshmukh, the ex-Finance Minister of India and ex-Chairman of the University Grants Commission served as its Vice-President.

In February 1958 he went on a trans-oceanic tour to America to speak on world peace and Vedanta, staying three months in Los Angeles, California travelling via the United Kingdom. This was the first tour outside India by a Shankaracharya in the history of the order. The tour was sponsored by Self Realization Fellowship of Los Angeles, the Vedantic Society founded by Paramhansa Yogananda in America.

He attended many national and international religious conferences and many other *yoga* workshops. He believed in the Vedantic ideal of "*Purnatva*" which literally translated means, "all-round perfection and harmony". He remained the Shankaracharya of the Govardhan Matha until his death in 1960.

In 1965 a Chair of Vedic Studies was founded at Banares Hindu University by Shri Arvind N. Mafatlala, a generous Mumbai business magnate and math devotee of the late Swami Sankaracarya.

Mathematics

Jagadguru Swami Sri Bharati Tirthaji Maharaja's book "Vedic Mathematics" opened the floodgates of similar literature, often derived from the Swami's 16 Sutras themselves. His treatise on this field of mathematics is a fundamental work on speed and accuracy in basic mathematics. The Vedic Math ideal is a mental calculation and one-line notation.

The foundations of Vedic Mathematics were mentioned in the Vedas themselves and even in the Vedanta scriptures. These had lain unused for many millennia, till the Swami rediscovered them.

His book, *Vedic Mathematics*, comprises many algorithms. He revealed his source in the ancient Hindu Vedas. Some are intuitively reconstructed from the *Atharva* Veda and from Parisistas (appendix) of the *Atharva* Veda. "The Upaveda of Sthapatya (engineering) comprises all kinds of architectural and structural human endeavor and all visual arts (and mathematics)." His work seems to be a whole Parisistas (appendix) itself.

The ancient Sanskrit writers did not use numerals when writing big numbers but preferred to use the letters of the Sanskrit Devanagari alphabet. In the Vedic Sutras the key word steps to solving many problems are given in a terse, decimal code of certain sets of rhyming syllables, within the verses of the Sûtra. The fact that the alphabetic code is in the natural order and can be immediately interpreted, is clear proof that the code language was resorted not for concealment but for greater ease in verification.

The Swami had written sixteen volumes on the Vedic Mathematics field explaining all the topics of mathematical study. Alas, many advanced formula were promised but not given in his first and only book. After his 1956 life's work manuscript on Vedic mathematics was lost in a fire at the home of a disciple, though he was going blind from cataracts, he rewrote the manuscript in 1957 in six weeks! It was to be proofread and published in the USA but was send back to India in 1960 after his death. In 1965, this manuscript was published by Motilal Banarsidass, Varanasi, India and reprinted four times in the 1970s.

His book, *Vedic Mathematics*, included sixteen terse formulas for mental mathematics. For arithmetic, we are given several algorithms for whole number multiplication and division, (flag or straight) division, fraction conversion to repeating decimal numbers, calculations with measures of mixed units, summation of a series, squares and square roots (duplex method), cubes and cube roots (with expressions for a digit schedule), and divisibility (by osculation). He gives a poem in Anusub metre, couched in the alphabetic Code-Language that has three meanings, a hymn to Lord Sri K[cGa, a hymn in praise of the Lord Shri Shankara, and the third the value of pi/ 10 to 32 decimal places, pi/ 10 = 0.31415926535897932384626433832792... with a "self-contained master-key" for extending the evaluation to any number of decimal places!

Several tests and techniques for featuring and solving certain algebraic equations with integer roots for quadratic, cubic, biquadratic, pentic equations, systems of linear equations, and systems of quadratic equations are demonstrated. For fractional expressions, a separation algorithm and fraction merger algorithms are given. Other techniques handle certain patterns of some special case algebraic equations. Just an introduction to differential and integral calculus is given.

Geometric applications are reviewed for linear equations, analytic conics, the equation for the asymptotes, and the equation to the conjugate-hyperbola. Five simple geometric proofs for the Pythagorean theorem are given. A 5-line proof of Apollonius' theorem is given.

Advanced topics promised included the integral calculus (the center of gravity of hemispheres, conics), Trigonometry, Astronomy (spherical triangles, earth's daily rotation, earth's annual rotation about the sun and eclipses), and Engineering (dynamics, statics, hydrostatics, pneumatics, applied mechanics).

In his final comments he asserted that the names for "Arabic numerals," "Pythagoras' Theorem," and "Cartesian" co-ordinates are historical misnomers.

Jayendra Saraswathi

Sri Jayendra Saraswathi Swamigal (born July 18, 1935 as Subramanyam Mahadeva Iyer) is the 69th Shankaracharya (guru and head or pontiff (Peetadhipathi)) of the Kanchi Kamakoti Peetham.

Subramanyam Mahadeva Iyer was nominated by his predecessor, Sri Chandrasekarendra Saraswati Swamigal as his successor and was given the title Sri Jayendra Saraswathi on March 22, 1954. He is one of the leading religious figures in Hinduism today.

On account of his sacerdotal office and his profound knowledge of the Hindu religion, he commands wide respect in India, particularly in religious Hindu circles. The Kanchi Math has grown into a strong organization under him. Further, the Kanchi Mutt is also widely patronised by many NRIs, particularly from the U.S.A. The Finance of the Kanchi Mutt runs into many millions and it runs many schools, eye clinics and hospitals, Shankara Nethralaya in Chennai and Guwahati, Assam, and the Children's Hospital, Hindu Mission Hospital and the Tamilnadu Hospital.

The Jayalalithaa government in Tamil Nadu enacted a law to ban religious conversion, in keeping with the Shankaracharya's oft-expressed concerns.. The Tamil Nadu government also started to enforce a preexisting ban on animal sacrifice in temples, echoing concerns raised by the pontiff.

He was arrested on November 11, 2004 and charged by state prosecutors to being a conspirator in the murder of a temple manager, Sankararaman. On January 10, 2005, he was able to secure bail from the Supreme Court of India although lower courts refused his bail application. On 26 October 2005, the Supreme Court of India transferred the case out of the state of Tamil Nadu state to the adjoining Union Territory of Pondicherry..

The Sankaracharya's arrest attracted widespread media coverage, prompting accusations of a trial by media. The interest of the media decreased after successive verdicts of the High Courts in Andhra Pradesh and Tamil Nadu as well as the Supreme Court of India. Particularly, the High Court of Andhra Pradesh found that the conduct of the media was improper.

Jyotirmath

Jyotirmath, also called Jyotir Math and Joshimath is a city and a municipal board in Chamoli District in the Indian state of Uttarakhand. It is home to one of the four cardinal *pîthas* established by Adi Shankara.

Demographics

As of 2001 India census, Joshimath had a population of 13,202. Males constitute 61% of the population and females 39%. Joshimath has an average literacy rate of 77%, higher than the national average of 59.5%: male literacy is 83%, and female literacy is 67%. In Joshimath, 12% of the population is under 6 years of age.

The Matha

Jyotirmath is the *Uttaramnaya matha* or northern monastery, one of the four cardinal institutions established by Adi Shankara, the others being those at Sringeri, Puri and Dwaraka. Their heads are titled "Shankaracharya". According to the tradition initiated by Adi Shankara, this matha is in charge of the Atharva Veda.

Jyotirmath, which is close to the pilgrimage town of Badrinath, has not always been an active matha. It is sometimes said incorrectly that the original northern matha was established at Badrinath. This place can be a base station for travellers going to Guru Gobind Ghat or the Valley of Flowers (There is a famous National Park there called the Valley of Flowers National Park).

In its most recent history, the Jyotirmath became inactive in the early 19th century. The formal occupation of the matha was restarted with the aid of the heads of some of the other mathas from about 1940 onward. However, there is an unresolved controversy over the succession to the headship of Jyotirmath. The best known of the claimants to be the current head or Shankaracharya is Svarûpânanda Sarasvatî who is also head of the Dwaraka matha. The other two claimants are Vasudevananda Sarasvatî and Madhavaurama.

Brahmananda Saraswati

Brahmananda Saraswati (20 December 1870-20 May 1953) was the Shankaracharya of Jyotir Math, a revered spiritual title in India, from 1941 to 1953.

Early Life

Brahmananda Saraswati was born into a Brahmin family in the village of Gana, near Ayodhya in Uttar Pradesh, India. He was called Rajaram in his younger days and was also known as Maha Yogiraj.

At the age of nine, Rajaram left his home unannounced to follow a spiritual path of renunciation but was soon after returned to his parents by a policeman. Upon returning home, he asked his parents for their permission to leave home and begin the life of a recluse. His parents wanted him to marry and live the life of a householder and asked their family guru, or panditji, to convince Rajaram to forget his dream of a recluse life. However, the family guru was so impressed with Rajaram's advanced state of wisdom and spiritual evolution, that he gave up any attempts to change the boy's mind. The parents then also acquiesced and gave their permission for Rajaram to leave. Two days later, Rajaram formally renounced his family life and left his boyhood home in search of solitude in the Himalayas.

Rajaram travelled by foot to the town of Haridwar and then on to Rishikesh, the gateway to the Himalayas. Here he began the search for a suitable guru or spiritual master. Rajaram met with many wise sages, but none of them met his requirements of life long celibacy and an intimate knowledge and experience of the Vedas.

Five years later at the age of fourteen, in a village in Uttar Kashi, Rajaram found his chosen Master and became a disciple of Dandi Swami Krishnanand Saraswati. At that time Rajaram was given the name of Brahma Chaitanya Brahmachari. He then became the favourite disciple in his master's ashram and, according his master's instructions, he retired tc a cave, resolving not to emerge until he had attained enlightenment.

Adult Life

At the age of twenty-five (25), having achieved his goal, the Brahmachari emerged from his cave and permanently rejoined his Master at his ashram.

In 1904, at the age of thirty-six (36) Brahmachari was initiated into the order of "Sannyas" by his Master at the great Indian celebration called Kumbh Mela. At that time, Brahmachari was formally ordained in the ascetic order and given the name Shri Swami Brahmanand Saraswati Maharaj.

Shankaracharya of Jyotir Math

In 1941, at the age of 70, after repeated requests and decades of meditation and living alone in silence in the forests and mountains of India, Swami Brahmananda Saraswati accepted the position of Shankaracharya (spiritual leader) of Jyotir Math, a position that had been vacant for about 150 years. The Adi Shankara (c. 8th century CE), the great reviver of Vedic Sanatana Dharma, had set up four principal seats of learning in India. Shankara's four principal disciples, Padma-Pada, Hasta-Malaka, Vartika-Kara and Trotaka were assigned to these four learning centers in the north, south, east and west of India, with the Jyotir Math learning center in the north being the most highly regarded of the four.

On various occasions Brahmananda Saraswati was visited by public figures such as Dr. Rajendra Prasad, the president of India and philosopher Dr. Sarvapalli Radhakrishnan, who succeeded Prasad as President of India. In 1950, President Radhakrishnan addressed Brahmananda Saraswati as Vedanta Incarnate (the embodiment of truth).

Disciples

Maharishi Mahesh Yogi became a devotee of Brahmananda Saraswati shortly before he was installated as Shankaracharya in 1941. The Maharishi later became the Shankaracharya's personal assistant. The Maharishi wrote a paper on Brahmananda Sarawsati, who he referred to as Guru Dev (greatest teacher). That paper was included in the 1955 book *Beacon Light of the Himalayas*.

In this paper the Maharishi says that: "In the English Language, his devotees felt that the expression "His Holiness" did not adequately describe this personified Divine Effulgence; and so the new expression "His Divinity" was used.

With such unique adoration of newer and fuller grandeur, transcending the glories of the expression of antiquity, was worshiped the holy name of Guru Deva, the living expression of Upanishadic Reality, the embodiment of the transcendent Divinity."

Devotees of the Maharishi also respect and revere Brahmananda Saraswati as their "Guru Dev" and as an outstanding representative of the Vedic tradition. It is in recognition of Guru Dev as the modern custodian of the Vedic tradition that a puja ceremony is performed by the Transcendental Meditation teacher during personal instruction.

An explanation of the purpose of the TM puja ceremony, the Sanskrit text of the ceremony, and its English translation was written and published by the Maharishi in the pamphlet, *The Holy Tradition*. The court in *Mainak v Yogi*, quoting and citing *The Holy Tradition*, found that this ceremony involved the making of offerings to a "deified" Guru Dev.

Five months before his death in 1953, Brahmananda Sarawsati had created a will naming one of his disciples, Shri Swami Shantananda Swamiji Maharaj as his successor.

Trust

Maharishi Mahesh Yogi, in his farewell message on January 11, 2008, announced the establishment of the Brahmananda Saraswati Trust, named in honor of his teacher, to support large groups totaling more than 30,000 peace-creating Vedic Pandits in perpetuity across India.

Vedanta

Vedanta was originally a word used as a synonym for that part of the Veda known also as the Upanishads. The name is a sandhied form of *Veda-anta* = "Veda-end" = "the appendix to the Vedas". Vedanta is considered to be source of all vedic literature. Original Vedanta contained four verses, later expanded to thousands. By the 8th century CE, the word also came to be used to describe a group of philosophical traditions concerned with the self-realisation by which one understands the ultimate nature of reality (Brahman). The word Vedanta teaches that the believer's goal is to transcend the limitations of self-identity. Vedanta is not restricted or confined to one book and there is no sole source for Vedantic philosophy. Vedanta is based on two simple propositions:

1. Human nature is divine.
2. The aim of human life is to realize that human nature is divine.

The goal of Vedanta is a state of self-realization or cosmic consciousness. Historically and currently, it is assumed that this state can be experienced by anyone, but it cannot be adequately conveyed in language.

Vedanta is also called Uttara Mimacsa, or the 'latter enquiry' or 'higher enquiry', and is often paired with Purva Mimacsa, the 'former enquiry'. Purva Mimamsa, usually simply called Mimamsa, deals with explanations of the fire-sacrifices of the Vedic mantras (in the Samhita portion of the Vedas) and Brahmanas, while Vedanta explicates the esoteric teachings of the ragyakas (the "forest scriptures"), and the Upanishads, composed from the 9th century BC until modern times.

History

While the traditional Vedic *Karma kanda*, or ritualistic components of religion, continued to be practiced through the Brahmins as meditative and propitiatory rites to guide society to self-knowledge, more jnana (gnosis)- or knowledge-centered understandings began to emerge. These are mystical streams of Vedic religion that focused on meditation, self-discipline and spiritual connectivity rather than on rituals. In earlier writings, Sanskrit 'Vedanta' simply referred to the Upanishads, the most speculative and philosophical of the Vedic texts.

However, in the medieval period of Hinduism, the word Vedanta came to mean the school of philosophy that interpreted the Upanishads. Traditional Vedanta considers scriptural evidence, or shabda pramana, as the most authentic means of knowledge, while perception, or pratyakssa, and logical inference, or anumana, are considered to be subordinate (but valid).

Formalization

The systematization of Vedantic ideas into one coherent treatise was undertaken by Badarayana in the Vedanta Sutra which was composed around 200 BCE.

Scholars know the Vedanta-sutra by a variety of names, including:

(1) Brahma-Sutra,

(2) Uariraka,

(3) Vyasa-sutra,

(4) Badarayaga-sutra,

(5) Uttara-mimaasa and

(6) Vedanta-daroana.

The cryptic aphorisms of the Vedanta Sutras are open to a variety of interpretations, resulting in the formation of numerous Vedanta schools, each interpreting the texts in its own way and producing its own sub-commentaries claiming to be faithful to the original. Consistent throughout Vedanta, however, is the exhortation that ritual be eschewed in favour of the individual's quest for truth through meditation governed by a loving morality, secure in the knowledge that infinite bliss awaits the seeker. Nearly all existing sects of Hinduism are directly or indirectly influenced by the thought systems developed by Vedantic thinkers. Hinduism to a great extent owes its survival to the formation of the coherent and logically advanced systems of Vedanta.

Source Texts

All forms of Vedanta are drawn primarily from the Upanishads, a set of philosophical and instructive Vedic scriptures. "The Upanishads are commentaries on the Vedas, their putative end and essence, and thus known as Vedanta or "End of the Veda". They are considered the fundamental essence of all the Vedas and although they form the backbone of Vedanta, portions of Vedantic thought are also derived from some of the earlier Aranyakas.

The primary philosophy captured in the Upanishads, that of one absolute reality termed as Brahman is the main principle of Vedanta. The sage Vyasa was one of the major proponents of this philosophy and author of the Brahma Sutras based on the Upanishads. The concept of Brahman – the Supreme Spirit or the eternal, self existent, immanent and transcendent Supreme and Ultimate Reality which is the divine ground of all Being-is central to most schools of Vedanta. The concept of God or Ishvara is also there, and the Vedantic sub-schools differ mainly in how they identify God with Brahman.

The contents of the Upanishads are often couched in enigmatic language, which has left them open to various interpretations. Over a period of time, several scholars have interpreted the writings in Upanishads and other scriptures like Brahma Sutras according to their own understanding and the need of their time. There are a total of six important interpretations of these source texts, out of which, three (Advaita, Vishishtadvaita and Dvaita) are prominent, both in India and abroad. These Vedantic schools of thought were founded by Shri Adi Shankara, Shri Ramanuja and Shri Madhvacharya, respectively. It should be noted, however, that the Indian pre-Shankara Buddhist writer, Bhavya, in the Madhyamakahrdaya Karika describes the Vedanta philosophy as "Bhedabheda". Proponents of other Vedantic schools continue to write and develop their ideas as well, although their works are not widely known outside of smaller circles of followers in India.

While it is not typically thought of as a purely Vedantic text, the Bhagavad Gita has played a strong role in Vedantic thought, with its representative syncretism of Samkhya, Yoga, and

Upanishadic thought. Indeed, it is itself called an "upanishad" and thus, all major Vedantic teachers (like Shankara, Ramanuja, and Madhvacharya) have taken it upon themselves to compose often extensive commentaries not only on the Upanishads and Brahma Sutras, but also on the Gita. In such a manner, Vedantists both old and new have implicitly attested to the Gita's importance to the development of Vedantic thought and practice.

Sub-schools of Vedanta

Advaita Vedanta

Advaita Vedanta was propounded by Adi Sankara and his grand-guru Gaudapada, who described Ajativada. According to this school of Vedanta, Brahman is the only reality, and the world, as it appears, is illusory. As Brahman is the sole reality, it cannot be said to possess any attributes whatsoever. An illusionary power of Brahman called Maya causes the world to arise. Ignorance of this reality is the cause of all suffering in the world and only upon true knowledge of Brahman can liberation be attained. When a person tries to know Brahman through his mind, due to the influence of Maya, Brahman appears as God (Ishvara), separate from the world and from the individual. In reality, there is no difference between the individual soul *jivatman* and Brahman. Liberation lies in knowing the reality of this non-difference (i.e. a-dvaita, "non-duality"). Thus, the path to liberation is finally only through knowledge (*jnana*).

Vishishtadvaita

Vishishtadvaita was propounded by Ramanuja and says that the *jivatman* is a part of Brahman, and hence is similar, but not identical. The main difference from Advaita is that in Visisht Advaita, the Brahman is asserted to have attributes, including the individual conscious souls and matter. Brahman, matter and the individual souls are distinct but mutually inseparable entities. This school propounds Bhakti or devotion to God visualized as Vishnu to be the path to liberation. Maya is seen as the creative power of God.

Dvaita

Dvaita was propounded by Madhwacharya. It is also referred to as tatvavada-The Philosophy of Reality. It identifies God with

Brahman completely, and in turn with Vishnu or his various incarnations like Krishna, Narasimha, Srinivasa etc. In that sense it is also known as sat-vaishnava philosophy to differentiate from the Vishishtadvaita school known by Sri-vaishnavism. It regards Brahman, all individual souls (*jivatmans*) and matter as eternal and mutually separate entities.

This school also advocates Bhakti as the route to sattvic liberation whereas hatred (Dvesha) and indifference towards the Lord will lead to eternal hell and eternal bondage respectively. Liberation is the state of attaining maximum joy or sorrow, which is awarded to individual souls (at the end of their sadhana), based on the souls' inherent and natural disposition towards good or evil. The achintya-adbhuta shakti (the immeasurable power) of Lord Vishnu is seen as the efficient cause of the universe and the primordial matter or prakrti is the material cause.

Dvaita also propounds that all action is performed by the Lord energising every soul from within, awarding the results to the soul but Himself not affected in the least by the results.

Dvaitadvaita

Dvaitadvaita was propounded by Nimbarka, based upon an earlier school called Bhedabheda, which was taught by Bhaskara. According to this school, the *jivatman* is at once the same as yet different from Brahman. The Jiva relation may be regarded as dvaita from one point of view and advaita from another. In this school, God is visualized as Krishna.

Shuddhadvaita

Shuddhadvaita was propounded by Vallabha. This system also identifies Bhakti as the only means of liberation, 'to go to Goloka' (lit., the world of cows; the Sankrit word 'go', 'cow', also means 'star'). The world is said to be the sport (Leela) of Krishna, who is *Sat-Chit-Ananda*.

Achintya Bhedabheda

Achintya Bhedabheda was propounded by Chaitanya Mahaprabhu (Bengal, 1486-1534). He was a follower of the Dvaita Vedanta of Sri Madhwacharya. This doctrine of inconceivable and simultaneous one-ness and difference states that the soul or energy of God is both distinct and non-distinct from God, whom he identified as Krishna, Govinda, and that this, although unthinkable, may be experienced through a process of loving devotion (*bhakti*). This philosophy of "inconceivable oneness and difference" is followed by a number of modern Gaudiya Vaishnava movements, including ISKCON.

Purnadvaita or Integral Advaita

According to his followers, Sri Aurobindo, in his *The Life Divine*, synthesized all the exant schools of Vedanta and gave a comprehensive resolution integrating cues from the Western metaphysics and modern science. He is said to have restored the umbilical cord of the Vedantic exegesis with the Vedas.

Modern Vedanta

The term "modern Vedanta" is sometimes used to describe the interpretation of Advaita Vedanta given by Swami Vivekananda of the Ramakrishna order of monks.

He stressed that:

- Although God is the absolute reality, the world has a relative reality. It should therefore not be completely ignored.
- Conditions of abject poverty should be removed; only then will people be able to turn their minds toward God.
- All religions are striving in their way to reach the ultimate truth. Narrow sectarian bickering should therefore be abandoned, and religious tolerance should be practiced — between different Hindu denominations, as well as Christianity, Judaism, Islam, Buddhism, etc.

Vivekananda travelled to the Parliament of the World's Religions in Chicago in 1893, and became an influential figure in synthesising Eastern and Western thought. He played a major role in the spread of Vedanta to Western nations. His travel to the West was criticised by some orthodox Hindus. His proponents claim that he made Vedanta living, by understanding how it could be applied to the modern world, and by investing it with his own spirit. For Vivekananda, Vedanta was not something dry or esoteric, but a living approach to the quest for self-knowledge.

In his interpretation of Advaita (as in Shankara's), there is still a place for Bhakti (devotion). Monks of the Ramakrishna order suggest that it is easier to begin meditation on a personal God with form and qualities, rather than the formless Absolute, of which everyone is said to be part. Saguna Brahman and Nirguna Brahman are viewed as obverse and reverse of the same coin.

List of Teachers

There have been many teachers of Vedanta in India and other countries over the centuries. A. C. Bhaktivedanta Swami Prabhupada Maharshi Swami Dayananda Saraswati (Arya Samaj), Hari Prasad Shastri, D. Krishna Ayyar, Swami Niranjanji Maharaj, Bhagavan Shri Ramana Maharshi, Narayana Guru, Shri Bhausaheb Maharaj, Shri Siddharameshwar Maharaj, Shri Nisargadatta Maharaj, Sri Ranjit Maharaj, Swami Rama Tirtha, Swami Vivekananda, Swami Sivananda, Swami Jyotirmayananda, Swami Brahmananda Saraswati, Swami Krishnananda, Swami Paramananda, Swami Chinmayananda, Swami Sri Dayananda Saraswathi of Arsha Vidya Gurukulam, Swami Sri Lilashahji Maharaj, Shri Maharishi Mahesh Yogi, Sri Aurobindo, Shri Swami Tapovan Maharaj, Sengalipuram Muthannaval, Mannargudi periyaval, Paruthiyur Krishna Sastri, Anantarama Dikshitar, Kanchi Mahaswamigal, Swami Ranganathananda were great Vedanta scholars. Swami Parthasarathy, Swami Dayananda Saraswati, Pujya Sri Prem Siddharth, Baba Ramdev, Nithyananda Swamigal, Muralidara Swamigal, Swami Krsnapriyananda Saraswati, Nome are distinguished, traditional teacher of Vedanta of the present day. Additionally Paramahansa Yogananda.

Influence in the West

The influential philosopher Georg Wilhelm Friedrich Hegel refers to Indian thought reminiscent of Advaita-Vedanta in his introduction to his *The Phenomenology of Spirit* and in his *Science of Logic.* Arthur Schopenhauer was influenced by the Vedas and Upanishads; in his own words: "If the reader has also received the benefit of the Vedas, the access to which by means of the Upanishads is in my eyes the greatest privilege which this still young century (1818) may claim before all previous centuries, if then the reader, I say, has received his initiation in primeval Indian wisdom, and received it with an open heart, he will be prepared in the very best way for hearing what I have to tell him."

(*The World as Will and Representation*) Among western figures who have been influenced by or have commented on Vedanta are Ram Dass, Friedrich Nietzsche, Max Muller, Voltaire, J.D. Salinger,

Aldous Huxley, T. S. Eliot, J.B. Priestley, Christopher Isherwood, Romain Rolland, Alan Watts, Eugene Wigner, Arnold Toynbee, Joseph Campbell, Hermann Hesse, Ralph Waldo Emerson, Henry David Thoreau, Will Durant, Nikola Tesla, Erwin Schrodinger and John Dobson. J. Robert Oppenheimer, theoretical physicist and director of the Manhattan Project, also was a professed Vedantist. In reference to the Trinity test in New Mexico, where his Los Alamos team tested the first atomic bomb, Oppenheimer famously recalled the Bhagavad Gita: "If the radiance of a thousand suns were to burst at once into the sky, that would be like the splendour of the mighty one. Now I am become Death, the destroyer of worlds."

Advaita Vedanta

Advaita Vedanta is a sub-school of the Vedanta (literally, *end or the goal of the Vedas*, Sanskrit) school of Hindu philosophy. Other major sub-schools of Vedanta are *Dvaita* and *Vi[ishmdvaita. Advaita* (literally, *non-duality*) is a monistic system of thought. "Advaita" refers to the identity of the Self (Atman) and the Whole (Brahman).

The key source texts for all schools of Vednta are the Prasthanatrayi—the canonical texts consisting of the Upanishads, the Bhagavad Gita and the Brahma Sutras. The first person to explicitly consolidate the principles of Advaita Vedanta was Adi Shankara, while the first historical proponent was Gaudapada, the guru of Shankara's guru Govinda Bhagavatpada.

Adi Shankara

Adi Shankara consolidated the Advaita Vedanta, an interpretation of the Vedic scriptures that was approved and accepted by Gaudapada and Govinda Bhagavatpada siddhnta (system). Continuing the line of thought of some of the Upanishadic teachers, and also that of his own teacher's teacher Gaudapada, (Ajativada), Adi Shankara expounded the doctrine of Advaita — a nondualistic reality.

Brahma satyaC jagat mithy, Jiva brahmaiva nparah — Brahman is the only truth, the world is illusion, and there is ultimately no difference between Brahman and individual self

This widely quoted sentence of his is also widely misunderstood. In his metaphysics, there are three tiers of reality with each one more real than the previous. The category *illusion* in this system is unreal only from the viewpoint of the absolutely real and is different from the category of the *Absolutely unreal.* His system of Vedanta introduced the method of scholarly exegesis on the accepted metaphysics of the Upanishads, and this style was adopted by all the later Vedanta schools. Another distinctive feature of his work is his refusal to be literal about scriptural statements and adoption of symbolic interpretation where he considered it appropriate.

In a famous passage in his commentary on the Brahmasutra's of Badarayana, he says "For each means of knowledge {Pramanam} has a valid domain. The domain of the scriptures {Shabda Pramanam} is the knowledge of the Self. If the scriptures say something about another domain-like the world around us-which contradicts what perception {Pratyaksha Pramanam} and inference {Anumana Pramanam} (the appropriate methods of knowledge for this domain) tells us, then, the scriptural statements have to be symbolically interpreted..."

Adi Shankara's contributions to Advaita are crucial. His main works are the commentaries on the *Prasthanatrayi* (Brahma Sutras, Bhagavad Gita and the Upaniads) and the *Gaudapadiya Karikas.* He also wrote a major independent treatise, called Upadeua Sahasri, expounding his philosophy.

Prerequisites

The Necessity of a Guru

Advaita Vedanta requires anyone seeking to study advaita Vedanta to do so from a Guru (*teacher*). The Guru must have the following qualities:

1. Zrotriya — must be learned in the Vedic scriptures and sampradaya
2. Brahmanicmha — literally meaning *established in Brahman;* must have *realised* the oneness of Brahman in everything and in himself.

The seeker must serve the Guru and submit questions with all humility in order to remove all doubts. By doing so, advaita says, the seeker will attain moksha (*liberation from the cycle of births and deaths*).

According to Adi Shankara, knowledge of brahman springs from inquiry into the words of the Upanishads, and the knowledge of brahman that shruti provides cannot be obtained in any other way. It is the teacher who through exegesis of shruti and skillful handling of words generates a hitherto unknown knowledge in the disciple. The teacher does not merely provide stimulus or suggestion.

Epistemology

Prama, in Sanskrit, refers to the correct knowledge, arrived at by thorough reasoning, of any object. Pramga (*sources of knowledge,* Sanskrit) forms one part of a tripumi (trio), namely,

1. Pramt[, the *subject;* the *knower* of the knowledge
2. Pramga, the *cause* or the *means* of the knowledge
3. Prameya, the *object* of knowledge.

In Advaita Vedanta, the following pramnas are accepted:

- Pratyakca – the knowledge gained by means of the *senses*
- Anumna – the knowledge gained by means of *inference*
- Upamna – the knowledge gained by means of *analogy*
- Arthpatti – the knowledge gained by superimposing the known knowledge on an appearing knowledge that does not concur with the known knowledge
- gama – the knowledge gained by means of *texts* such as Vedas (also known as ptavkya, Zabda pramga).

Krya and Krana

The krya (*effect*) and krana (*cause*) form an important area for investigation in all the systems of Vedanta. Two kranatvas (*ways of being the cause*) are recognised:

1. Nimitta kranatva – *Being the instrumental cause.* For example, a potter is assigned Nimitta kraGatva as he acts as the maker of the pot and thus becomes the pot's *instrumental cause.*
2. Updna kranatva – *Being the material cause.* For example, the mud is assigned Updna kraGatva as it acts as the material of the effect (the pot) and thus becomes the pot's *material cause.*

3

Advaita Vedanta

Jagadguru Sri Adi Sankaracharya was the greatest exponent of the doctrine of Advaita Vedanta and a savior of Vedic Dharma. Salutations to Sankara, who is an ever shining star on the sky of Indian philosophy.

The existence of Vedic Dharma in India today is due to Sankara. The forces opposed to Vedic religion were more numerous and powerful at the time of Sankara than they are today.

Still, single-handed, within a very short time, Sankara overpowered them all and restored the Vedic Dharma and Advaita Vedanta to its pristine purity in the land pure knowledge and spirituality.

Sankaracharya occupies a very important position in the history of Indian philosophy. It can be affirmed, without any fear of contradiction, that Bharata Varsha would have ceased to be Bharata Varsha several centuries ago and would never have survived the murderous sword, the devastating fire and the religious intolerance of the successive invaders, if Sankara had not lived the life he lived and taught the lessons he taught. And those lessons are still pulsating in every cell and in every protoplasm of the true aspirant and the true Hindu.

What is Advaita Vedanta?

The doctrine of advaita Vedanta as expounded by Sankara can be summed up in half a verse: "*Brahma Satyam Jagan Mithya Jiva Brahmaiva Na Aparah*" — Brahman (the Absolute) is alone real; this world is unreal; and the Jiva or the individual soul is non-different from Brahman. This is the quintessence of his philosophy.

According to Sri Sankara, whatever is, is Brahman. Brahman Itself is absolutely homogeneous. All difference and plurality are illusory.

Tenets of Advaita Vedanta:

- Brahman (the Absolute) is alone real; this world is unreal; and the Jiva or the individual soul is non-different from Brahman.
- The Atman is self-evident (Svatah-siddha). It is not established by extraneous proofs. It is not possible to deny the Atman, because It is the very essence of the one who denies It.
- Brahman is not an object, as It is Adrisya, beyond the reach of senses, mind or intellect. It is not another. It is all-full, infinite, changeless, self-existent, self-delight, self-knowledge and self-bliss. It is Svarupa, essence. It is the essence of the knower. It is the Seer (Drashta), Transcendent (Turiya) and Silent Witness (Sakshi). It is always the Witnessing Subject. It can never become an object as It is beyond the reach of the senses. Brahman is non-dual, one without a second. It has no other beside It.
- Sat-Chit-Ananda constitute the very essence or Svarupa of Brahman, and not just Its attributes.
- The world is not an illusion according to Sankara. The world is relatively real (Vyavaharika Satta), while Brahman is absolutely real (Paramarthika Satta). The unchanging Brahman appears as the changing world because of a superimposition of non-Self (objects) on Self (subject-Brahman). This is called Avidya.
- The Jiva or the individual soul is only relatively real. Its individuality lasts only so long as it is subject to unreal Upadhis or limiting conditions due to Avidya. The Jiva identifies itself with the body, mind and the senses, when it is deluded by Avidya or ignorance. Just as the bubble becomes one with the ocean when it bursts, so also the Jiva or the empirical self becomes one with Brahman when it gets knowledge of Brahman. When knowledge dawns in it through annihilation of Avidya, it is freed from its individuality and finitude and realizes its essential Satchidananda nature. It merges itself in the ocean of

bliss. The river of life joins the ocean of existence. This is the Truth.

- Because samsara (or duality) exists due to ignorance or Avidya, Knowledge (Jnana) alone can make an individual realize his true nature. Karma Yoga, Bhakti Yoga, Raja Yoga etc., are necessary only to purify the individual and to help remove this Avidya. All other paths culminate in Jnana.
- Brahma Jnana is not about acquiring any external knowledge (as Brahman can't be an object of knowledge), it just about removing the Avidya or Maya.

Adi Shankaracharya

About Adi Shankaracharya

Adi Shankaracharya was the first philosopher who consolidated Advaita Vedanta, one of the sub-schools of Vedanta. He believed in the greatness of the holy Vedas and was a major proponent of the same. Not only did he infuse a new life into the Vedas, but also advocated against the Vedic religious practices of ritualistic excesses. He founded four Shankaracharya Peethas in the four corners of India, which continue to promote his philosophy and teachings. Adi Sankaracharya biography reveals that he was also the founder of Dashanami monastic order and the Shanmata tradition of worship.

Childhood of Adi Shankaracharya

Adi Shankaracharya was born as Shankara in around 788 AD in a Brahmin family in Kaladi village of Kerala. He was born to Sivaguru and Aryamba a number of years after their marriage. It is said that Aryamba had a vision of Lord Shiva, in which he promised her that He would incarnate Himself in the form of her first-born child. The life history of Adi Shankracharya tells us that he showed great intelligence right from his childhood. He mastered all the Vedas and the Vedanta in gurukul itself and could recite the epics and Puranas by heart.

Adopting Sanyasa (Monastic Life)

Adi Shankaracharya was attracted towards sanyasa right from his childhood. One day, while bathing in the Purna River, Shankaracharya was attacked by a crocodile. Seeing his mother's incapability to rescue him, he asked her to give him the permission to renounce the world. Left with no other option, she agreed to it. Shankaracharya recited the mantras of renunciation and immediately, the crocodile left him. Thus started the life of Shankara as an ascetic. He left Kerala and moved towards South India in search of a Guru.

Meeting Govinda Bhagavatpada and Enlightenment

On the banks of Narmada River, Shankara met Govinda Bhagavatpada. Impressed by his knowledge of the Vedas and the Vedanta, he took Shankaracharya under his tutelage. Under the guidance of his Guru, Shankara mastered Hatha, Raja and Jnana Yoga. Thereafter he received initiation in the knowledge of Brahma. Thus was born Adi Shankaracharya, whose aim in life was to spread the Vedic teachings of the Brahma Sutras throughout the world.

Adi Sankaracharya Teachings

The philosophy and teachings of Adi Sankaracharya were based on the Advaita Vedanta. He preached 'Non-Dualism'. It means that each and every person has a divine existence, which can be identified with the Supreme God. The mere thought that human being is finite with a name and form subject to earthly changes, is to be discarded. The bodies are diverse, but the soul of all the separate bodies is the same, the Divine One.

The Four Adi Shankaracharya Peethas:

- Vedanta Jnana Peetha, Sringeri (South India)
- Govardhana Peetha in Jagannath Puri (East India)
- Kalika Peetha, Dwaraka (West India).

Shankaracharya Peethas

Adi Shankaracharya

Adi Shankaracharya was one of the most notable philosophers as well as Savants of India. In his short lifespan of thirty-two years, he became one of the greatest teachers of the Vedas. He was a major proponent of the Vedanta tenet that 'Lord Brahma and men are of one essence and every individual should try to develop this vision of oneness'. As per him, God is one and the only way to achieve salvation is through the study of the Vedas. He founded four Shankaracharya Peethas (spiritual centers) in the four corners of India, which uphold his teachings.

Shankaracharya Ashrams in India

Adi Shankaracharya established four peeths or maths in the four corners of India. Known as Amnaya Peethas, Shankaracharya Ashrams count amongst the most revered pilgrim destinations in the country. The heads of these four institutions are considered the principal Shankaracharyas in India.

Vedanta Jnana Peetha, Sringeri (South India)

Sringeri is situated in Karnataka, on the embankment of river Tunga. Great sages like Vibhan-daka, Rishyashringa, etc have meditated here in the ancient times. The serene and calm environs of Sringeri charmed him and he established his first Vedanta Jnana Peetha here. He installed there the idol of Sri Sharada, the Goddess of Learning, and named Sureshwara as the Head of that Sharada Peetha.

The three other Adi Shankracharya Maths in India are as follows-

- Govardhana Peetha in Jagannath Puri (Orissa)
- Kalika Peetha, Dwaraka (Gujarat)
- Jyotih Peetha, Badarikashrama (Uttarakhand/Uttaranchal)
- yotih Peetha, Badarikashrama (North India).

Adi Shankaracharya

About Adi Shankaracharya

Sri Adi Shankaracharya (meaning 'first shankara' in his lineage) was the first and most famous philosopher who consolidated Advaita Vedanta, He believed in the greatness of the holy Vedas and was a major proponent of the same. Not only did he infuse a new life into the Vedas, he advocated the greatness and importance of the important Hindu scriptures, the Vedas (most particularly on the Upanishads, also known as Vedanta), spoke to a spirituality founded on reason and without dogma or ritualism, and gave new life to Hinduism at a time when Buddhism and Jainism were gaining popularity.

He founded four Shankaracharya Peethas in the four corners of India, which continue to promote his philosophy and teachings.

On a closer introspection of the life history of Sri Shankaracharya, we find that he also started the monastic order known as Dashanami and the Shanmata convention of worship. Given here is Adi Shankaracharya biography, which will give you valuable insight into the life of this great poet and philosopher.

Childhood of Adi Shankaracharya

Adi Shankaracharya was born as Shankara in around 788 AD in a Brahmin family in Kaladi, a small village of Kerala. He was born to Sivaguru and Aryamba. It is said that Aryamba had a vision of Lord Shiva, in which he promised her that He would incarnate Himself in the form of her first-born child. The life history of Adi Shankracharya tells us that he showed great intelligence right from his childhood.

Shankara lost his father when quite young, and his mother performed his upanayana ceremony with the help of her relatives. Shankara excelled in all branches of traditional vaidika learning. A few miracles are reported about the young Shankara. As a brahmin, he went about collecting alms from families in the village. A lady who was herself extremely poor, but did not want to send away the boy empty-handed, gave him the last piece of Amla fruit she had at home.

Shankara, sensing the abject poverty of the lady, composed a hymn (kanakadhara stotram) to Sri, the goddess of wealth, right at her doorstep. As a result, a shower of golden Amlas rewarded the lady for her piety. On another occasion, Shankara is said to have re-routed the course of the purna river, so that his old mother would not have to walk a long distance to the river for her daily ablutions.

He mastered all the Vedas and the Vedanta in gurukul itself and could recite the epics and Puranas by heart. Adi Shankara's teachings were thoroughly adopted by his disciples later on.

Adopting Sanyasa (Monastic Life)

Adi Shankaracharya was attracted towards sanyasa right from his childhood. One day, while taking a bath in the Purna River, Shankaracharya was attacked by a crocodile. Seeing his mother's incapability to rescue him, he asked her to give him the permission to renounce the world. Left with no other option, she agreed to it. Shankaracharya recited the mantras of renunciation and immediately, the crocodile left him. Thus started the life of Shankara as an ascetic. He left Kerala and moved towards South India in search of a Guru.

Meeting Govinda Bhagavatpada and Enlightenment

On the banks of Narmada River, Shankara met Govinda Bhagavatpada. Impressed by his knowledge of the Vedas and the Vedanta, he took Shankaracharya under his tutelage. Under the guidance of his Guru, Shankara mastered Hatha, Raja and Jnana Yoga. Thereafter he received initiation in the knowledge of Brahma. Thus was born Adi Shankaracharya, whose aim in life was to spread the Vedic teachings of the Brahma Sutras throughout the world.

Adi Shankaracharya Teachings

The philosophy and teachings of Adi Shankaracharya were based on the Advaita Vedanta. He preached 'Non-Dualism'. It means that each and every person has a divine existence, which can be identified with the Supreme God. Though bodies are diverse, the soul is one. The moment someone believes that the concept of life is finite; they are discarding an entirely higher and different dimension of life and knowledge. Self-realization is the key to attain Moksha and connect with God.

In addition to writing his own commentaries, Shankara sought out leaders of other schools, in order to engage them in debate. As per the accepted philosophical tradition in India, such debates helped to establish a new philosopher, and the loser in the debate has to become a disciple of the winner.

Shankara's debate with visvarupa was unique. The referee at the debate was visvarupa's wife, Bharati, who was herself very well-learned, and regarded as an incarnation of Goddess saraswati. At stake was a whole way of life. The agreement was that if visvarupa won, Shankara would consent to marriage and the life of a householder, whereas if Shankara won, visvarupa would renounce all his wealth and possessions and become a sannyasi disciple of Shankara.

The debate is said to have lasted for whole weeks, till in the end, visvarupa had to concede defeat and become a sannyasi. Bharati was a fair judge, but before declaring Shankara as the winner, she challenged Shankara with questions about kamasastra, which he knew nothing about. Shankara therefore requested some time, during which, using the subtle yogic process called parakaya-pravesha, he entered the body of a dying king and experienced the art of love with the queens. Returning to visvarupa's home, he answered all of Bharati's questions, after which visvarupa was ordained as a sannyasi by the name of suresvaracharya.

Though he died young, he left an invaluable treasure of spiritual knowledge for future generations.

The Four Adi Shankaracharya Peethas

Shankara continued to travel with his disciples all over the land, all the while composing philosophical treatises and engaging opponents in debate. It is said that none of his opponents could ever match his intellectual prowess and the debates always ended with Shankara's victory. No doubt this is true, given the unrivaled respect and popularity that Shankara's philosophical system enjoys to this day.

In the course of his travells, He established mathas:

- Vedanta Jnana Peetha, Sringeri (South India)
- Govardhana Peetha in Jagannath Puri (East India)
- Kalika Peetha, Dwaraka (West India)
- Jyothi Peetha, Badarikashrama (North India).

Salient Features of Advaita Vedanta

Three Levels of Truth:

- The transcendental or the *Pramrthika* level in which Brahman is the only reality and nothing else;
- The pragmatic or the *Vyvahrika* level in which both Jiva (living creatures or individual souls) and Ishvara are true; here, the material world is completely true, and,
- The apparent or the *Prthibhsika* level in which even material world reality is actually false, like illusion of a snake over a rope or a dream.

Brahman

According to Adi Shankara, God, the Supreme Cosmic Spirit or Brahman (pronounced; nominative singular *Brahma*) is the One, the whole and the only reality. Other than Brahman, everything else, including the universe, material objects and individuals, are false. Brahman is at best described as that infinite, omnipresent, omnipotent, incorporeal, impersonal, transcendent reality that is the divine ground of all Being. Brahman is often described as neti neti meaning "not this, not this" because it cannot be correctly described as this or that.

It is the origin of this and that, the origin of forces, substances, all of existence, the undefined, the basis of all, unborn, the essential truth, unchanging, eternal, the absolute. How can it be properly described as something in the material world when itself is the basis of reality? Brahman is also beyond the senses, it would be akin a blind man trying to correctly describe colour.

It (grammatically neutral, but exceptionally treated as masculine), though not a substance, is the basis of the material world, which in turn is its illusionary transformation. Brahman is not the effect of the world. Brahman is said to be the purest knowledge itself, and is illuminant like a source of infinite light.

Due to ignorance (*avidy*), the Brahman is visible as the material world and its objects. The actual Brahman is attributeless and formless. It is the Self-existent, the Absolute and the Imperishable (not generally the object of worship but rather of meditation). Brahman is actually indescribable. It is at best "Satchidananda" (merging "Sat" + "Chit" + "Ananda", i.e., Infinite Truth, Infinite Consciousness and Infinite Bliss). Also, Brahman is free from any kind of differences. It does not have any *sajtiya* (homogeneous) differences because there is no second Brahman. It does not have any *vijtiya* (heterogeneous) differences because there is nobody in reality existing other than Brahman. It has neither *svagata* (internal) differences, because Brahman is itself homogeneous.

Though Brahman is self-proved, Adi Shankara also proposed some logical proofs:

- *Shruti* — the Upanishads and the Brahma Sutras describe Brahman in almost exact manner as Adi Shankara. This is the testimonial proof of Brahman.
- Psychological — every person experiences his soul, or atman. According to Adi Shankara, Atman = Brahman. This argument also proves the omniscience of the Brahman.
- Teleological — the world appears very well ordered; the reason for this cannot be an unconscious principle. The reason must be due to the Brahman.

- Essential – Brahman is the basis of this created world.
- Perceptible feeling – many people, when they achieve the *turiya* state, claim that their soul has become one with everything else.

Georg Feuerstein summarizes the advaita realization as follows: "The manifold universe is, in truth, a Single Reality. There is only one Great Being, which the sages call Brahman, in which all the countless forms of existence reside. That Great Being is utter Consciousness, and It is the very Essence, or Self (Atman) of all beings."

My

My According to Adi Shankara, *Maya* is the complex illusionary power of Brahman which causes the Brahman to be seen as the material world of separate forms. Maya has two main functions—one is to "hide" Brahman from ordinary human perception, and the other is to present the material world in its (Brahmam) place. Maya is also said to be indescribable, though it may be said that all sense data entering ones awareness via the five senses are Maya, since the fundamental reality underlying sensory perception is completely hidden.

It is also said that Maya is neither completely real nor completely unreal, hence indescribable. Its shelter is Brahman, but Brahman itself is untouched by the illusion of Maya, just like a magician is not tricked by his own magic. Maya is temporary and is transcended with "true knowledge," or perception of the more fundamental reality which permeates Maya.

Since according to the Upanishads only Brahman is real, but we see the material world to be real, Adi Shankara explained the anomaly by the concept of this illusionary power My.

Status of the World

Adi Shankara says that the world is not real (true), it is an illusion, but this is because of some logical reasons. Let us first analyse Adi Shankara's definition of Truth, and hence why the world is not considered real (true).

- Adi Shankara says that whatever thing remains eternal is true, and whatever is non-eternal is untrue. Since the world is created and destroyed, it is not real (true).

- Truth is the thing which is unchanging. Since the world is changing, it is not real (true).
- Whatever is independent of space and time is real (true), and whatever has space and time in itself is real (true).
- Just as one sees dreams in sleep, he sees a kind of super-dream when he is waking. The world is compared to this conscious dream.
- The world is believed to be a superimposition of the Brahman. Superimposition cannot be real (true).

On the other hand, Adi Shankara claims that the world is not absolutely unreal (false). It appears unreal (false) only when compared to Brahman. In the pragmatic state, the world is completely real—which occurs as long as we are under the influence of Maya. The world cannot be both true and false at the same time; hence Adi Shankara has classified the world as indescribable. The following points suggest that according to Adi Shankara, the world is not false (Adi Shankara himself gave most of the arguments, *Sinha, 1993*):

- If the world were unreal (false), then with the liberation of the first human being, the world would have been annihilated. However, the world continues to exist even if a human attains liberation.
- Adi Shankara believes in Karma, or good actions. This is a feature of this world. So the world cannot be unreal (false).
- The Supreme Reality Brahman is the basis of this world. The world is like its reflection. Hence the world cannot be totally unreal (false).
- False is something which is ascribed to nonexistent things, like Sky-lotus. The world is a logical thing which is perceived by our senses.

Consider the following logical argument. A pen is placed in front of a mirror. One can see its reflection. To one's eyes, the image of the pen is perceived. Now, what should the image be called? It cannot be true, because it is an image. The truth is the pen. It cannot be false, because it is seen by our eyes.

Shvara

Shvara (pronounced, literally, the Supreme Lord) — According to Advaita Vedanta, when man tries to know the attributeless Brahman with his mind, under the influence of Maya, Brahman becomes the Lord. Ishvara is Brahman with Maya — the manifested form of Brahman. Adi Shankara uses a metaphor that when the "reflection" of the Cosmic Spirit falls upon the mirror of Maya, it appears as the Supreme Lord. The Supreme Lord is true only in the pragmatic level — his actual form in the transcendental level is the Cosmic Spirit.

Ishvara is Saguna Brahman or Brahman with innumerable auspicious qualities. He is all-perfect, omniscient, omnipresent, incorporeal, independent, Creator of the world, its ruler and also destroyer. He is causeless, eternal and unchangeable — and is yet the material and the instrumental cause of the world. He is both immanent (like whiteness in milk) and transcendent (like a watch-maker independent of a watch). He may be even regarded to have a personality. He is the subject of worship. He is the basis of morality and giver of the fruits of one's Karma. However, He himself is beyond sin and merit. He rules the world with his Maya — His divine power.

This association with a "false" knowledge does not affect the perfection of Ishvara, in the same way as a magician is himself not tricked by his magic. However, while Ishvara is the Lord of Maya and she (i.e., Maya) is always under his control, the living beings (*Jiva*, in the sense of humans) are the servants of Maya (in the form of ignorance). This ignorance is the cause of the unhappiness and sin in the mortal world. While Ishvara is Infinite Bliss, humans are miserable. Ishvara always knows the unity of the Brahman substance, and the Mayic nature of the world. There is no place for a Satan in Hinduism, unlike Abrahamic religions. Advaitins explain the misery because of ignorance. Ishvara can also be visualized and worshipped in anthropomorphic form as deities such as Shiva, Vishnu or Devi.

Now the question arises as to why the Supreme Lord created the world. If one assumes that Ishvara creates the world for any incentive, this slanders the wholeness and perfection of Ishvara. For example, if one assumes that Ishvara creates the world for gaining something, it would be against His perfection. If we assume that He creates for compassion, it would be illogical, because the emotion of compassion cannot arise in a blank and void world in the beginning (when only Ishvara existed). So Adi Shankara assumes that Creation is a sport of Ishvara. It is His nature, just as it is man's nature to breathe.

The sole proof for Ishvara that Adi Shankara gives is Shruti's mentions of Ishvara, as Ishvara is beyond logic and thinking. This is similar to Kant 's philosophy about Ishvara in which he says that "faith" is the basis of theism. However, Adi Shankara has also given few other logical proofs for Ishvara, but warning us not to completely rely on them:

- The world is a work, an effect, and so must have real cause. This cause must be Ishvara.
- The world has a wonderful unity, coordination and order, so its creator must have been an intelligent being.
- People do good and sinful work and get its fruits, either in this life or after. People themselves cannot be the giver of their fruits, as no one would give himself the fruit of his sin. Also, this giver cannot be an unconscious object. So the giver of the fruits of Karma is Ishvara.

Status of God

To think that there is no place for a personal God (Ishvara) in Advaita Vedanta is a misunderstanding of the philosophy. Ishvara is, in an ultimate sense, described as "false" because Brahman appears as Ishvara only due to the curtain of Maya. However, as described earlier, just as the world is true in the pragmatic level, similarly, Ishvara is also pragmatically true. Just as the world is not absolutely false, Ishvara is also not absolutely false. He is the distributor of the fruits of one's Karma.

In order to make the pragmatic life successful, it is very important to believe in God and worship him. In the pragmatic level, whenever we talk about Brahman, we are in fact talking about God. God is the highest knowledge theoretically possible in that level. Devotion (Bhakti) will cancel the effects of bad Karma and will make a person closer to the true knowledge by purifying his mind. Slowly, the difference between the worshipper and the worshipped decreases and upon true knowledge, liberation occurs.

Tman

The swan is an important motif in Advaita. It symbolises two things: first, the swan is called *hamsah* in Sanskrit (which becomes *hamso* if the first letter in the next word is/h/). Upon repeating this *hamso* indefinitely, it becomes *so-aham*, meaning, "I am That". Second, just as a swan lives in water but its feathers are not soiled by water, similarly a liberated Advaitin lives in this world full of maya but is untouched by its illusion.

The soul or the self (Atman) is identical with Brahman. It is not a part of Brahman that ultimately dissolves into Brahman, but the whole Brahman itself. Now the arguers ask how the individual soul, which is limited and one in each body, can be the same as Brahman? Adi Shankara explains that the Self is not an individual concept. Atman is only one and unique. Indeed Atman alone is {Ekaatma Vaadam}. It is a false concept that there are several Atmans {Anekaatma Vaadam}.

Adi Shankara says that just as the same moon appears as several moons on its reflections on the surface of water covered with bubbles, the one Atman appears as multiple atmans in our bodies because of Maya. Atman is self-proven, however, some proofs are discussed—eg., a person says "I am blind", "I am happy", "I am fat" etc. The common and constant factor, which permeates all these statements is the "I" which is but the Immutable Consciousness. When the blindness, happiness, fatness are inquired and negated, "I" the common factor which, indeed, alone exists in all three states of consciousness and in all three periods of time, shines forth.

This proves the existence of Atman, and that Consciousness, Reality and Bliss are its characteristics. Atman, being the silent witness of all the modifications, is free and beyond sin and merit. It does not experience happiness or pain because it is beyond the triad of Experiencer, Experienced and Experiencing. It does not do any Karma because it is Aaptakaama. It is incorporeal and independent.

When the reflection of atman falls on Avidya (ignorance), atman becomes *Jiva* — a living being with a body and senses. Each Jiva feels as if he has his own, unique and distinct Atman, called jivatman. The concept of Jiva is true only in the pragmatic level. In the transcendental level, only the one Atman, equal to Brahman, is true.

Adi Shankara exposed the relative and thus unreal nature of the objective world and propounded the truth of the Advaita {One without a second} by analysing the three states of experience of the atman — waking (Vaishvanara), dreaming (taijasa), and deep sleep (prajna).

Salvation

Advaitins believe that suffering is due to Maya, and only knowledge (called Jnana) of Brahman can destroy Maya. When Maya is removed, there exists ultimately no difference between the Jiva-Atman and the Brahman. Such a state of bliss when achieved while living is called *Jivan mukti*. While one is in the pragmatic level, one can worship God in any way and in any form, like Krishna or Ayyappa as he wishes, Adi Shankara himself was a proponent of devotional worship or Bhakti. But Adi Shankara believes that while Vedic sacrifices, puja and devotional worship can lead one in the direction of jnana, true knowledge, they cannot lead one directly to Moksha.

Theory of Creation

In the relative level, Adi Shankara believes in the Creation of the world through *Satkaryavada*. It is like the philosophy of Samkhya, which says that the cause is always hidden into its effect—and the effect is just a transformation of the cause. However, Samkhya believes in a sub-form of *Satkaryavada* called Parinamavada (evolution) — whereby the cause really becomes an effect. Instead, Adi Shankara believes in a sub-form called *Vivartavada*. According to this, the effect is merely an apparent transformation of its cause — like illusion. eg., In darkness, a man often confuses a rope to be a snake. But this does not mean that the rope has actually transformed into a snake.

At the pragmatic level, the universe is believed to be the creation of the Supreme Lord Ishvara. Maya is the divine magic of Ishvara, with the help of which Ishvara creates the world. The serial of Creation is taken from the Upanishads. First of all, the five subtle elements (ether, air, fire, water and earth) are created from Ishvara.

Ether is created by Maya. From ether, air is born. From air, fire is born. From fire, water is born. From water, earth is born. From a proportional combination of all five subtle elements, the five gross elements are created, like the gross sky, the gross fire, etc. From these gross elements, the universe and life are created. This series is exactly the opposite during destruction.

Some people have criticized that these principles are against *Satkaryavada*. According to *Satkaryavada*, the cause is hidden inside the effect. How can Ishvara, whose form is spiritual, be the effect of this material world? Adi Shankara says that just as from a conscious living human, inanimate objects like hair and nails are formed, similarly, the inanimate world is formed from the spiritual Ishvara.

Status of Ethics

Some claim that there is no place for ethics in Advaita, because everything is ultimately illusionary. But on analysis, ethics also has a firm place in this philosophy—the same place as the world and God. Ethics, which implies doing good Karma, indirectly helps in attaining true knowledge. The traditional ethical system put forth by Advaitins is that the basis of merit and sin is the Shruti (the Vedas and the Upanishads). Truth, non-violence, service of others, pity, etc are Dharma, and lies, violence, cheating, selfishness, greed, etc are adharma (sin). However, no authoritative definition of Dharma was ever formulated by any of the major exponents of Advaita Vedanta. Unlike ontological and epistemological claims, there is room for significant disagreement between Advaitins on ethical issues.

The Impact of Advaita

Advaita rejuvenated much of Hindu thought and also spurred debate with the two main theistic schools of Vedanta philosophy that were formalized later: Vishishtadvaita (qualified nondualism), and Dvaita (dualism). Advaita further helped to merge the old Vedic religion with popular south-Asian cults/deities, thus making a bridge between higher types of practice (such as jnana yoga) and devotional religion of simple householders.

Vedanta Resources

Vedanta Resources plc (LSE: VED) is a global diversified and integrated metals and mining group headquartered in London, England. Headed by Indian billionaire Anil Agarwal, most of Vedanta's operations are located in India. Several of Vedanta's projects are mired in controversy and local unrest due to allegations that they will have a damaging impact on the environment, and on the livelihoods of local people.

Vedanta was first listed on the London Stock Exchange in December 2003 and became a constituent of the FTSE 100 Index in June 2006.

History

The business was founded by Anil Agarwal in 1976 as *Sterlite Industries* operating in the industrial sector. *Vedanta Resources* was established in 1986 to bring together a variety of businesses owned by the Agarwal family including *Sterlite Industries*. *Vedanta Resources* was first listed on the Bombay Stock Exchange in 1988 and on the London Stock Exchange in 2003. In 2004 it acquired a 51% stake in Konkola Copper Mines in Zambia.

The United States Geological Survey reported that as of 2005, the company supplies 75 per cent of Indian zinc requirements.

Founder

The founder of Vedanta Resources and Sterlite Industries is the billionaire Anil Agarwal.

Operations

The Company's principal operations are located in India, with a major market share in the metals: aluminium, copper, zinc and lead. There are also substantial copper operations in Zambia and Tasmania, Australia.

Subsidiaries

Vedanta's subsidiary Sterlite Industries is one of India's largest mining companies while Konkola Copper Mines is the largest mining company in Zambia.

Other subsidiary companies of Vedanta Resources include Hindustan Zinc Limited, Bharat Aluminium Company, Madras Aluminium Company and Sterlite Energy Limited.

Vedanta Resources also has a major stake in iron ore producer, Sesa Goa.

Criticism

Environmental Damage

Vedanta has come under attack from human rights and activist groups due to their operations in Niyamgiri Hills in Orissa, India that are said to threaten the lives of the Dongria Kondh that populate this region. The Niyamgiri hills are also claimed to be an important wildlife habitat in Eastern Ghats of India as per a report by the Wildlife Institute of India as well as independent reports/studies carried out by civil society groups In January 2009, thousands of locals formed a human chain around the hill in protest at the plans to start bauxite mining in the area.

Vedanta's Alumina Refinery in Lanjigarh was critiqued by the Orissa State Pollution Control Board (the statutory environmental regulation body) for air pollution and water pollution in the area. This includes increasing pH value of the river Vamshadhara below the refinery and the high level of SPM in the stack emissions.

In October 2009 it was reported that the British Government has criticised Vedanta for its treatment of the Dongria Kondh tribe in Orissa, India.. The company refused to co-operate with the British Government and with an OECD investigation.

Safety Concerns

2007 Mining Deaths

Unsafe mining operations led to 1,246 injuries and 18 deaths involving own employees and contractors.

Balco, Korba, Chhattisgarh

A chimney under construction by Gannon Dunkerley & Company at the Balco smelter in Korba, Chhattisgarh collapsed on 23 September 2009 killing at least 40 workers. Balco and GDCL management have been accused of negligence in the incident.

Litigation

Armenia

In early 2007, the Armenian government began an investigation of AGRC, a subsidiary of Vedanta Resources, *vis-a-vis* compliance with licensing and tax regulations following independent media claims that AGRC submitted incorrect data in production reports relating to royalty payments and was in violation of licensing laws. AGRC was also served a preliminary notice of penalties and fines to the tune of about $50 million (or 80 per cent of its net assets).

India

In respect of bauxite mines at Lanjigarh, Orissa, public interest litigations were filed in 2004 by Indian non-government organisations led by the Peoples Union for Civil Liberties to the Supreme Court sub-committee regarding the potential environmental impact of the mines. The Ministry of Environment and Forests received reports from expert organisations and has submitted its recommendations to the Supreme Court.

The sub-committee has found "blatant violations" of environmental regulations and grave concerns about the impact of the Niyamgiri mine on both the environment and the local tribal population. The committee recommended to the Court that mining in such an ecologically sensitive area should not be permitted.

Vedanta Society

Vedanta Society, and its variant Vedanta Centre, are terms covering organizations, groups, or societies formed for the study, practice, and propagation of Vedanta.

The first Vedanta Society was founded by Swami Vivekananda in New York in November 1894., who later on asked Swami Abhedananda to lead the organization in 1897. Many of the existing Vedanta Societies are affiliated, either formally or informally, with the Ramakrishna Order, the monastic order, which lead to the formation of Ramakrishna Mission.

Prior to its inception, Swami Vivekananda had given his famous "Brothers and Sisters of America!", public lecture at Parliament of Religions, Chicago in September 1893; after its success he spent following two years lecturing in various parts of eastern and central United States, appearing chiefly in Chicago, Detroit, Boston, and New York. In June 1895, for two months he conducted private lectures to a dozen of his disciples at the Thousand Island Park.

The branches of the Ramakrishna Order located outside India are generally known as Vedanta Societies, and are under the spiritual guidance of the Ramakrishna Order.

The work of the Vedanta Societies in the west has primarily been devoted to spiritual and pastoral activities, though many of them do some form of social service. Many of the Western Vedanta societies have resident monks, and several centers have resident nuns.

List of Vedanta Societies and Centers

Africa

South Africa: Ramakrishna Centre of South Africa · external link

Zambia: Ramakrishna Vedanta Centre, Lusaka

Australia

- Ramakrishna Sarada Vedanta Society of New South Wales, Sydney ·
- Vedanta Centre of Sydney external link.

Asia

Japan: Nippon Vedanta Kyokai, Zushi, Japan · external link

Europe

France: Centre Vedantique Ramakrishna, Gretz · external link.

Germany: Vedanta-Gesellschaft e. V., Sieg · external link.

Italy: Ramakrishna Mission Italia · external link.

The Netherlands: Ramakrishna Vedanta Sociey, Amstelveen · external link.

Russia: Ramakrishna Society Vedanta Centre, Moscow · external link.

Switzerland: Centre Vedantique, Geneva external link.

United Kingdom: Ramakrishna Vedanta Centre, Bucks · external link.

North America

Alberta: Vedanta Society of Calgary · external link.

British Columbia: Vivekananda Vedanta Society of British Columbia, Vancouver ·

Ontario: Vedanta Society of Toronto, Ontario · external link.

USA

Arizona: Vedanta Society of Phoenix · external link.

California: Ananda Ashrama, La Crescenta;

- external link
- Vedanta Society of Berkeley

- external link;
    - Vedanta Society, San Jose.
- Vedanta Society of Northern California, San Francisco · external link
- Vedanta Society of Sacramento · external link
- Vedanta Society of Southern California, Hollywood · external link.
    - Ramakrishna Monastery, Trabuco Canyon
    - Vedanta Society, San Diego
    - Vedanta Society, Santa Barbara
    - Vivekananda House, South Pasadena.

Colorado: Northern Colorado Vedanta Society, Fort Collins · external link

Delaware: Vedanta Society of Delaware Valley · external link

Florida: Vedanta Center of St Petersburg · external link

Georgia: Vedanta Center of Atlanta · external link

Illinois: Vivekananda Vedanta Society, Chicago · external link

Iowa: Vedanta Society of Iowa, Cedar Rapids · external link

Maryland: Vedanta Center of Greater Washington DC · external link

Massachusetts: Ramakrishna Vedanta Society, Boston · external link

Michigan: Vedanta Monastery and Retreat, Ganges ·

Missouri: Vedanta Society of St Louis · external link

New York: Ramakrishna-Vivekananda Center, New York · external link

North Carolina: Ramakrishna Vedanta Society of North Carolina · external link

Oregon: Vedanta Society, Portland · external link

Rhode Island: Vedanta Society, Providence · external link

Texas: Ramakrishna Vedanta Society of North Texas, Dallas · external link

Washington: Vedanta Society of Western Washington, Seattle· external link

South America

Brazil: Ramakrishna Vedanta Ashrama, Sao Paulo external link :

- o Centro Ramakrishna Vedanta, Belo-Horizonte, Brazil · external link
- o Centro Ramakrishna Vedanta, Curitiba-Parana, Brazil · external link
- o Centro Ramakrishna Vedanta, Rio de Janeiro external link.

Argentina: Ramakrishna Ashrama, Buenos Aires · external link

4

Ramanuja

Ramanuja; Traditionally 1017–1137, also known as Ramanujacharya, Ethirajar, Emperumannar, was a theologian, philosopher, and scriptural exegete. He is seen by Zr+vaicGavas as the third and most important teacher (*Acarya*) of their tradition (after Nathamuni and Yamunacharya), and by Hindus in general as the leading expounder of Vi[icmadvaita, one of the classical interpretations of the dominant Vedanta school of Hindu philosophy.

Establishing Dates

The traditional biographies of Ramanuja place his life in the period of 1017–1137, yielding a lifespan of 120 years. However, the unusual length and roundness of this lifetime has led scholars to propose that Ramanuja was born 20–60 years later, and died as many as 20 years earlier than the traditional dates. Any chronology depends crucially on the major historical event mentioned in the traditional biographies: the persecution of Vaishnavas under the Chola king Kulothunga and Ramanuja's subsequent 12-year exile in Melkote, in Karnataka.

In 1917, T. A. Gopinatha Rao proposed a chronology based on the traditional lifetime of 1017–1137. He identified the Chola king with Kulothunga Chola I (reigned 1070–1120), and dated the exile to Melkote from 1079 to 1126 CE (Rao 1923 cited in Carman 1974:45). However, this would extend the period of exile to 47 years, and in any case, Kulothunga I was not known for being an intolerate Shaivite.

A different chronology was proposed by T. N. Subramanian, an official in the Madras government (Subramanian 1957 cited in

Carman 1974:45). This chronology identifies the Chola King with Kulothunga Chola II, who reigned from 1133–50 and was-also arguably-known for his persecution of Vaisnavites. It puts Ramanuja's exile from c. 1137 to 1148. Subramanian's hypothesis is aided by a fragment from the late Tamil biography *Ramanujarya Divya Caritai*, which states that Ramanuja completed his most important work, the *Zr+bhcya*, in 1155–56. Nevertheless, temple inscriptions in Karnataka indicate the presence of Ramanuja and his disciples before 1137. Carman (1974:45) hypothesizes that the traditional biographers conflated two different visits to Mysore into one. This later chronology has been accepted by several scholars, yielding a tentative lifetime of 1077–1157.

Whatever the precise dates of Ramanuja's lifetime, it seems clear that all three of the great Zrivaic Gava *âcâryas* lived under the relatively stable and ecumenical climate of the Chola empire, before its decline in the late 12th and 13th centuries.

Historical Background

By the 5th century, the South Indian religious scene was diverse, with popular religion existing alongside Vedic sacrifice and non-Vedic traditions like Buddhism and Jainism. Indeed, the title character of the sixth century Tamil Buddhist epic Manimekalai is advised at one point to study the various Hindu schools of philosophy, such as Sankhya and Vaisheshika as well as Buddhism, Ajivika, Carvaka, and Jainism. It was in this context that fears of a Buddhist or Jain takeover spurred a large Hindu revival that reached its peak in the 7th century and continued nearly into the 2nd millennium.

The popular aspects of this revival took the shape of several mystical and passionate bhakti movements, represented on the Vaishnavite side by the twelve alvars. The alvars came from a variety of social strata; their ranks include shudras and one woman. The intense devotionalism of their poetry and insistence that caste and sex are no barrier to a relationship with the Divine is uncharacteristic of classical Vedic thought, which laid a strong emphasis on the performance of the social and religious duties proper to one's place in the social structure. Some of these were collected into a definitive canon known as the *Nalayira Divya Prabandha* ("divine composition of 4000 verses"), by Nathamuni in the 10th century, and came to be seen as a source of revelation equal in authority to the Vedas in the Zrivaic Gava community. On the philosophical side, this period saw the rise of the Vedanta school of philosophy, which focused on the elucidation and exegesis of the speculative and philosophical Vedic commentaries known as the Upanishads. The Advaita, or non-dualist interpretation of Vedanta was developed in this time by Adi Shankara and later by Manana Miœra. It argued that the Brahman presented in the Upanishads is the static and undifferentiated absolute reality, and that the ultimately false perception of difference is due to avidya, or ignorance.

The goal of proving the Vedantic legitimacy of the popular conception of a personal deity and a genuine personal identity essentially characterizes Ramanuja's project, and the Advaitin school presents a natural object for his polemics. It is this synthesis between the classical Sanskrit writings and the popular Tamil poetry that is the source of one of the names of Ramanuja's system: *Ubhaya Vedanta*, or "Vedanta of both kinds."

Evaluating Sources

In dealing with the lives of the Vedantic teachers, there is little in the way of actual history, and it is thus necessary to make reference to the many hagiographical works—both in verse and prose—that form a major genre in both Sanskrit and South Indian vernaculars.

The earliest such hagiographies in prose is the *ryirappami Guruparamparaprabhava* (the "six thousand" splendour of the succession of teachers) (not to be confused with the well-known commentary on the Divya Prabandha of the same length, also commonly referred to as the "Six Thousand"). This was written by Pilpaakiya Peruma Jiyar in the 13th century in a highly Sanskritized dialect of Tamil known as MaGipravala. Perhaps earlier was a Sanskrit work of poetry, the *Divya Suri Carita* or Acts of the Divine Sages, probably written in the 12th century by Garuavaha Ga PaG ita, a contemporary disciple of Ramanuja's.

In later times, a number of traditional biographies proliferated, such as the 16th or 17th century Sanskrit work *Prapannm[ta* and, following the split of the Zrivaic Gava community into the Vamakalais and Telkalais, various sectarian works. The *Muvyirappami Guruparamparaprabhava* or the "Three Thousand" Splendour of the Succession of Teachers by Brahmatantra Svatantra

Jiyar represents the earliest Vamakalai biography, and reflects the Vamakalai view of the succession following Ramanuja *ryirappami Guruparamparaprabhava*, or "Six Thousand" Splendour of the Succession of Teachers referred in the previous paragraph represents the Tenkalai biography.

The various biographies differ in emphasis, facts, and sometimes even entire episodes. In general, the later biographies tend to be more fanciful and elaborate, and the Vamakalai and Telkalai biographies reflect their sectarian outlook: for instance, the Telkalai biographies tend to emphasize episodes that reflect more liberal attitudes toward caste on Ramanuja's part, while the Vamakalai biographies generally minimize them. These generalizations are often inaccurate, but the differences in the biographies do at any rate reflect the difficulty of coming up with a single historical narrative. Nonetheless, the traditional biographies agree in most of the facts of Ramanuja's life, and thus an outline of Ramanuja's life and achievements can be sketched.

Formative Years

Ramanuja was born Ilaya Perumal in a Brahmin family in the village of Perumbudur, Tamil Nadu, India in 1017 CE. His father was Asuri Keshava Somayaji Deekshitar and mother was Kanthimathi in sect of Vadama. To quote from Shyam Ranganathan's article on Ramanuja at the Internet Encyclopedia of Philosophy, "From a young age he is reputed to have displayed a prodigious intellect and liberal attitudes towards caste.

At this time he became friendly with a local, saintly Sudra (member of the servile caste) by the name of Kancipurna, whose occupation was to perform services for the local temple idol of the Hindu deity Vishnu. Ramanuja admired Kancipurna's piety and devotion to Vishnu and sought Kancipurna as his guru-much to the horror of Kancipurna who regarded Ramanuja's humility before him as an affront to caste propriety."

Shortly after being married in his teenage years, and after his father died, Ramanuja and his family moved to the neighboring city of Kancipuram. There Ramanuja found his first formal teacher, Yadavaprakasha, who was an accomplished professor of the form of the Vedanta philosophy that was in vogue at the time-a form of Vedanta that has strong affinities to Shankara's Absolute Idealistic Monism (Advaita Vedanta) but was also close to the Difference-

and-non-difference view (Bhedabheda Vedanta). ("Vedanta" means the 'end of the Vedas' and refers to the philosophy expressed in the end portion of the Vedas, also known as the Upanishads, and encoded in the cryptic summary by Badharayana called the Vedanta Sutra or Brahma Sutra. The perennial questions of Vedanta are: what is the nature of Brahman, or the Ultimate, and what is the relationship between the multiplicity of individuals to this Ultimate. Vedanta comprises one of the six orthodox schools of Hindu philosophy.) "

From a young age, his intelligence and ability to comprehend highly abstract philosophical points were legendary. He took initiation from Yadavaprakasa, a renowned Advaitic scholar. Though his new guru was highly impressed with his analytical ability, he was quite concerned by how much emphasis Ramanuja placed on bhakti. After frequent clashes over interpretation, Yadavaprakasa decided the young Ramanuja was becoming too much of a threat and plotted a way to kill him.

However, Ramanuja's cousin Govinda Bhatta (a favourite of Yadavaprakasa) discovered the plot and helped him escape. An alternative version is that one of Yadavaprakasa's students plotted to kill Ramanuja as a means of pleasing their teacher, but Sri Ramanuja escaped in the afore-mentioned manner. Yadavaprakasa was horrified when learnt about the conspiracy. Ramanuja returned to Yadavaprakasa's tutelage but after another disagreement, Yadavaprakasa asked him to leave. Ramanuja's childhood mentor, Kancipurna, suggested he meet with Kancipurna's own guru, Yamunacharya. After renouncing the life of a house-holder, Ramanuja travelled to Srirangam to meet an aging Yamunacharya, a philosopher of the remergent Vishishtadvaita school of thought. Yamunacharya had died prior to Ramanuja's arrival. Followers of Ramanuja relate the legend that three fingers of Yamunacharya's corpse were curled. Ramanuja saw this and understood that Yamunacharya was concerned about three tasks.

Ramanuja vowed to complete these—

- Teach the doctrine of Saranagati (surrender) to God as the means to moksha.
- Write a Visisht Advaita Bhashya for the Brahma Sutras of Vyasa which had previously been taught orally to the disciples of the Visisht Advaita philosophy.

- That the names of Paraœara, the author of Vishnu Purana, and saint Œaþhakopa should be perpetuated.

Legend goes that on hearing the vow, the three fingers on the corpse straightened. Ramanuja accepted Yamunacharya as his *Manasika Acharya* and spent 6 months being introduced to Yamunacharya's philosophy by his disciple, Mahapurna although he did not formally join the community for another year. Ramanuja's wife followed very strict brahminical rules of the time and disparaged Mahapurna's wife as being of lower subcaste. Mahapurna and his wife left Srirangam.

Ramanuja realized that his life as a householder was interfering with his philosophical pursuit as he and his wife had differing views. He sent her to her parent's house and renounced family and became a sanyasin. Ramanuja started travelling the land, having philosophical debates with the custodians of various Vishnu temples. Many of them, after losing the debates, became his disciples. Ramanuja standardized the liturgy at these temples and increased the standing and the membership of the srivaishnava school of thought. He wrote his books during this time. Ramanuja, who was a Vaishnavite, might have faced threats from some Shaivite Chola rulers who were religiously intolerant. Ramanuja and a few of his followers moved to the Hoysala kingdom of Jain king Bittideva and queen Shantala Devi in Karnataka. Bittideva converted to Srivaishanavism, in some legends after Ramanuja cured his daughter of evil spirits, and took the name Vishnuvardhana meaning "one who grows the sect of Vishnu". However, the queen and many of the ministers remained Jain and the kingdom was known for its tolerance. Ramanuja re-established the liturgy in the Cheluvanarayana temple in Melukote In Mandya District and Vishnuvardhana re-built it and also built other Vishnu temples like Chennakesava Temple and Hoysaleswara Temple.

Five acharyas

Swami Ramanuja incorporated teachings from 5 different people who he considered to be his acharyas

1. Peria Nambigal who performed his samasrayana
2. Thirukkotiyur Nambigal : who revealed the meaning of Charama slokam to swami on his 18th trip
3. Periya Thirumalai Nambigal : Ramayana

4. Tirumalai Aandaan : Bhagavad Vishayam
5. Azhwar Thiruvaranga Perumal Arayar

Visisht Advaita Philosophy

Ramanuja's philosophy is referred to as Vishishtadvaita because it combines Advaita (oneness of God) with Vishesha (attributes).

Differences with Shankara

Adi Shankara had argued that all qualities or manifestations that can be perceived are unreal and temporary. Ramanuja believed them to be real and permanent and under the control of the *Brahman*. God can be one despite the existence of attributes, because they cannot exist alone; they are not independent entities. They are *Prakaras* or the modes, *Sesha* or the accessories, and *Niyama* or the controlled aspects, of the one *Brahman*.

In Ramanuja's system of philosophy, the Lord (Narayana) has two inseparable *Prakaras* or modes, namely, the world and the souls. These are related to Him as the body is related to the soul. They have no existence apart from Him. They inhere in Him as attributes in a substance. Matter and souls constitute the body of the Lord. The Lord is their indweller. He is the controlling Reality. Matter and souls are the subordinate elements. They are termed *Viseshanas*, attributes. God is the *Viseshya* or that which is qualified.

Ramanuja opines, wrong is the position of the *Advaitins* that understanding the *Upanishads* without knowing and practicing dharma can result in Brahman knowledge. The knowledge of Brahman that ends spiritual ignorance is meditational, not testimonial or verbal.

In contrast to Shankara, Ramanuja holds that there is no knowledge source in support of the claim that there is a distinctionless (homogeneous) Brahman. All knowledge sources reveal objects as distinct from other objects. All experience reveals an object known in some way or other beyond mere existence. Testimony depends on the operation of distinct sentence parts (words with distinct meanings). Thus the claim that testimony makes known that reality is distinctionless is contradicted by the very nature of testimony as a knowledge means. Even the simplest perceptual cognition reveals something (Bessie) as qualified by something else (a broken hoof, "Bessie has a broken hoof," as known perceptually). Inference depends on perception and makes the same distinct things known as does perception. He also holds that the Advaitin argument about prior absences and no prior absence of consciousness is wrong. Similarly the Advaitin understanding of a-Vidya (not-Knowledge), which is the absence of spiritual knowledge, is incorrect. "If the distinction between spiritual knowledge and spiritual ignorance is unreal, then spiritual ignorance and the self are one."

The Seven Objections to Shankara's Advaita

Ramanuja picks out what he sees as seven fundamental flaws in the Advaita philosophy to revise them. He argues:

The nature of Avidya. Avidya must be either real or unreal; there is no other possibility. But neither of these is possible. If Avidya is real, non-dualism collapses into dualism. If it is unreal, we are driven to self-contradiction or infinite regress.

The incomprehensibility of Avidya. Advaitins claim that Avidya is neither real nor unreal but incomprehensible, {anirvachaniya.} All cognition is either of the real or the unreal: the Advaitin claim flies in the face of experience, and accepting it would call into question all cognition and render it unsafe.

The grounds of knowledge of Avidya. No pramana can establish Avidya in the sense the Advaitin requires. Advaita philosophy presents Avidya not as a mere lack of knowledge, as something purely negative, but as an obscuring layer which covers Brahman and is removed by true Brahma-Vidya. Avidya is positive nescience not mere ignorance. Ramanuja argues that positive nescience is established neither by perception, nor by inference, nor by scriptural testimony. On the contrary, Ramanuja argues, all cognition is of the real.

The locus of Avidya. Where is the Avidya that gives rise to the (false) impression of the reality of the perceived world? There are two possibilities; it could be Brahman's Avidya or the individual soul's {Jiva.} Neither is possible. Brahman is knowledge; Avidya cannot co-exist as an attribute with a nature utterly incompatible with it. Nor can the individual soul be the locus of Avidya: the existence of the individual soul is due to Avidya; this would lead to a vicious circle.

Avidya's obscuration of the nature of Brahman. Sankara would have us believe that the true nature of Brahman is somehow covered-over or obscured by Avidya. Ramanuja regards this as an absurdity: given that Advaita claims that Brahman is pure self-luminous consciousness, obscuration must mean either preventing the origination of this (impossible since Brahman is eternal) or the destruction of it-equally absurd.

The removal of Avidya by Brahma-Vidya. Advaita claims that Avidya has no beginning, but it is terminated and removed by Brahma-Vidya, the intuition of the reality of Brahman as pure, undifferentiated consciousness. But Ramanuja denies the existence of undifferentiated {nirguna} Brahman, arguing that whatever exists has attributes: Brahman has infinite auspicious attributes. Liberation is a matter of Divine Grace: no amount of learning or wisdom will deliver us. The removal of Avidya. For the Advaitin, the bondage in which we dwell before the attainment of Moksa is caused by Maya and Avidya; knowledge of reality (Brahma-Vidya) releases us. Ramanuja, however, asserts that bondage is real. No kind of knowledge can remove what is real. On the contrary, knowledge discloses the real; it does not destroy it. And what exactly is the saving knowledge that delivers us from bondage to Maya? If it is real then non-duality collapses into duality; if it is unreal, then we face an utter absurdity.

Bhagavad Ramanuja taught his followers to highly respect all Sri Vaishnavas irrespective of caste.

Cited from Sri Ramanuja, His Life, Religion, and Philosophy, published by Sri Ramakrishna Math, Chennai, India.

Writings

Ramanuja may have written 9 books. They are also referred to as the nine precious gems, the *Navarathnas*.

- His most famous work is known as the Sri Bhasya or Brahma Sutra Bhasya. It is a commentary on the Brahma Sutras, known also as the *[Vedanta Sutras]* of [Badarayana].
- Gadhya Thrayam (three prose hymns). All three are important works in Vaishnava philosophy:
    - o Vaikunta Gadyam describing in great detail Vaikuntha, the realm of Vishnu and recommending meditating on it.
    - o Sriranga Gadyam, a prayer of surrender to the feet of Ranganatha

- o Saranagati Gadyam, an imagined dialogue between Ramanuja and Shri (Lakshmi) and Narayana where he petitions Lakshmi to recommend Narayana to give him grace. Narayana and Lakshmi accept his surrender.
- Vedartha Sangraha (a resume of Vedanta). It sets out Ramanuja's philosophy, which is theistic (it affirms a morally perfect, omniscient and omnipotent God) and realistic (it affirms the existence and reality of a plurality of qualities, persons and objects).
- Vedanta Saara (essence of Vedanta) an appendix to Sri Bhasya
- Vedanta Deepa (the light of Vedanta), another appendix/ commentary to Sri Bhasya.
- Gita Bhashya (his commentary on the Bhagavad Gita)
- Nithya Grantham (About the day to day activities to be performed by all Sri Vaishnavas).

Samadhi Mandir

Ramanuja's *thiruvarasu* (sacred burial shrine) is the Ramanuja shrine (*sannidhi*) located inside the Sri Ranganathaswamy temple (*periyakoyil* or simply *koyil*) Srirangam, Tamil Nadu within the temple complex, where he attained his Acharyan Thiruvadi (the lotus foot of his Acharya). His mortal remains (*thirumeni*) have been interred inside the Sri Ramanuja shrine and on top of it his wax look-alike deity has been consecrated and it is anointed with *chandan* (sandalwood paste) and saffron (*kungumappoo*).His shrine is open to the general public for *darshan*.

Stone Idol of Ramnujacharya as it is generally seen and worshipped in every Srivaishnava temple, along with the main deities of the temple in India

A Living Tradition

Ramanuja's achievements are visible to this day. Iyengar Brahmins in South India follow his philosophical tradition. The Tamil prabhandas are chanted at Vishnu temples on par with the Sanskrit vedas. Persons of all communities, and not just Brahmins, are given roles in rituals at Srirangam and other leading temples. The philosophic discourses have been passed on to subsequent generations by great successors like Pillai Lokacharya, Vedanta

Desika and Manavala Mamuni who lived in the 13th and 14th centuries. Several accounts suggest that Ramanuja was an incarnation of Sri Adisesha.

There are however stories of tragedy as well. In 1564.C.E, a pontiff of a mutt commited to Ramanuja's philosophy by name venkatacharya who was visiting puri in orissa which also had an important buddist vihara, was challenged at that place by a theravada buddist pontiff from srilanka namely sree sangabodhi dharmadasar in a polemical debate. The "vaishnavite seer" was defeated and being unable to bear the humiliation of the loss had jumped into the river mahanadi and committed suicide.

Srivaishnavas hold 108 sacred temples sung by azhwars as dhivyakshetras. In almost all the divyakshetrams, the prabhandha seva or the chanting of Tamil Vedas start with the invocation to Sri Manavala Mamuni as follows:

Srisailesa dhaya pathram dheebhakthyadhi gunarnavam Yatheendra pravanam vandhe Ramyajamataram munim.

The above sloka was first recited by none other than Swami Ranganatha of Srirangam after listening to Mamuni's rendering of the Eedu Muppatharayairam, the celebrated commentary of Nampillai on Nammazhvar's thiruvaimozhi. In this reverential verse the Lord describes Mamuni as His preceptor.

At homes and temples, the chanting concludes with Srimathe *Ramyajamamathru muneendhraya Mahathmane Sriranga vasine bhooyath nithyasri nithya mangalam.* This is an auspicious verse showing special love towards Srirangam and Mamuni Also, in the Vadakalai/Ubhayakalai sampradaya, this thaniyan is chanted at the start of the prabhandas:

Ramanuja dhaya pathram gnana vairagya bhushanam, srimath venkata natharyam vande Vedanta desikam

Sri Ranganatha and Periya Piratti have also shown their love for Srimad Vedanta Desikar with Sri Ranganayaki Thayar herself proclaiming Sri Desikan as Kavitharkika Simham

Sri Ramanujacharya Life History

Sri Ramanuja (1017-1137 CE), the most important philosopher-saint of Sri Vaishnavam and one of the most dynamic characters of Hinduism. He was a philosophical as well as a social reformer, displaying a catholicity that was nearly unparalleled in Hindu religious history before him. He revitalized Indian philosophy and popular religion so much that nearly every aspect of Hinduism has been influenced by his work. His life and works show a truly unique personality, combining contemplative insight, logical acumen, catholicity, charismatic energy, and selfless dedication to God.

The less known fact even among Srivaishnavas about this well known Acharya by whose name Srivaishnava philosophy is called 'Ramanuja Darsanam' and who is hailed as "Sri Vaishnava Siddhanta Nirdhaarana Saarva bouma" is that he was a 'Vadama' by birth. (Authority:" Periya Thrumudi Adaivu, Pazhanadai Vilakkam and Visishtaadvaita Catechism"-quoted in GLE)

His Avatara and Early Days

Ilaya Perumal was born to Kesava Perumal Somayaji Dikhsitar and Kanthimathi Ammal at Sriperumpudur. Just as Sage Vasishta on seeing the brilliance in the face of the child named him as Lakshmana saying "Lakshmano Lakshmi Sampannaha", Periya Thiru malai Nambi struck by the Tejas of the child, named him after Lakshmana as Ilaya Perumal. (PPM) aka Ilayalwar.

There is a sloka in Yadhavaachala Mahatmyam which says:

Ananthah Prathamam Roopam Lakshmanascha Tathah Parah |

Balabadram Thritheeyasthu Kalou Kaschit Bhavishyathi ||

(meaning) It is the same who was Adhisesha first, Lakshmana after and Balarama in the third who is born as Sri Ramanuja in the Kali yuga. This Kaschit is taken by our Poorva Acharyas as referring to Ramanuja (PPM)

His Birth: Chitrai-Tiruvadhirai)

His date of birth is placed differently by different authorities. As per PPM, he was born in Kaliyuga year 4119 which corresponds to 1017 AD. PPM fixes even the exact date as 13th April 1017 AD, interms of English Calendar.

PRA, though notes the year as 4118 Kali, maintains the year as 1017 AD only and gives additional information that the Rasi was Karkataka and the time of birth was exactly at noon.

VAC, MKS and MSR also agree on the year 1017. PTA gives a few more details like the Yogam being Ayushman, Karanam being Bhadra, Gotra being Harita, Saakha being Yajus, Sutra being Apasthambha and Sect being Vadama.

PPM and ATA mention the year as Pingala, month Chitrai and the constellation Tiruvadirai. PPM adds that it was a Sukla Paksha Panchami, a Friday.

It will be for the Research minded scholars to piece together all these details to arrive at the correct date, time etc.

Vriddha Padma Purana presages his incarnation thus:-

" Long, long afterwards, the Lord himself will come down on earth as a Tridanda Sannyasin, to restore the good law. At that time heretics and men of perverted intellects will confuse the minds of the people. Aasuric Saastraas, based upon fallacious arguments and various schools of thought, very attractive and almost indistinguishable from the Vedanta, will turn away mens' hearts from Vishnu and cause them to forget His glory. That glorious incarnation will, through the good fortune of the Lord's devotees, come down upon earth, to explain and amplify the teachings of the great Sage Baadaraayana and the divine singer of the Gita. The holy one would compose a Bhaashya on the Vyaasa Sutras, to save men from the confusion and despair caused by spurious doctrines and lead them to the True faith".

While still a boy, he lost his father and was living with his mother at Kanchipuram under the protection of one 'Tiruk kachi Nambi' This Nambi was believed to converse and was on 'speaking terms' with Lord Varadaraja in the Archa form.

Events in the Life of Sri Ramanuja:

(1) Within 16 years of age, he had mastered all the Vedas and Sastras. At age 17, he married Rakshakaambaal (Tanjammal, in Tamil) (PPM)

(2) Ilaya Perumal was placed under the Advaitic Sannyasi called YADAVA PRAKASA at Tirupput kuzhi for training in Advaita Purva Paksha Sastra of Vedanta. Once during this period, Alavandar who desired nominating Ilaya Perumal to succeed himself visited Tirupput kuzhi, met with him but had no opportunity to speak to him and had to return to Srirangam.

Very many occasions arose when the Saivite Guru clashed

with Ilaya Perumal when the Guru misinterpreted Vedantic statements. Ilaya Perumal fearlessly pointed out the errors in the Guru's interpretations and corrected him. This enraged the Guru. Fearing that one day, Ilaya Perumal would demolish Advaita philosophy, he plotted to kill Ilaya Perumal by drowning him in Ganga while on a pilgrimage tour of the country with his disciples.

Learning of the design through one Govinda, another disciple who was also related to him, Ilaya Perumal slipped out into the forest at dead of night. Miraculously, an aged hunter couple appeared and guided him. As Ilaya Perumal who was in a trance, opened his eyes, he found himself at the outskirts of Kanchipuram and the couple had disappeared. He realized that it was Lord Varadaraja and Perundevi Thayar who had come in the guise of the hunter couple. He stayed at Kanchi for a while to assist Tiruk Kachi Nambi in his daily chores of service to Lord Varadaraja.

News came that Alavandar was very sick and he desired to meet with Ilaya Perumal. Just as Tirukkachi Nambi and Ilaya Perumal arrived, they saw the funeral procession of Alavandar. During the last rites, they noticed that three fingers of Alavandar remained folded signifying three of his last unfulfilled wishes.

As Ilaya Perumal swore:

(i) that he would write a commentary on Veda Vyasa's Brahma Sutra

(ii) that he would perpetuate the memory of Vyasa and Parasara and

(iii) that he would strive to propagate Visisht Advaita on the lines of the 4000 holy collects of Alwars, the fingers unfolded one by one automatically and stretched out to normal position signifying that these were his last wishes. Since he could not meet with Alavandar, he returned to Kanchi without even going into the temple at Srirangam (PPM).

Tirukkachi Nambi obtained from Lord Varadaraja the famous 'Six Words' and passed them on to Ilayalwar. The six words provided the guidelines for Ilayalwar to follow.

They were:-

(i) that Lord Narayana is the Paramatma.

(ii) that the individual souls were different from Paramatma.

(iii) that Prapatti is the means to attain salvation.

(iv) that the last remembrance of the Lord on the part of the departing soul was not necessary.

(v) that Moksha can be obtained only on laying off the mortal coils (Videha Mukti) &

(vi) that Ilaya Perumal should take refuge at the feet of Periya Nambi.

Accordingly, he met with Periya Nambi at Madurantakam, where under the shade of Vakula tree Periya Nambi performed Pancha Samskara to him. As he was initiated into the esoteric of Dvaya Mantra at Madurantakam, the place came to be known as "Dvayam Vilaindha Tiruppathi" (PPM) Both returned to Srirangam and did Kalakshepams on Brahma Sutra etc. for sometime. It was at this time that Lord Ranganatha called him "Nammudaiyavar" (He is ours). (PPM)

Ilaya Perumals was not a happy married life. His wife never understood either his greatness nor appreciated his catholicity and always acted on her own wavelength and there was no compatibility as between them. Several instances are cited wherein the lady ensconced in her own in her own pet ideas of being holy or otherwise showed scant respect to Bhagavatas and this greatly annoyed Ilayalwar. When he was about 30 years of age, Ilayalwar took Sannyas with the name of 'Ramanuja Muni'. He was the king among Sannyasis. Hence, he is called ' Yati Rajar'-a honorific invested by Lord Devaathi Rajan.

The seat of Acharya at Srirangam was lying vacant without a successor to take over. He was prevailed upon to assume charge. But, before doing so, he wanted to equip himself with the secrets of the three great Mantras. For this purpose, he approached one " Tiruk Koshtiyur Nambi" who made him come several times before actually instructing him. He cautioned Ramanuja that he should not give out the secrets to all and sundry and if he did so, he would go to hell.

Immediately on receiving the instructions, Ramanuja climbed up to the top of the steeple of the temple and proclaimed to the large gathering of his disciples assembled there the purport of the instruction.

The popular belief that he gave out the Mantras is not correct; What he actually gave out was that he had found out the way to attain Moksha through the three great Mantras and invited those who sincerely wished to follow him and get initiated. Also, he did not advise all and sundry as assumed by some. By the time of this episode, he had already gathered a huge following of disciples who congregated at the main entrance to the temple and he was thus addressing his own disciples (as explained in a separate posting in this series).

his is another less known fact about the well known Acharya Tirukkoshtiyur Nambi was so enraged and demanded an explanation. Ramanuja replied that he did not give out the secrets and even if he had transgressed the specific warning of the Guru, only he himself would go to hell but the multitude of humanity that listened to his clarion ' wake-up' call would be saved spiritually. The Guru was overwhelmed by this reply. Embracing Ramanuja appreciating his broad mindedness, he called him 'Emperumanar'- " O! My lord" and declared that Sri Vaishnavism would thenceforward be known as " Ramanuja Darsanam"-' the light of Ramanuja'

Yadava prakasa, his old Guru had by then returned to Kanchi, became Ramanuja's disciple assuming the name of 'Govinda Yogi'

Ramanuja used to go round the streets for his Biksha. An evil minded fellow had mixed poison in the biksha. His wife while serving the biksha fell at Ramanujas feet with tears in her eyes. Ramanuja understood that there was something wrong. When the Sishyas sorted out the biksha for cooking, they found out that poison was mixed with it. Ramanuja went on a fast with a view to cleanse the mind of the evil-doer. On hearing this, Tirukkoshtiyur Nambi rushed all the way to Srirangam.

When Ramanuja heard of the coming of his Guru, he rushed to the banks of River Kaveri to receive him. It was the height of summer. Ramanuja ran towards him in the hot Sun to receive him and fell at his feet on the burning sands on the banks of river Kaveri. Nambi did not ask him to get up. Such was his Acharya Bhakti.

At that time, Kidambi Aachaan, who was nearby told Nambi " Your action (in not asking Ramanuja to get up) is worse than the poison mixed in the bikshai". Such was the Acharya bhakti of Ramanujas Sishya !(Like master, like pupil !). Tirukkoshtiyur Nambi exclaimed, " After all, now I can cast off my physical body since

I have found one who would take the greatest care of Ramanuja" Ramanuja travelled throughout the country spreading the message of Visisht Advaita. Once a votary of the ' illusion theory' Yagna Murthi by name confronted him for 16 days in endless arguments and counter arguments. Finally, he accepted defeat and became a disciple of Ramanuja assuming the name of 'Arulala Perumal Emperumanar' and wrote 'Gnana Saram and Prameya Saram'.

One of the most important disciples who was totally devoted to Ramanuja was Kuresan also known as ' Kurattalwan'. Once, Kuresan participated in the shradda ceremony performed for his mother by the famous Tiruvarangathu Amudanar. This Amudanar was in charge of the Srirangam temple. When Amudanar inquired what Kuresan desired as reward for his participation, Kuresan replied that the administration of the temple should be handed over to Ramanuja. Amudanar, who had already known the greatness of Ramanuja was only too glad to hand over the key to Ramanuja. It is this Tiruvarangattu Amudanar who subsequently wrote the Ramanuja Noorrantadhi of 108 verses which was included in the holy collects to make up the total of 4,000.

After Mastering the Bodhaayana Vritti of Sage Vyaasa, he wrote several works like Vedanta Sangraham explaining the various viewpoints of Sankara, Yadhava, Bhaskara and others, Vedanta Deepam, Geetha Bashyam etc.

During Panguni Uttram, he did Prapatti before the Divya Dhampathi in Serthi and submitted his famous Gadhyatrayam (comprising Saranagathi Gadhyam, Sriranga Gadhyam and Sri Vaikunta Gadhyam),

Later, he wrote a Grantha called Nityam detailing the Tiruvaradhana Kramam.

While he was on his Sancharam, it is believed that the Lord himself appeared before him at Tiruk Kurum Kudi as a Srivaishnava got Samasrayanam from Udaiyavar (PPM)

When he visited Saraswati Peetam, Goddess Saraswati was so impressed with his commentary on Brahma Sutram that she named it "Sri Bhashyam" and conferred on him the title of "Bhashyakaarar". It must be noted that while the other commentaries are known by the names of their authors like 'Sankara Bashyam' written by Aadhi Sankara, the commentary of Ramanuja is always referred to with the venerable honorific 'Sri' denoting its unsurpassed quality and clarity and known as ' Sri Bashyam' (PPM)

When he visited Tirumala, a miracle happened. Some argued that the Lord of Tirumalai was Shaiva param. It is surprising that such a claim should have arisen about the Lord who had been worshipped as Lord Vishnu by all the Alwars and Acharyas besides Elango Adigal and other Tamil Pulavars for several centuries. This was because the Lord had earlier entrusted His insignia to a King called Tondamaan. The Lord desired to take back from Tondamaan, these insignia viz., Sankhu, Tiruvaazhi, Soolam, Damarukam etc. They were placed in the Sannidhi the previous night. And, when the doors were opened the next morning, the Lord gave Darshan adorning all his insignia (PPM). Ramanuja was hailed as " Appanukku Sangaazhi Alittha Perumaal" Poet Arunagiri himself sang clearing all doubts in this regard saying "Ulageenra Pachai umaiyanan, Vada Venkadathil Uraibhavan, Uyar Sanga Chakra kara Thalan". Ramanuja "was the greatest synoptic thinker which the world ever produced to systematize Visisht Advaitic philosophy, faithfully interpreting the ancient knowledge in tune with the letter and spirit of the text in the light of revelation and experience tested by stern logic".

His magnum opus is his wonderful commentary on Vedavyasa's Brahma Sutram and a simpler commentary thereon called Vedanta Saram. Kuresan was very helpful in publishing his works. Thus, he fulfilled his FIRST PROMISE to Alavandar. It is this Kuresan (aka) Sri Vatsanka Misra who wrote the famous Pancha Sthava consisting of Athi Maanusha Sthava, Sri Sthava, Varadaraja Sthava, Vaikunta Sthava and Sundarabaahu Sthava.

He asked Kuresan to name his two sons after Veda Vyasa and Parasara and thus fulfilled his SECOND PROMISE to Alavandar. It was this Parasara Bhattar who subsequently wrote the famous commentary on Vishnu Sahasra Nama as ordained by Ramanuja.

Another disciple of Ramanuja was Pillaan. Once, when Ramanuja was alone mentally reciting a particular hymn of Tiruvoimozhi, Pillaan entered his room and inquired if he was meditating on a particular hymn. And, it was indeed the one Ramanuja was actually meditating on!. Ramanuja decided that Pillaan was the person best suited to write a commentary on Tiruvoimozhi.

As ordered, he wrote the famous 'Aaraayirappadi' (the commentary known as the 6000 Padi also known as Bhagavad Vishayam) and called Pillaan as 'Tirukkurugai Piraan' after the name of Nammalwar. He was also known as Kurugesar and Braathru Thozhappar. Thus, he fulfilled his to Alavandar. He was one of the Sri Bhashya ubhaya Simhasana Adhipathis. (PPM)

Kulothunga Chola was a staunch devotee of Siva. He commanded Ramanuja to come to his court with a view to enlisting his support to establish the superiority of Siva over all other deities (including Vishnu). If the support was not forthcoming, the king was planning to kill Ramanuja. Sensing the danger, Kuresa went to the court disguised as Ramanuja along with another disciple called Periya Nambi. The king ordered him to sign a document to the effect that 'Siva is the greatest'.

Kuresa added that ' Sivam was no doubt great but Dronam was greater than Sivam'-both expressions referring to units of measurement. The enraged king ordered both of them to be blinded when he came to know that he was Kuresa who was impersonating Ramanuja. Periya Nambi was tortured to death while Kuresa survived. Kuresa, though he himself was blinded, was happy that he had saved Ramanuja. It is this Kulothunga who is reported to have thrown away the idol of Govindaraja in the sea. Ramanuja recovered it and had it installed at Tirupati.

While on an itinerary, Ramanuja noticed an officer of state, by name Danur daasa, a hunter by birth was over-concerned and over-protective about the beauty of his wife who was walking along on the hot sands on the banks of the river Kaveri. Ramanuja offered to show him something more beautiful than his wife and took him to the proximity of the image of Lord Ranganatha. Danur daasa was enraptured by the charm of the Lord and became a disciple of Ramanuja assuming the name of ' Uranga Villi Daasar'. Ramanuja never entertained any caste distinctions and was conferring his benedictions even on the lowliest of the lowly whom he called 'Tiruk Kulattar'.

Ramanuja went to Tiru narayana puram in search of white clay paste used for applying caste marks by Vaishnavites. The idol of the temple there had been taken away by the muslim invaders and was being used at play as a doll by the muslim princess in Delhi. Ramanuja went to Delhi and when he endearingly called

Come on! My dear child 'Selva Pillaiye Vaarum', the idol miraculously came onto his lap. Ramanuja reinstalled it in the temple.

Once some kids were playing on the road pretending to construct a temple, installing an idol of the Lord, offering fruits and flowers etc all the time using the dust on the road for the purpose.

They offered some mud as prasadam to Ramanuja who was passing along, he received it with due respect. He remembered in this connection the words of Poigai Alwar who said that the Lord took whatever name and form his sincere devotees wished and in the instant case though the kids were only playing, they sincerely believed in what they were doing.

Another disciple of Ramanuja was Vaduga Nambi who put the sandals of his Guru along with those of the Lord. When questioned, he replied that the Acharya's sandals were for him as holy as those of the Lord.

When Lord Ranganatha was coming on his rounds on the streets of Srirangam, Vaduga Nambi remarked that the eyes that had seen the charm in the eyes of Ramanuja would not be able to appreciate the beauty of the eyes of even the Lord.-'En Amudinai Kanda Kangal Marronrinai Kaanaave.' Such was his devotion to his Acharya.

Ramanuja arranged to make a lifelike idol of himself and embracing it invested it with his powers and had it installed in Tirumalai at Tirupati. The only temple consecrated in Tirumalai, other than that of Lord Venkateswara, is that of Ramanuja. The Archa moorthi of Ramanuja known as "Thaan Ugantha Tirumeni" was installed in Tirunarayanapuram.

Once, when he visited Tondanoor in Hoysala State, he happened to meet a Jain king called Devarayan. His daughter was possessed by a demon and none could get rid of her predicament. When Ramanuja's Sripaada Theertham (water consecrated by association with his feet) was sprinkled on her, she was cured of the devil. The King pleaded to be accepted as Ramanujas Sishya. Ramanuja accepted and named him "Vishnu Vardhana".

Ramanuja nominated 74 Acharyas to succeed him. It is he who instituted the 13 day "iyal oshti in Srirangam." (PPM)

His Ascent to Paramapadam

With his head on the lap of Embar and his feet on the lap of Vaduga Nambi, Ramanuja breathed his last in 1137 AD listening to the recitation of the Divya Prabandam.

Born in PINGALA year, he left for his heavenly abode also in PINGALA year that followed 120 years from the year of his Avatara. Thus, he lived TWO full cycles of Tamil years after his birth

PLV places the date in Saaka era 1009, Pingala, in the month of Magha, the 10th day of Sukla Paksha under the constellation of Tiruvadirai and at noon (as in the time of his birth).

TKG notes that Lord Ranganatha and Periya Piraatti bathed and purified themselves as relatives do.

PRA avers that he died on a Saturday.

VAC places the date as 4238 Kali yuga which corresponds to 1137 AD.

PTA, however, states that he lived for 128 years and died in the year Durmati in the month of Vaisaka.

Again, Research scholars may fin ways to piece together all these information to arrive at the correct date.

His physical body is preserved even today in a sitting posture in the Sannidhi (Sanctum Sanctorum) dedicated to him on the southwest corner on the fifth round within the Srirangam temple as ordered by Lord Ranganatha himself.

The whole world is aghast at the feat of preservation of the mummies of Egypt and the body of St. Xavier in Goa in India and make so much fuss about them.

Even some Srivaishnavas are not aware that here in Srirangam their holiest place hailed as ' Bhuloka Vaikuntam' (Heaven on Earth) lies preserved the body of Sri Ramanuja in all its pristine state unostentatiously, without any fanfare or publicity and without using any of the chemical preservatives employed by the Egyptian and Goan models.

Swami Desika in Sloka 10 of his Yathiraja Saptadhi pays obeisance to Bhagavad Ramanuja thus before proceeding with his eulogy.

Pranaamam Lakshmana Munih Prathi Grihnaathu Maamakam I

Prasaadhayathi yat Sookthih Svadheena Pathikaam Sruthim I I

I beseech Sri Ramanuja whose Srisookthis claimed the acclaim of the Lord and adorned the Upanishads to kindly accept my Pranams. There is another famous Sloka which says:-

Thasmai Ramaanujaaryaaya Namah Parama Yoginae I

Yah Sruthi Smrithi Sutraanaam Antharjvaramaso Samathaa I I

I bow to that Sri Ramanuja, the great Yogi who became the very soul of Vedas, Upanishads and other Sutras.

Vishishtadvaita

Vishisht Advaita Vedanta is a sub-school of the Vedanta (literally, *end or the goal of Knowledge,* Sanskrit) school of Hindu philosophy, the other major sub-schools of Vedanta being *Advaita* and *Dvaita. Vishisht Advaita* (literally "Advaita with uniqueness/ qualifications") is a non-dualistic school of Vedanta philosophy. It is non-dualism of the qualified whole, in which Brahman alone exists, but is characterised by multiplicity. It can be described as qualified monism or attributive monism.

Asesha Chit-Achit Prakaaram Brahmaikameva Tatvam-Brahman as qualified by the sentient and insentient modes (aspects or attributes) is the only reality.

It is a school of Vedanta philosophy which believes in all diversity subsuming to an underlying unity. Ramanuja, the main proponent of Visisht Advaita philosophy contends that the Prasthana Traya ("The three courses") i.e. Upaniads, Bhagavad Gita, and Brahma Sutras are to be interpreted in way that shows this unity in diversity, for any other way would violate their consistency.

Philosophers

The Visisht Advaitic thought is considered to have existed for a long time, and it is surmised that the earliest works are no longer available.

The names of the earliest of these philosophers is only known through Ramanuja's Vedanta Sangraha. In the line of the philosophers considered to have expounded the Visisht Advaitic system, the prominent ones are Bodhayana, Dramida, Tanka, Guhadeva, Kapardi and Bharuci. Besides these philosophers, Ramanuja's teacher Yamunacharya is credited with laying the foundation for what culminates as the Sri Bhashya.

Bodhayana is considered to have written an extensive *vritti* (commentary) on the Purva and Uttara Mimamsas. Tanka is attributed with having written commentaries on Chandogya Upanishad and Brahma Sutras. Natha-muni of the ninth century AD, the foremost Acharya of the Vaishnavas, collected the Tamil prabandhas, classified them, made the redaction, set the hymns to music and spread them everywhere.

He is said to have received the divine hymns straight from Nammalvar, the foremost of the twelve Alwars, by yogic insight in the temple at Alwar Thirunagari, which is located near Tirunelveli in South India. Yamunacharya renounced kingship and spent his last days in the service of the Lord at Srirangam and in laying the fundamentals of the Vishishtadvaita philosophy by writing four basic works on the subject.

Ramanuja is the main proponent of Visisht Advaita philosophy. The philosophy itself is considered to have existed long before Ramanuja's time. Ramanuja continues along the line of thought of his predecessors while expounding the knowledge expressed in the Upanishads, Brahma Sutras and Bhagavad Gita. Vedanta Desika and Pillai Lokacharya, disciples in the tradition of Ramanuja, had minor disagreements on some aspects of Vishishtadvaita, giving rise to the Vadakalai and Thenkalai schools of thought, as explained below.

Swaminarayan, the founder of the Swaminarayan Sampraday (original name is Uddhav Sampraday) also propagated this philosophy and based the Swaminarayan Sampraday on these ideals.

Key Principles of Vishisht Advaita

The understanding of the 3 principles of Vishisht Advaita namely, Tattva, Hita and PurushArtha are essential pre-requisites for an aspirant of that knowledge which leads to liberation.

- Tattva: The knowledge of the 3 real entities namely, Jiva (the sentient); Jagat (the insenient) and Ishvara (*Vishnu-Narayana* or *Parabrahman*)
- Hita: The means of realisation i.e. through Bhakti (devotion) and Prapatti (self-surrender)
- PurushArtha: The goal to be attained i.e. moksha or liberation from bondage.

Epistemology

Pramnas

Prama, in Sanskrit, refers to the correct knowledge, arrived at by thorough reasoning, of any object. Pramga (*sources of knowledge,* Sanskrit) forms one part of a tripumi (trio), namely,

1. Pramt[, the *subject;* the *knower* of the knowledge
2. Pramga, the *cause* or the *means* of the knowledge
3. Prameya, the *object* of knowledge.

In Visisht Advaita Vedanta, the following three pramGas are alone accepted as valid means of knowledge:

- Pratyakca – the knowledge gained by means of *perception*
- Anumna – the knowledge gained by means of *inference*
- abda – the knowledge gained by means of *Œruti.*

Perception refers to knowledge obtained by cognition of external objects based on sensory perception.

In the modern day usage this will also include evidence obtained by means of observation through scientific instruments since they are only an extension of perception.

Inference refers to knowledge obtained by deductive reasoning and analysis.

Sruti refers to knowledge obtained from scriptures which primarily are Upanishads, Brahma Sutras and Bhagavad Gita.

Rules of Epistemology

The following rules of hierarchy apply to the issues when there is apparent conflict between the 3 modes of acquiring knowledge:

- [abda or Zruti Pramga occupies the highest position in matters which cannot be settled or resolved by Pratyakca or Anumana.
- Anumana occupies the next position. When an issue cannot be settled through sensory perception alone, it is settled based on Anumana i.e. whichever argument is more logical.
- When Pratyakca yields a definitive position on a particular issue, such a perception cannot be ignored to interpret [abda in a way which violates that perception.

Metaphysics

Ontology

The ontology in Vishisht Advaita consists of explaining the relationship between Ishvara (*Parabrahman*), the sentient beings (*chit-brahman*) and the insentient Universe (*achit-brahman*). In the broadest sense, Ishvara is the Universal Soul of the pan-organistic body consisting of the Universe and sentient beings. The description of the three ontological entities is given below:

Ishvara

Ishvara (denoted by Vishnu-Narayana) is the Supreme Cosmic Spirit who maintains complete control over the Universe and all the sentient beings, which together also form the pan-organistic body of Ishvara. The triad of Ishvara along with the universe and the sentient beings is Brahman, which signifies the completeness of existence. Ishvara is Parabrahman endowed with innumerable auspicious qualities (Kalyana Gunas).

Ishvara is perfect, omniscient, omnipresent, incorporeal, independent, creator of the universe, its active ruler and also the eventual destroyer. He is causeless, eternal and unchangeable — and is yet the material and the efficient cause of the universe and sentient beings. He is both immanent (like whiteness in milk) and transcendent (like a watch-maker independent of a watch). He is the subject of worship. He is the basis of morality and giver of the fruits of one's Karma. He rules the world with His Maya — His divine power. Ishvara is considered to have a 2-fold characteristic: he is the indweller of all beings and all beings also reside in Ishvara.

Antarvyapi

When Ishvara is thought of as the indweller of all beings, he is referred to as the paramatman, or the innermost self of all beings. Ishvara is also the self for the non-conscious Universe.

He who inhabits water, yet is within water, whom water does not know, whose body water is and who controls water from within—He is your Self, the Inner Controller, the Immortal.

He who inhabits the sun, yet is within the sun, whom the sun does not know, whose body the sun is and who controls the sun from within—He is your Self, the Inner Controller, the Immortal-
Brihadaranyaka Upanishad 3.7.4-14

Bahuvyapi

When Ishvara is thought of as the all encomposing and the residence of all beings i.e. all beings reside in Ishvara, he is referred to as the paramapurusha. The sentient beings and the insentient universe which form part of the pan-organistic body of Ishvara are encapsulated by Ishvara.

Chit

Chit is the world of sentient beings, or of entities possessing consciousness. It is similar to the Purusha of Samkhya system. The sentient beings are called Jivas and they are possessors of individual consciousness as denoted by "I". The scope of Chit refers to all beings with an "I" consciousness, or more specifically self-consciousness. Therefore all entities which are aware of their own individual existence are denoted as *chit*. This is called *Dharmi-jnana* or *substantive consciousness*. The sentient beings also possess varying levels of *Dharma-bhuta-jnana* or *attributive consciousness*

The jivas possess three different types of existence:

- *Nityas*, or the eternally free Jivas who were never in Samsara
- *Muktas*, or the Jivas that were once in Samsara but are free
- *Baddhas*, or the Jivas which are still in Samsara.

Achit

Achit is the world of insentient entities as denoted by matter or more specifically the non-conscious Universe. It is similar to the Prakriti of Samkhya system

Brahman

There is a subtle difference between Ishvara and Brahman. Ishvara is the substantive part of Brahman, while jivas and jagat are its modes (also secondary attributes), and kalyanagunas (auspicious attributes) are the primary attributes. The secondary attributes become manifested in the effect state when the world is differentiated by name and form. The kalyanagunas are eternally manifest.

Brahman is the description of Ishvara when comprehended in fullness i.e. a simultaneous vision of Ishvara with all his modes and attributes.

The relationship between Brahman and Jivas, Jagat is expressed by Ramanuja in numerous ways.

He calls this relationship as one of:

- Sarira/Sariri (*body/indweller*);
- Prakara/Prakari (*attribute or mode/substance*);
- Sesha/Seshi (*Owned/owner*);
- Amsa/Amsi (*part/whole*);
- Adharadeya/Sambandha (*supporter/supported*);
- Niyamya/Niyanta (*controlled/controller*);
- Rasksya/Raksaka (*redeemed/redeemer*);

These relationships can be experienced holding Brahman as the father, son, mother, sister, wife, husband, friend, lover and lord. Hence, Brahman is a personal being.

What does Nirguna Brahman mean?

Ramanuja argues vehemently against understanding Brahman as one without attributes. Brahman is Nirguna in the sense that impure qualities do not touch it. He provides three valid reasons for staking such a claim:

Sruti/Sabda Pramana: All sruti and sabda's denoting Brahman always list either attributes inherent to Brahman or not inherent to Brahman. The Sruti's only seek to deny Brahman from possessing impure and defective qualities which affect the world of beings. There is evidence in the Sruti's to this regard. The Sruti's proclaim Brahman to be beyond the tri-gunas which are observed. However, Brahman possess infinite number of transcendental attributes, the evidence of which is given in vakhyas like "satyam jnanam anantam Brahma"

Pratyaksha Pramana: Ramanuja states that "a contentless cognition is impossible". And all cognition must necessarily involve knowing Brahman through the attributes of Brahman.

Anumana Pramana: Ramanuja states that "Nirgunatva" itself becomes an attribute of Brahman on account of the uniqueness of no other entity being Nirguna.

Theory of Existence

Vishisht Advaita adheres to a system of complete reality. The three ontological entities i.e. Ishvara, Chit and Achit are fundamentally real. It upholds the doctrine of *Satkaryavada* as against *Asatkaryavada*.

Briefly

- Satkaryavada is pre-existence of the effect in the cause. It maintains that karya (effect) is sat or real. It is present in the karana (cause) in a potential form, even before its manifestation.
- Asatkaryavada is non-existence of the effect in the cause. It maintains that karya (effect) is asat or unreal until it comes into being. Every effect, then, is a new beginning and is not born out of cause.

More specifically, the effect is a modification of what exists in the cause and doesnot involve new entities coming into existence. This is called as *parinamavada* or evolution of effect from the cause. This doctrine is common to the Samkhya system and Vishisht Advaita system. The Samkhya system adheres to Prakriti-Parinama vada whereas Vishishtadvaita is a modified form of Brahma-Parinama vada.

Krya and KraGa

The kraGa (*cause*) and krya (*effect*) in Vishishtadvaita is different form other systems of Indian Philosophy. Brahman is both the kraGa (*cause*) and the krya (effect). Brahman as the cause does not become the Universe as the effect.

Brahman is assigned two kraGatvas (*ways of being the cause*):

1. Nimitta kraGatva – *Being the Efficient/Instrumental cause.* For example, a goldsmith is assigned Nimitta kraGatva as he acts as the maker of jewellery and thus becomes the jewellery's *Instrumental cause.*
2. Updna kraGatva – *Being the material cause.* For example, the gold is assigned Updna kraGatva as it acts as the material of the jewellery and thus becomes the jewellery's *material cause.*

The Universe and Sentients always exist, much like Brahman. However, they undergo transformation. They begin from a subtle state and undergo transformation. The subtle state is called a causal state, while the transformed state is called the effect state. The causal state is when Brahman is internally not distinguishable by name and form. The effect state is when the internal distinction becomes pronounced. It can be said that Vishishtadvaita follows Brahma-Prakara-Parinama Vada. That is to say, it is the modes

(Jivas and Jagath) of Brahman which is under evolution. The cause and effect only refer to the pan-organistic body transformation. Brahman as the Universal Self is unchanging and eternal.

Brahman having the subtle (sukshma) chit and achit entities as his *Saareeram/ Prakaaram (body/mode)* before manifestation is the same Brahman having the expanded (stula) chit and achit entities as *Saareeram/ Prakaaram (body/mode)* after manifestation.

The essential feature is that the underlying entity is the same, the changes are in the description of that entity.

For eg. *Jack was a baby. Jack was a small kid. Jack was a middle-aged person. Jack was an old man. Jack is dead*

The body of a single personality named Jack is described as continuously changing. Jack doesnot become "James" because of the change.

Ethics

Souls and Matter are only the body of God. Creation is a real act of God. It is the expansion of intelligence. Matter is fundamentally real and undergoes real revelation. The Soul is a higher mode than Matter, because it is conscious. It is also eternally real and eternally distinct. Final release, that comes, by the Lord's Grace, after the death of the body is a Communion with God. This philosophy believes in liberation through one's Karmas (actions) in accordiance with the Vedas, the Varna (caste or class) system and the four Ashramas (stages of life), along with intense devotion to Vishnu. Individual Souls retain their separate identities even after moksha. They live in Fellowship with God either serving Him or meditating on Him. The philosophy of this school is Sri Vaishnavism, a branch of Vaishnavism.

Interpretation of Mahavakyas

All Vedantic schools need to substantiate the meaning espoused by Mahavakyas which occur throughout Upanishadic literature. The interpretation of these *Grand Pronouncements* serve as the cornerstone for establishing each school of thought. The most significant among them is: Translated literally, this means *All this is Brahman*. The ontology of Vishishtadvaita system consists of:

1. Ishvara is *Para-brahman* with infinite superlative qualities, whose substantive nature imparts the existence to the modes

2. Jivas are *chit-brahman* or sentient beings (which possess consciousness). They are the modes of Brahman which show consciousness.
3. Jagat is *achit-brahman* or matter/Universe (which are non-conscious). They are the mode of Brahman which are not conscious.

Brahman is the composite whole of the triad consisting of Ishvara along with his modes i.e. Jivas and Jagat. Hence, "all this is Brahman" denotes the triad of entities

Translated literally, this means the *Self is Brahman*. From the earlier statement, it follows that on account of everything being Brahman, the self is not different from Brahman.

The vakya establishes the identity of the Jiva and Brahman. The issue here is if the identity involves establishing a unique identity or a universal identity. The difference is as follows:

1. *Unique Identity:* Atman is Brahman; Nothing else is Brahman; Brahman is reality and therefore everything else is illusion
2. *Universal Identity:* Atman is Brahman in the same way as everything else is Brahman.

Ramanuja chooses to take the position of universal identity. He interprets this passage to mean the subsistence of all attributes in a common underlying substratum. This is referred to as *samanadhikaranya*. Thus Ramanuja says the purport of the passage is to show the unity of all beings in a common base. Ishvara (*Parabrahman*) who is the Cosmic Spirit for the pan-organistic body consisting of the Universe and sentient beings, is also simultaneously the innermost self (Atman) for each individual sentient being (Jiva). All the bodies, the Cosmic and the individual, are held in an adjectival relationship (aprthak-siddhi) in the one Isvara. Tat Tvam Asi declares that oneness of Isvara.

When multiple entities point to a single object, the relationship is established as one of substance and its attributes.

Similarly, when the upanishads declare Brahman is the Universe, Purusha, Self, Prana, Vayu, and so on, the entities are attributes or modes of Brahman. If the statement tat tvam asi is taken to mean as only *the self is brahman*, then sarvam khalv idam brahma will not make sense.

Understanding Neti-Neti

This is an upanishadic concept which is employed while attempting to know Brahman. The purport of this exercise is understood in many different ways and also influences the understaning of Brahman. In the overall sense, this phrase is accepted to refer to the indescribable nature of Brahman who is beyond all rationalisations. All descriptions of such an entity will necessarily have to be partial or fall short of the actual.

The typical interpretation of Neti-Neti is *not this, not this* or *neither this, nor that.* In Visisht Advaita, the phrase is taken in the sense of *not just this, not just this* or *not just this, not just that.* This means that Brahman cannot be restricted to one specific or a few specific descriptions. Consequently, Brahman is understood to possess infinite qualities and each of these qualities are infinite in extent.

Purpose of Human Existence

The purpose or goal of human existence is called as Purush Artha. According to the Vedas, there are four goals namely Artha (wealth), Kama (pleasure), Dharma (righteousness) and Moksha (permanent freedom from worldly bondage). According to this philosophy, the first three goals are not an end by themselves but need to be pursued with the ideal of attaining Moksha.

Moksha

Moksha is a state where the Jiva achieves one-ness with Brahman in terms of all knowership and possessing qualities free from all wordly evils and defects. The Jiva however does not possess the power to manifest/create and unmanifest/destroy. Neither does it have the power to grant Moksha.

The union of Atman and Brahman is likened to a situation where tiny lamps come under the blaze of the Sun. The lamp and Sun are still identifiable as different sources of light and yet the light arising from them is indistinguishable.

Moksha does not involve destruction of the self ("I") consciousness of the Jiva.

Bhakti as the Means to Attain Moksha

Bhakti Yoga is the sole means of liberation in Visisht Advaita. Through Bhakti (devotion), a Jiva ascends to the realm of the Lord, where it continues to delight in His service. Karma Yoga and Jnana Yoga are natural outcomes of Bhakti, total surrender, as the devotee acquires the knowledge that the Lord is the inner self. A devotee realizes his own state as dependent on, and supported by, and being led by the Lord, who is the Master. One is to lead a life as an instrument of the Lord, offering all his thought, word, and deed to the feet of the Lord. One is to see the Lord in everything and everything in Him. This is the unity in diversity achieved through devotion.

Thenkalai and Vadakalai schools of thought

Vedanta Desikan, one of the foremost learned scholars of medieval India, wrote more than a hundred works in Sanskrit and Tamil. All are characterised by their versatility, deep spiritual insight, ethical fervour and excellent expressions of devotional emotion in delightful style. His Paduka-sahasram is a classic example. He was a great teacher, expositor, debater, poet, philosopher, thinker and defender of the faith of Vaishnavism. The Vadakalai sect of Sri Vaishnavism associate themselves with Vedanta Desikan.

Pillai Lokacharya is associated with the Tenkalai sect of Sri Vaishnavism. He was a contemporary of Vedanta Desika. He is said to have born as an *amsa* ("essence") of Kanchi Devaraja (Varadaraja) Perumal to document and immortalize Ramanuja's message in the month of Aippaci under the star Thiruvonam (Sravana), in the year 1205 CE.. He is said to have lived for 106 years, during which time, he also helped to safeguard the idol of Ranganatha at Srirangam from Muslim invaders.

Pillai Lokacharya confirmed the basics of the Sri Vaishnava system in his 18 works popularly known as *Ashtadasa Rahasyangal* ("the eighteen secrets") also called the Rahasya granthas ("doctrines that explain the inner meanings"). Manavala Mamuni expanded on and popularized Lokacharya's teachings arguments in Tamil.

Traditions Following Vishshtadvaita:

- Sri sampradaya of south India.
- Swaminarayan Sampraday of Gujarat.

Visisht Advaita and Sri Vaishnavism

The Absolute Supreme Reality referred to as Brahman, is a Transcendent Personality with infinite superlative qualities. He is

Narayana, also known as Lord Vishnu. He is also the other two members of the Trimurti, namely, Creator Brahma and Shiva, the Lord of Deluge.

A man who has discrimination for his charioteer and holds the reins of the mind firmly, reaches the end of the road; and that is the supreme position of Vishnu.-1.3.9 Katha Upanishad.

Beyond the senses are the objects; beyond the objects is the mind; beyond the mind, the intellect; beyond the intellect, the Great Atman; beyond the Great Atman, the Unmanifest; beyond the Unmanifest, the Purusha. Beyond the Purusha there is nothing: this is the end, the Supreme Goal. -1.3.10,11 Katha Upanishad.

In terms of theology, Ramanujacharya puts forth the view that both the Supreme Goddess Lakshmi and Supreme God Narayana together constitute Brahman-the Absolute. Sri Lakshmi is the female personification of Brahman and Narayana is the male personification of Brahman, but they are both inseparable, co-eternal, co-absolute and are always substantially one. Thus, in reference to these dual aspects of Brahman, the Supreme is referred to in the Sri Vaishnava Sampradaya as Sriman Narayana.

Comparison with Western Non-dualism

Baruch Spinoza, the 17th century Dutch rationalist philosopher, in his magnum work Ethics establishes the nature of God. Spinoza's pan-organistic God (i.e. God revealed as orderly nature) is comparable to Brahman (having the individual selves' and Universe as its body)

Spinoza makes the following propositions on the nature of God in his work "Ethics". These positions closely reflect the VishistAdvaitic position on the nature of Brahman:

Proposition XI. God, or substance consisting of infinite attributes, of which each expresses eternal and infinite essentiality, necessarily exists.

Proposition XV. Whatsoever is, is in God, and without God nothing can be, or be conceived.

Proposition XVII. God acts solely by the laws of his own nature and is not constrained by anyone.

Proposition XVIII. God is the indwelling and not the transient cause of all things.

Proposition XIX. God and all the attributes of God are eternal.

Proposition XXX. Intellect, in function finite, or in function infinite, must comprehend the attributes of God and the modifications of God, and nothing else

Vedanta Desika

Vedanta Desika (1269 – 1370) was a Sri Vaishnava Guru. He was a poet, devotee, philosopher and master-teacher.

Life

Desikan was born in Thoopul, near Kanchipuram, (according to legend, on the order of Lord Srinivasa and Padmavathi Thayaar, the God and Goddess of the Tirumala Venkateswara Temple), as the son of Ananta Suri and Totaramba. He was named "Venkatanatha" and belonged to the Vishwamithra gothra (lineage). He was educated and trained by a scholarly maternal uncle of his, Kidambi Appullalar who was a direct disciple of Nadadoor Ammal (Grand Nephew of Ramanuja).

Appullarlar also initiated Venkatanatha's Upanayanam (sacred thread ceremony) at the age of seven and made him master the Vedas, Divyaprabandam, Puranas and Sastras. By the age of twenty he was a great scholar without par in the history of Vaishnavism. He got married at the age of 21 to Tirumangai (also known as "Kanakavalli"). Vedanta Desikan rose to the status of an "Acharya" by the age of 27.

Works

His writings include devotional works on deities and Acharyas, treatises on Vishishtadvaita, commentary on the Bhagavad Gita, secret doctrines of Vaishnavism, original Tamil poems, epic poems and allegorical dramas in Sanskrit, dialectical works such as Satadushani directed against rival religious schools, treatises on daily life and several other miscellaneous treatises. His gloss on the meanings of the Vedas, reconciling the teachings of the Alvars and the Prasthanatrayi created history because it exposed the Divya Prabhandham of the Alvars to a much wider audience and elevated it to a status equivalent to that of the Vedas in the eyes of the Tamil Vaishnava people.

The poem "Sudarshnashtakam" on Lord Sudarshana the deity that represents the disc-shaped weapon that Vishnu carries in his right hand, and a similar poem "Hayagriva Stotram" on Hayagriva are his most famous works. He composed close to fifty other Stotrams (sacred prayer poems similar to psalms) on different Vaishnava gods on various occasions.

The Eight-Lettered Mantra

In talking about the eight-lettered mantra of Narayana, he mentioned several things which can also have an eightfold classification, like eight kinds of devotion, eight siddhis, eight functions of the intellect and so on. In the same strain he described eight flowers for the worship of God; these are: non-violence; sense-control; universal compassion; infinite patience; wisdom; austerity; meditation; and truth. He composed three hymns exclusively on Lord Ranganatha of Srirangam.

The Hamsa-Sandesha

Hamsa-Sandesha (IAST HaCsasande[a) or "The Message of the Swan" – is a medieval love poem set in southern India. Lovesick Rama, the epic hero, petitions a swan to carry a message to his beloved Sita, who has been abducted by the demon king, Ravana. As the swan's route winds through South India, it honours the land which Rama and Sita made sacred, whose beautiful landscape and peoples it describes in full.

The Swan shoots like an arrow across the ocean to the island of Lanka and there he sustains the pining and near-suicidal Sita with his message. But more than this, the poet also pays deep homage to Kalidasa's 'Cloud Messenger'. This work is four things: an fine poem in its own right; a suggestive retelling of the Ramayana; a pilgrim's guide to the holy sites of South India; and a work that develops the poetics of Kalidasa's Meghaduta and gives them a devotional and heroic twist.

Paaduka Sahasram

Paaduka Sahasram or "1000 Verses on the Sandals of the Lord" is considered to be Desikan's Magnum Opus. The whole work is a monument for supreme devotion and superb poetry, all in one night's intuition,-an overnight miracle of one thousand verses! It was done by him just as a fulfillment of a competition committed to as a challenge by his disciples who were provoked by members of the Tenkalai school.

All this was composed by Desika (as he puts it, by the Grace of the paduka of the Divine) in just one quarter of the night, actually the third quarter. The earlier two quarters were devoted by him, as soon as he accepted the commitment, to yoga and yoga-nidra (=sleep induced by yoga and resulting in intuition). The opposite school kept awake the whole night and brought forth 300 of the 1000 promised, on the lotus feet of the Lord.

Brahma Sutras

The Brahma sutras, also known as *Vedanta Sutras,* constitute the *Nyaya prasthana,* the logical starting point of the *Vedanta* philosophy (Nyaya = logic/order). No study of Vedanta is considered complete without a close examination of the *Prasthana Traya* (Prasthanatrayi), the texts that stand as the three starting points. The Brahma Sutras are attributed to Badarayana.

While the Upanishads (*Uruti prasthana,* the starting point of revelation) and the Bhagavad-Gita (*Smriti prasthana,* the starting point of remembered tradition) are the basic source texts of Vedanta, it is in the Brahma sutras that the teachings of Vedanta are set forth in a systematic and logical order.

While the earlier commentators like Adi Shankara treat Badarayaga, the author of the Brahma Sûtra, as the Jnana-Shakti Avatara (knowledge-power incarnation) of God, Vaishnavite tradition identifies him with Krishna Dwipayana Vyasa, the author of the Mahabharata.

Commentaries

Many commentaries have been written on this text, the earliest extant one being the one by Adi Shankara. His commentary set forth the non-dualistic (*Advaita*) interpretation of the Vedanta, and was commented upon by Vacaspati and Padmapâda. These sub-commentaries, in turn, inspired other derivative texts in the Advaita school.

Ramanuja also wrote a commentary on the Brahma sutra, called Sri Bhasya, which lays the foundations of the Vishishtadvaita tradition. In this, he firmly refutes the Advaita view as proposed by Adi Shankara in his commentary.

Other commentators on the Brahma Sutras, belonging to other schools of Vedanta, include Bhaskara, Yadavaprakaua, Keuava,

Nilakaoha, Madhvacharya, Vallabha, Vijnanabhiksu, Nimbarka, and Baladeva Vidyabhushana.

Overview

The Brahma Sutras are also known by other names: *Vedanta Sutras, Uttara Mimamsa-sutras, Uariraka Sutras, Uariraka Mimâmsâ-sutras*. Vaishnavas also call this the *Bhikshu sutras*.

The Brahma Sutras attempt to reconcile the seemingly contradictory and diverse statements of the various Upanishads and the Bhagavad Gita, by placing each teaching in a doctrinal context. The word *sutra* means thread, and the Brahma sutras literally stitch together the various Vedanta teachings into a logical and self-consistent whole.

However, the Brahma Sutras are so terse that not only are they capable of being interpreted in multiple ways, but they are often incomprehensible without the aid of the various commentaries handed down in the main schools of Vedanta thought.

The Vedanta Sutras supply ample evidence that at a very early time, i.e. a period before their own final composition, there were differences of opinion among the various interpreters of the Vedanta. Quoted in the Vedanta Sutras are opinions ascribed to Audulomi, Karshnagni, Kauakatsna, Jaimini and Badari, in addition to Vyasa.

The Brahma Sutras consist of 555 aphorisms or sutras, in four chapters (*adhyaya*), each chapter being divided into four quarters (*Pada*). Each quarter consists of several groups of sutras called *Adhikaraòas* or topical sections. An *Adhikaraoa* usually consists of several sutras, but some have only one sutra.

The first chapter (*Samanvaya*: harmony) explains that all the Vedanta texts talk of Brahman, the ultimate reality, which is the goal of life. The very first sutra offers an indication into the nature of the subject matter. VS 1.1.1 *athato brahma jijnasa*-Now: therefore the inquiry (into the real nature) of Brahman.

The second chapter (*Avirodha*: non-conflict) discusses and refutes the possible objections to Vedanta philosophy.

The third chapter (*Sadhana*: the means) describes the process by which ultimate emancipation can be achieved. The fourth chapter (*Phala*: the fruit) talks of the state that is achieved in final emancipation.

These *sutras* systematize the jnanakaoda (path of wisdom, as opposed to *Karmakaoda,* the path of action) of the Veda, by combining the two tasks of concisely stating the teaching of the Veda and argumentatively establishing the specific interpretation of the Veda adopted in the sutras.

The sutras also discuss the role of karma and God and critically address the various doctrines associated with Buddhism, Jainism, Yoga, Nyaya, Vaisheshika, Shaiva, Shakta, Atheism, and Sankhya philosophies

5

Madhvacharya

Shri Madhvacharya was the chief proponent of Tattvavada (True Philosophy), popularly known as Dvaita or dualistic school of Hindu philosophy. It is one of the three most influential Vedanta philosophies. Madhva was one of the important philosophers during the Bhakti movement. He was a pioneer in many ways, going against standard conventions and norms. Madhvacharya is the third incarnation of Vayu, aka Mukhyaprana, after Hanuman and Bhima.

Birth and Childhood

Acharya Madhva was born on Vijayadashami day of 1238 CE at *Pajaka*, a tiny hamlet near Udupi. Narayana Panditacharya who later wrote Madhva's biography has recorded the names of Acharya's parents as Madhyageha Bhatta as name of the father and Vedavati as Acharya's mother. They named him *Vasudeva Naduilya* at birth. Later he was also refferred to as Purnaprajna, Anandatirtha and finally Madhvacharya.

Even as a child, Vasudeva exhibited precocious talent for grasping all things spiritual. He was drawn to the path of renunciation and even as a young boy of eleven years, he chose initiation into the monastic order from Achyuta-Pragna, a reputed ascetic of the time, near Udupi, in the year Saumya (1249 CE). The preceptor Achyuta-Pragna gave the boy Vasudeva the name of 'Purnaprajna' at the time of his initiation into *sanyasa*.

A little over a month later, little Purnaprajna is said to have defeated a group of expert scholars of *Tarka (logic)* headed by Vasudeva-pandita. Overjoyed at his precocious talent, Achyuta Preksha consecrated him as the head of the empire of Vedanta and conferred upon him the title of *Anandatirtha*. Thus Purna-prajna is the Acharya's name given to him at the time of Sanyasa (renunciation). The name conferred on him at the time of consecration as the Master of Vedanta is 'Ananda-Tirtha'. *Madhva*, a name traceable to the vedas (Balithasuktham), was the *nom-de-plume* assumed by the Acharya to author all his works. Madhva showed that vedas talk about him as "Madhva" and utilized that name for himself. However, he used Ananda Tirtha or Suka Tirtha to author his works. Madhva was the name by which he was to later be revered as the founders of *Tattvavada* or *Dvaita-mata*.

Tour of South India

Still in his teens, Madhva set out on a tour of South India. He visited several places of pilgrimage like Anantasayana, Kanyakumari, Ramesvara and Sriranga. Wherever he went, he preached his Tattvavada or religious truth to the people. He attacked superstitions and declared that they should not be mixed with spirituality. While his Tattvavada initiated frenzied discussion among scholars all over India, it also attracted severe criticism and attacks from the orthodoxy.

But Madhva remained unperturbed and soon after returning to Udupi, he proceeded to write his commentary (Bashya) of the Bhagawadgita. The authentic records show that he wrote 37 works on Tattvavada and they are collectively called as Sarvamula granthas. He established his school of thought by giving concrete proofs using three platforms called prathyaksha, anumaana and aagama.

Visit to Badri

In course of time, the urge to spread his philosophy far and wide took him north. In Badri, he bathed in the holy Ganga and also observed a vow of silence of 48 days. From there, he travelled to Vyasa-Badri where he met Vyasa at his hermitage and presented him with his commentary of the Gita. Veda Vyasa changed the word that claimed "I have written with all His capacity" to "I have written with little of His capacity"

Upon his return from there, he authored his celebrated commentaries on the Brahma Sutras. Though he authored several works, he never wrote any work with his own hands. Instead, his disciples transcribed his dictation onto palm leaves. Satya-Tirtha was one of the disciples who served as the scribe for most of his works.

In the meantime, his influence had spread far and wide throughout the country. Scholars all over India paid tribute to his unique analysis and commentaries of the scriptures. The circle of his disciples grew bigger and several got initiated into sanyasa under him. Achyuta Pragna who had until then been skeptical about Acharya's philosophy soon became a whole hearted adherent of Tattvavada.

Installation of Krishna and Return to Badri

After his return from Badri, Madhvacharya stayed in Udupi for some time and wrote his bhashyas or authoritative commentaries on all the ten Upanishads. He also composed glosses on forty hymns of the Rig Veda and wrote a treaties Bhagavata-tatparya highlighting the essential teachings of the puranas. Apart from these, he authored several topical handbooks and a on devotional song.

It was also during this time that he installed the deity of Krishna which he found in the western ocean near the Udupi sea-coast. After sometime, after appointing some disciples to take care of worshiping the deity of Krishna that he had installed, he undertook his second tour to Badri.

On the way, he had to cross the River Ganga. The other bank was then under the rule of a Muslim king. Unmindful of the threats of the Muslim soldiers against crossing the river, the Acharya boldly crossed the river and reached the other bank. He was taken before the Muslim ruler who was taken aback at the boldness of the ascetic. The Acharya said: 'I worship that Father who illumines the entire universe; and so do you. Why should I fear then either your soldiers or you?'. Hearing such words, the Muslim king was greatly impressed. He was filled with reverence for this unique monk. He made offers of several gifts and riches which Madhva politely declined and continued on his way to Badri. Once there, he met with Vyasa and Narayana yet again. On his way back to Udupi, he visited Kashi where he defeated an elderly Advaita ascetic, Amarendra Puri in a philosophical debate.

Then came Kurukshetra where a strange episode is said to have occurred. The Acharya got a mound there excavated and demonstrated to his disciples the buried mace of (the epic hero)

Bhima therein; and once again had it buried under the ground. Later on he visited Goa on the way back to Udupi. Here he is said to have enthralled audiences with his music. His musical expertise is attested by contemporaneous writers.

Last Days

After returning home from his second tour, the Acharya took to initiating social reforms in and around Udupi. A section of orthodoxy however, was still active and opposed to his views. Pundarika-Puri, an advaita ascetic was also humbled by the Acharya in a debate. It was around this time that Padmatirtha, a monk jealous of Madhva's erudition and popularity, arranged to have his works stolen from the custody of Pejattaya Shankara Pandita in Kasaragod. Madhva now travelled to Kasargod and defeated Padma-Tirtha in a philosophical debate. The essence of this debate was reduced to writing by his disciples and published as the *Vada* or *Tattvoddyota*. The stolen works were eventually returned to Madhva in a felicitation ceremony arranged by Jayasimha of Kumbla, the king of sothern Tulu Nadu

The acharya also had an intense debate for about 15 days with Pejattaya Trivikrama Panditacharya, the royal preceptor of the time, and emerged victorious. Trivikrama Panditacharya eventually became a disciple himself and went on to write a commentary called Tattva-dipika on the Acharya's Brahma-sutra-bhashya and thus paid his tribute to the guru.

The Acharya too was equally fond of Trivikrama pandita. In deference to the request of the devoted pupil, he wrote an extensive commentary in verse, viz, Anu-vyakhyana on the Brahma-sutras. The Acharya was dictating this work-to four disciples simultaneously, on each of the four chapters, without any break. At the same time, the composition of the work Nyayavivarana was also completed.

Nearing his seventies now, Madhvacharya initiated his brother into the monastic order. He was to be known as Sri Vishnutirtha, the first pontiff of the present day Sodhe Matha and Subramanya Matha. About the same time, Sobhana-bhatta received initiation into sanyasa from the Acharya. He later came to be known as Padmanabha Tirtha.

Both before and after the initiation of these two, several disciples form various regions of the country got their initiation into sanyasa from the Acharya. Among them, the names of eight disciples who chose to stay on in Udupi as pontiffs of different mathas are as under, in the order of their initiation:

1. Hrisikesa-Tirtha (Palimaru matha)
2. Narasimha-Tirtha (Adamaru-matha)
3. Janardana-Tirtha (Krsnapura-matha)
4. Upendra-Tirtha (Puttige-matha)
5. Vamana-Tirtha (Sirur-matha)
6. Vishnu-Tirtha (Sode-matha)
7. Srirama-Tirtha (Kaniyuru-matha)
8. Adhoksaja-Tirtha (Pejavaramatha).

The other two celebrated sanyasin-disciples of the Acharya are-9. Padmanabha-Tirtha 10. Narahari-Tirtha

When Padmanabha-Tirtha was initiated into sanyasa is not definitely known. There were several who had got initiation before him. It appears that he should have been initiated into the order some time between the dates when these eight pontiffs were initiated into the order.

After initiating several into the monastic order and installing pontiffs to the various mathas, he toured all over the district and engaged himself in educating the general public. He also composed the literary work "Krsnamrtamaharnava".

His discourse to Brahmins at Ujire, where he delved upon the spiritual aspect of ritualism came to be published under the title of Khandartha-nimaya (Karmanimaya).

Next he visited Panchalingesvara temple at Paranti, which he found in a dilapidated condition, without any worship or festivity. He made arrangements for the resumption of proper worship there according to the rituals prescribed by the ancient scriptures (agamas).

In the 79th year of his life, he decided to take leave of his disciples and proceeded to assign to them the responsibility of carrying on the tradition of his Tattvavada.

Having done that, on the ninth day of the bright half of the month of Magha in the Kali year 4418(1317 CE), he betook himself to Badri, all alone. The day on which he thus proceeded to Badri is celebrated as Madhvanavami to this day.

Tradition

The disciples of the Acharya, both pontifical and lay, continued his tradition with devout zeal. Hundreds of dialectical treatises came to be written. Among the writers belonging to this school we may roughly classify some outstanding ones in the following chronological order: Vishnu Tirtha, Padmanabha-Tirtha, Narahari-Tirtha, Trivikrama-panditacharya, Narayana Panditacharya, Vamana-Panditacharya, (Traivikramaryadasa), Jayatirtha (Tikacharya), Vijayadhvaja-Tirtha, Visnudasacharya, Vyasatirtha, Vadiraja, Vijayindra-Tirtha, Raghavendra Swami, Yadupati-acharya, etc.

His philosophy Tattvavada also eventually inspired the Haridasa cult who heralded the Bhakti movement for centuries to come. Seminal contributions were also made by the Haridasas in fields of music and literature. Narahari Tirtha, one of the direct disciples is also responsible for the resurgence of Yakshagana and other forms such as Kuchipudi.

Raghavendra Swami of Mantralaya was a saint in this tradition who lived in the 16th CE and is revered and worshiped to this day. Several Dvaita mathas and Raghavendra mathas in particular, continue to be established all over India and also in some places in US, UK and other countries. All these Madhva mathas continue to further the propagation of Vedic studies and are also involved in social and charitable activities.

Madhva, commenting on the Vedanta-sutra (2.1.6), quotes the Bhavicya PurGa as follows: "The Zg Veda, Yajur Veda, Sama Veda, Atharva Veda, Mahabharata [which includes the Bhagavad-Gita], Pancaratra, and the original RmyaGa are all considered Vedic literature.... The Vaic Gava supplements, the PurGas, are also Vedic literature." We may also include corollary literatures like the Saahitas, as well as the commentaries of the great teachers who have guided the course of Vedic thought for centuries.

Works of Madhvacharya

The extant works of Dvaita philosopher Sri Madhvacharya are many in number. The works span a wide spectrum of topics concerning Dvaita and Hindu philosophy. They comprise commentaries on the Vedas, Upanishads, Bhagavadgita, Brahma Sutras and other works.

Commentaries on the Gita

Gita Bhashya: This work focusses on explaining the meaning of Gita. This is said to be the first work of Sri Madhvacharya after his taking up sanyasa, and at a very young age. Like all his other works, there is extremely brevity of expression, profusion of quotations from other authoritative sources (the exception being Brahmatarka, which is quoted in most other works), and is very definitive.

Gita Tatparya: This work compliments the Bhashya in two ways-it gives some alternate meanings to Gita (perhaps an indication to the truth in the quotation given in the Bhashya that Gita has at least 10 meanings) and reviews and criticizes some other commentaries on Gita, notably the advaita commentary on Gita.

Commentaries on the Brahmasutras

Brahmasutra Bhashya: This is a commentary on the Brahmasutras and covering every suutra. According to the Dvaita sampradaya, there are 564 sutras. More details can be seen from.

This has multiple commentaries, including some of the earliest disciples of Sri Madhvacharya —

- Sattarkadiipaavali from Sri Padmanabha Tirtha
- Tattvapradiipa from Sri Trivikrima Panditacharya
- Tattvaprakaashikaa from Sri Jayatirtha.

Sri Madhvacharya's treatment of Brahmasutras has many unique points:

Brahmasutras are considered decisive [nirnayaka] of purport of the entire scriptures. This is unlike other traditions which consider the suutras as just an aid or a part of the process to arrive at the purport. And for this reason, Brahmasutras are part of paravidya in dvaita, while it is not in other Sampradayas.

Brahmasuutras are recited with an 'OM' at the beginning and the end.

Brahmasuutras' range of coverage is the entire shabdash Astra, not just that Upanishads.

According to Advaita, one of the prerequisites to studying Brahmasutras or doing brahmajijn Asa (i.e. an enquiry into nature of Brahman) requires a thorough understanding of the karmamiimaasma. According to Vishishtaadvaita, Brahmasutras comprise one unit of shaastra, along with karmamiimaamsa and daivii miimaamsaa. According to Dvaita, Brahmasuutras are a unit in themselves, and having devotion to Vishnu and detachment in regular materialism etc, form the minimum prerequisite.

There is no stress on understanding of karmakanda:

- Anu Bhashya
- Anu Vyakhyana
- Nyaya Vivarana.

Commentaries on the Upanishads:

- Ishavasya Upanishad Bhashya
- Kena Upanishad Bhashya
- Kathopanishad Upanishad Bhashya
- Mundaka Upanishad Bhashya
- Satprashna Upanishad Bhashya
- Mandukya Upanishad Bhashya
- Aitareya Upanishad Bhashya
- Taittireya Upanishad Bhashya
- Brihadaranyaka Upanishad Bhashya
- Chandogya Upanishad Bhashya.

Commentaries on the Vedas, Puranas and Mahabharata:

- Bhagavata Tatparya
- Mahabharata Tatparya Nirnaya
- Rig Veda Bhashya.

Works related to Tattvavada (Philosophy of Truth):

- Pramana Lakshana
- Katha Lakshana
- Upadhi Khandana
- Prapanch Mithyatva-anumana Khandana
- Mayavada Khandana
- Tattva Samkhyana
- Tattva Viveka
- Tattvoddyota
- Karma Nirnaya
- Vishnu Tattva Vinirnaya.

6

Rise of Tamil Bhakti Movement

Background

As far as religious history of early India is concerned While archaeological material suggests that certain elements of Indian religions were present in the archaeological cultures dating prior to the Vedas, the hymns of the Rig Veda give us for the first time, an idea of how prayers were offered deities to please them. However, 'the simple prayers of the Rig Veda gave place gradually to complex rituals dominated by Brahmanas and one can notice the growth of a close relationship between the Brahmanas and the rulers and warriors on this situation.

Not only the wandering ascetics who moved away from the established society but also the Buddhist and the Jainas did not accept the dominance of the Brahrnanas and the rigid social and moral order which the Brahmanas advocated. There thus grew the heterodox movements which received support not only from rulers and rich merchants but also from other sections of people. In the pre-Gupta period Buddbism reached the height of its glory, spread to countries outside India and Buddhist centres were constructed on a large scale.

Meanwhile certain changes were taking place within Brahmanism as well as within heterodox sects. From the religious point of view the most important change was that the devotee was considered as being bound to the supreme god head by devotion (bhakti) and the god head was worshipped in the form of images. Vaishnavism and Shaivism as parts of Brahrnanical religion attracted many devotees; image worship became widespread among the Buddhists who worshipped not only the Buddha or Bodhisatva but also a host of other deities, the Jainas too worshipped the images of Tirthankaras, various minor deities, stone ayagapatas and other objects.

The Brahmanas used image worship to build up pantheons of deities by assimilating gods and goddesses from diverse sources. This is how many female deities (shakti) became Prominent in Brahmanical religions from the Gupta period onward. In fact, there was no homogeneity in Brahmanical religions and religious practices and beliefs varied widely.

Different sects of Savism, such as the Pasupatas, the Kaula-Kapalikas and the Kalamukhas were opposed to the dominance of the Brahmanas. They had their own religious orders centred around mathas or monastries and they received support from many royal families.

At the same time, Brahmanas who cultivated the Vedas and continued to perform Vedic sacrifices received royal support and agrahara settlements of the Brahmanas came to be a major link in the spread of Brahmanical ideas and practices throughout the country. The temple also became an institution which drew people together and served effectively in the spread of ideas.

Although in the complex religious situation of early medieval India the Brahmanas were gaining ascendancy, one should keep in mind also the following terms:

1) The orthodox Brahmanical order continued to be challenged particularly by movements within Shaivism, by poet saints and by those who practised tantric form of worship.
2) Most religions irrespective of whether it was Brahmanism, Buddhism or Shaivism, developed institutional bases in the form of temples and monasteries.
3) Ruling powers and elite sections of society supported institutions and Brahmanas, monks, acharyas or religious heads and others by grants of land, wealth and by other means. By these acts of patronage, the ruling powers and elite sections of society strengthened their own social base.

These are the various aspects which have been taken up in this Unit.

Alvars

The Alvars spelt as Azhwars were Tamil poet saints of south India who lived between the sixth and ninth centuries and espoused 'emotional devotion' or bhakti to Visnu-Krishna in their songs of longing, ecstasy and service. Sri Vaishnava orthodoxy posits the number of alvars as ten, though there are other references that include Andal and madhurakavi, making the number twelve.

The devotional outpourings of Alvars, composed during the early medieval period of Tamil history, helped revive the bhakti movement, through their hymns of worship to Vishnu and his avatars. The collection of their hymns is known as *Divya Prabandha* and is considered equal to the sanskrit body of work called vedas and related revelatory texts, detailing knowledge of Nature, God and the relationship between the two.

The Bhakti literature that sprang from Alvars has contributed to the establishment and sustenance of a culture that broke away from the ritual-oriented Vedic religion and rooted itself in devotion as the only path for salvation. In addition they helped to make the Tamil religious life independent of a knowledge of Sanskrit. As part of the legacy of the Alvars, five Vaishnava philosophical traditions (Sampradayas) have developed at the later stages.

Etymology

Alvars or 'Azhwars' literally means 'people who are immersed'. They are so called because they were immersed in their devotion and love to their Lord, Vishnu.

Legacy

The twelve Alvars were all inspired and ardent devotees who transmitted their divine infatuation to millions. They have left behind an imperishable legacy of devotional Tamil poetry-naalaayira Divya Prabhandham (considered to be the essence of the Vedas, in Tamil, and all in praise of Lord Vishnu). These have been rarely equalled either in quantity or in quality ever after.

The one held in greatest esteem among the Alvars is Nammalvar. He lived during the seventh century CE. His contribution to the four thousand prabandhams is as many as 1352. His hymns are considered by the Vaishnavites to contain the essence of the Vedas. His works-*Thiru Aasiriyam, Thiru Virudham, Periya Thiruvandhadhi* correspond to the Yajur, Rig and Atharva

Vedas respectively. His other work *Periya Thirumozhi* (Divine words) is the one of the key works of Vaishnavism.

Periyalvar delighted in worshipping Vishnu as mother, nurse, devotee and lady love. Andal, who grew up in Periyalvar's home, is attributed the *Tiruppaavai,* a most beautiful collection of 30 verses giving expression to the purest love of God.

Thirumangai Alvar has done mangalasasanam (sung in praise) of maximum number of Divya Desams.

Caste

The revered alvars came from all castes, a symbolic notion in Sri Vaishnavism to show that devotion to God transcends above caste. Nammalvar, or Satakopan, belonged to the Vellala caste. Tirumangai Alvar belonged to the Kallara tribe. Thirumalisai Alvar belonged to Paraiyar untouchable caste. Tiruppani Alvar belonged to Panar untouchable caste, Kulashekhara was a ruler. Vishnu Chitta, or Periyalvar, was a Brahmin.

Aandaal

Aandaal is an 8th century (or earlier) Tamil saint and one of the twelve Alvars (saints) and the only woman Alvar of Vaishnavism. She is credited with the great Tamil works of Thirupavai and Nachiar Tirumozhi that are still recited by devotees during the Winter festival season of Margazhi. Aandaal is known for her unwavering devotion to Lord Vishnu. The Srivilliputhoor Temple is dedicated to her and marks her birth place. Adopted by her father, the famous saint Periyalvar who found her as a baby, Aandaal avoided earthly marriage, the normal and expected path for women of her culture, to "marry" Lord Vishnu, both spiritually and physically. In many places in India, particularly in Tamilnadu, Aandaal is treated more than a saint and as a form of God herself.

Early Life

Aandaal is believed to have been discovered under a Tulsi (Basil) plant in the temple garden of Srivilliputtur, by a person named Vishnucitta who later became one of the most revered saints in Hinduism, Periyalvar. The child was named Kodhai (meaning, a beautiful garland, in Tamil) and she was raised by Vishnucitta. Goda (Sanskrit version of Kodhai) grew up in an atmosphere of love and devotion.

Vishnucitta doted on her in every respect, singing songs to her about Lord Vishnu; teaching her all the stories and philosophy he knew; and sharing with her his love for Tamil poetry. As Goda grew into a beautiful maiden, her love and devotion for the Lord grew to the extent that she decided to marry none but the Lord Himself. As days progressed, her resolve strengthened and she started to live in a dream world with her beloved Lord and was constantly fantasizing about marrying Him.

Vishnucitta had the responsibility of delivering flower garlands to the Lord's temple, everyday. Goda made these garlands and sent it to her beloved Lord through her father. Eventually she started acting unusual by wearing the flower garland which was meant to be offered to the Lord. This is generally considered sacrilege in Hinduism because the scriptures teach the devotees not to offer to the Lord, a thing that has already been used by a human being.

However, Goda felt she should test to see how the garland suited her and only if it did, she should offer it to the Lord. One day, she was caught red-handed by her father in this strange act, and as an orthodox devotee he was extremely upset. He rebuked her and told her not to repeat the sacrilegious act in the future. Frightened and apologetic, Goda made a new garland for the offering that day. Legend says that that very night the Lord appeared to Vishnucitta in his dream and asked him why he had discarded Goda's garland instead of offering it to Him.

The Lord is believed to have told Vishnucitta that He had whole-heartedly accepted Goda's offering all this time. This moved Vishnucitta so much even as he started to realize the Divine Love that existed between the Lord and his daughter. From this day on, Goda is believed to have been respected by the devotees and came to be known as "Aandaal", the girl who "ruled" over the Lord. She is also known by a phrase "Soodi kodutha Sudarkodi" which means "The bright creeper-like woman who gave her garlands after wearing them".

Marrying the Lord

As Aandaal blossomed into a fifteen-year-old beautiful young woman of marriageable age (girls were married at a much younger age in those days), her father prepared to get her married to a suitable groom. Aandaal, however, was stubborn and insisted that she would marry only the Lord at Srirangam. This perplexed and worried her father. Legend has it that he had a vision give by the Lord, once again, and was instructed to send Aandaal to Srirangam; the lord simultaneously commanded the priests at Srirangam, in their dreams, to prepare for the wedding. Aandaal who was anxious to reach Srirangam was unable to control herself in her urgency to meet her beloved Lord. She ran into the sanctum sanctorum of the Lord and is believed to have merged with Him completely at that point.

Literary Works

Aandaal composed two works in her short life of fifteen years. Both these works are in Tamil verse form and are exceptional in their literary, philosophical, religious, and aesthetic content. Her contribution is even more remarkable considering that she was a girl of fifteen when she composed these verses and her prodigiousness amazes readers till date.

Her first work is the Thiruppavai, a collection of thirty verses in which Aandaal imagines herself to be a Gopi or cowherd girl during the incarnation of Lord Krishna. She yearns to serve Him and achieve happiness not just in this birth, but for all eternity, and describes the religious vows (pavai) that she and her fellow cowherd girls will observe for this purpose.

The second is the Nachiar Tirumozhi, a poem of 143 verses. Tirumozhi, literally meaning "Sacred Sayings", is a Tamil poetic style. "Nachiar" means Goddess, so the title means "Sacred Sayings of the Goddess." This poem fully reveals Aandaal's intense longing for Vishnu, the Divine Beloved. Utilizing classical Tamil poetic conventions and interspersing stories from the Sanskrit Vedas and Puranas, Aandaal creates imagery that is possibly unparalleled in the whole gamut of Indian religious literature. However, conservative Vaishnavite institutions do not encourage the propagation of Nachiar Tirumozhi as much as they encourage Tiruppavai. This is because Nachiar Tirumozhi is belongs to an erotic genre of spirituality that is similar to Jayadeva's Gita Govinda.

The impact of these works on the daily religious life of the South Indian has been tremendous. Just like the Ramayana and the Mahabharata, the Thiruppavai is recited with great religious fervor by women, men, and children of all ages, particularly in Tamil Nadu. The daily services in most Vaishnava temples and households include this recitation. Both of these works, particularly the Thiruppavai, has been studied extensively by innumerable scholars. It has also been translated into a number of languages over the centuries.

Status in the Society

Aandaal is now one of the best-loved poet-saints of the Tamils. Pious tradition reckons her to be the veritable descent of Bhumi Devi (Mother Earth) in bodily form to show humanity the way to His lotus feet. She is present in all Sri Vaishnava temples, in India and elsewhere, next to her Lord, as she always desired. During the month of Margazhi, discourses on the Tiruppavai in Tamil, Telugu, Kannada, Hindi and English take place all over India.

Nayanars

The Nayanars or Nayanmars were Shaivite devotional poets of Tamil Nadu, active between the fifth and the tenth centuries CE. The Tamil Shaiva hagiography *Periya Puranam*, a volume of the *Tirumurai*, written during the thirteenth century CE, narrates the history of each of sixty-three Nayanars and the history of nine Thokai Adiyar.

Cuntarar's eighth century work *TirutoGmar tokai* lists 60 Shaiva saints but gives none of the legends associated with them. In the tenth century Nambiyandar Nambi composed the *TirutoGmar Antadi*, a sequence of interlocking verses the title of which can be rendered as the *Necklace of Verses on the Lord's Servants*. In this work Nambi add Cuntarar, himself and his parents to the sequence, creating what is now the canonical list of sixty-three saints, each with a brief sketch of their legend.

Nayanars were from varied backgrounds, ranging from kings and soldiers to untouchables. The foremost Nayanars are Appar, Cuntarar and Campantar. Together with the twelve Vaishnava Alvars, the Nayanars are sometimes accounted South India's 75 Apostles of Bhakti because of their importance in the rise of the Hindu Bhakti movement.

The Sixty-three Nayanmars:

1. Anaya
2. Adipaththa

3. Aiyadigal Kaadavarkon, Pallava King Aiyadigal Perumaanaar
4. Amaraneedi Nayanar
5. Appudhi Adigal
6. Arivattaya
7. Chandeshvara Nayanar
8. DhandiyadigaL
9. Enatinatha
10. Eripaththa
11. Eyarkon Kalikkaama
12. Gananatha
13. Idankazhi
14. Ilayankudi maranar
15. Isaignaniyaar-Female Nayanar
16. Iyarpagaiar
17. Kaari
18. Kalikkamba
19. Kaliya
20. Kanampulla
21. Kannappa Nayanar
22. Karaikkal Ammeiyar, Female Nayanar
23. Kazharchinga
24. Kazharir-rarivaar, Chera King, also Cheraman Perumal
25. Kochengat Cholan, A Chola King
26. Kootruva
27. Kotpuli
28. Kulachchirai
29. Kungiliyak Kalaya
30. Manakkanychaara Nayanar
31. Mangayarkkarachiyar, Female Nayanar
32. Meiporul Nayanar
33. Murkha
34. Murti
35. Munayaduvaar
36. Muruga

37. Nami Nandi Adigal
38. Narasingha Munayaraya
39. Nesa Nayanar
40. Ninra Seer Nedumaara
41. Perumizhalaik Kurumba
42. Pusalar
43. Pugal Chola, A Chola King
44. Pugazh Thunai Nayanar
45. Saakkiya
46. Sadaiya Nayanar
47. Saththi
48. Seruthtunai
49. Sirappuli
50. Siruttonda
51. Somaachi
52. Sundarar
53. TirugnaanaSambandar
54. Tirukkuripput Tonda
55. Tirumular
56. Thirunalai Povar Nayanar, popularly known as Nandanar
57. Tirunavukkarasar, popularly known as Appar
58. Thiruneelakandar
59. Tirunilakanda Yaazpaana
60. Tirunilanakka
61. Uruttira Pasupati
62. Vaayilaar
63. Viralminda nayanar.

Emergence of Bhakti in Brahmanism

Brahmanism had to accept the growing importance of new gods like Siva and Vishnu side by side with Vedic gods like Indra and Varuna. It also assimilated many other popular deities like Vasudeva, Skanda and so on. All these led to the growth of the Bhakti cult.

Around the fourth century B.C. the cult of Vasudeva was becoming popular. This is suggested by reference to it by classical authors like Megasthenes who came to the court of Chandgragupta Maurya.

The worshippers of Vasudeva submitted to Bhakti as the proper religious approach and called themselves Bhagavatas. Several epigraphs of the early Christian era bear testimony to the prevalence of the Vasudeva cult in central India and the Deccan.

Simultaneously with the cult of Vasudeva arose the sect of Pasupatas, devotees of Pasupati or Siva, a fertility deity. This cult was kept alive in non-brahmanic circles from the days of the Harappan culture.

The popularity of these new gods increased during the Sunga and Kanvaa periods. Patanjali, who lived in the Sunga period, in his Mahabhashya refers to the exhibition and sale of the images of Siva, Skanda and Vishakha. These gods appear on the coins of the Kushana kings, especially Huvishka. An important characteristic of later Brahmanism was its capacity to adopt new trends.

This became necessary to meet the challenge of the 'hentical sects' which were opposed to Brahmanism. Besides adopting new gods, Brahmanism gradually shifted its emphasis from Vedic ritual to Bhakti, which implied the cultivation and development of a personal relationship between God and the devotee. Thus a monotheistic concept of God,, with either Siva or Vishnu as his manifestation and Bhskti (loyalty and devotion) to him was gaining strength. Soon Bhakti became the dynamic force of later Brahmanism also called Hinduism.

Syncretism of Deities

An important characteristic of the new Brahmanism was its genius to syncretise many local deities and to evolve a monotheistic great God. Syncretism in this context will mean that deities worshipped at different places and by different people were recognised as identical and were worshipped as manifestation of the same supreme deity. Thus Vasudeva was identified with Vishnu, a minor Vedic god and Narayana, a god of obscure origin mentioned in the Brahmana literature.

Then Vishnu was closely connected with the name of Krishna, who represented the fusion between martial hero and a flute-playing pastoral deity. Vishnu could assimilate many other cults-the cult of the 'divine boar' which prevailed among some of the tribes of Malwa, the cult of Parasurama, a Brahamna hero; and Rama, the great hero of the Ramayana. Then Vishnu rose to the status of the Universal God in the Bhagavad Gita.

Similarly, Siva came to be syncretised with the Vedic Rudra and Bhairava, a tribal god and was worshipped in the form of the phallic emblem or linga. With Siva were later associated certain other deities such as Skanda and the elephant-headed Ganesa.

These theistic cults stressed the merit of worship rather than the performance of Vedic sacrifice.

Adaptation of Tribal Rituals

Yet another important feature of later Brahmanism was its adaptation of the tribal rituals keeping the Vedic Yajna rites supreme only in theory. In course of time the merit derived out of these new rituals were equated with the merit of the Vedic Yajna. Further, the sacred spots of the tribals were included as new places of pilgrimage (Tirtha) with suitable myths to make them respectable. The Ithihasas and Puranas are full of such material or stories which inspire bhakti (devotion) to a personal god.

Royal Support to Temples and Theism

The Puranas highlighted the merits acquired by visiting great cult centres like Mathura and Varanasi which were major places of pilgrimage. This gave a stimulus to the institution of the temple. In fact, the Puranas and other texts of the period list numerous places of pilgrimage (tirthas) which drew devotees in large numbers because visiting tirthas would ensure merit.

The temple which housed the deity, became a place of worship and thus drew devotees away from home to an institution which became a public centre. The Gupta age marked the beginning of temple construction. It laid the foundation of the typical styles of Indian temple architecture. Among the few Gupta temples which survive, the Dasavatara temple of Devagarh, the Vishnu temple at Tigawa, and the Siva temple at Bhumara are known for their beauty.

The epic and Puranic stories relating to Rama and Krishna were represented in the temple sculptures. Excellent specimens of them are still found in the Devagarh temple. The Gupta emperors patronised both Shaivism and Vaishnavism. However, the personal religion of most of the Gupta rulers was Vaishnavism which led to the creation of a number of important Vaishnava centres and Vaishnava sculptures in the Gupta period. The idea of the awataras or incarnations of Vishnu in which Vishnu is born on earth as a boar, a fish, or a human being for rescuing earth from a crisis, also seems to have been systematised in the Gupta period.

In the sixth and seventh centuries A.D. Shaivism seems to have replaced Vaishnavism as recipient of royal patronage in northern India. Shaivism counted among its followers supreme plers, foreign as well as indigenous, such as Mihirakula, Yashodharman, Sasanka and Harsha. Pasupata or Shaiva acharyas are frequently mentioned in contemporary records which include inscriptions, and many literary works like those of Varahamihira, Bana and Hiuen Tsang.

Spread of Bhakti to the South

All the major north Indian religions-Brahmanism, Jainism and Buddhism-travelled southwards. The Brahmanas brought with them the Vedic Yajna cult and the two theistic cults, Vaishnavism and Shaivism. The kings were in favour of the Vedic rituals as they conferred ritual status on them. The theistic cults struck root among the people. However, eventually the devotional theistic cults were to prove stronger than any other religious force in the south, and this was recognized even by royal patrons who extended support to Vaishnavism, Shaivism and their sects.

Among the early chalukya kings of Vatapi some professed Bhagavatism and others, the Pasupata cult. The famous bas-reliefs of Badami testify to the popularity of the theistic cults in the Deccan in the sixth-seventh centuries A.D. Similarly, the Pallavas of Kanchi patronised the two theistic cults as shown by the monolithic rathas (chariots) at Mahabalipuram and many bas-reliefs on them.

Bhakti, centring around the worship of specific deities, began to spread fast in the south through the brahmana settlements and temple centres where the exposition of the epics and the Puranas was institutionalized by means of munificent land grants. Thus Bhakti was popularised among the common people. It is to be noted that the way in which the Brahmanas transformed the earlier religious forms into temple-centred theistic culture in the north was repeated in the south also.

Bhakti Movement in South India

The final form of theistic Bhakti was largely the result of the influence of the Tamil devotionalism. This devotionalism was a product of the fusion between ecstatic local tribal cults (e.g. Velan Veriyadal) and northern theistic schools. This cross fertilization started at Tiruppati and Kalahasti, which then constituted the northern door of the Tamil country.

Then it developed around Kanchipuram, the Pallava capital and soon reached the region of Madurai, the Pandyan capital. The Tiru Murugu Arruppadai, a famous devotional work on Muruga, the local tribal god who was syncretised with Skanda in this work, is the earliest example of this cross fertilization.

Soon this Tamil devotionalism developed into a great movement when it was adapted to the two theistic cults, Shaivism and Vaishnavism. Then Tamil Bhakti movement was characterized not only by intense ecstatic piety for the deity, but also an aggressive militancy against the heterodox cults which were growing in popularity among the people with royal support.

This movement was spearheaded in the sixth century A.D. by gifted poet-saints who traversed the country many times with great missionary zeal. All their way they sang their hymns, danced and debated with the heterodox cults. Among these hymnal poet-saints the Shaiva saints are called Nayanmar and the Vaishnava saints as Alvars.

This great wave of religious enthusiasm attained its peak in the early seventh century and its triumph was largely achieved in the two centuries that followed. The hymns of the saints of this period are marked by an outspoken hatred against the Buddhists and the Jainas. As a result, public debates, competition in the performance of miracles and tests of the truth of I their doctrines by means of ordeal became the order of the day..I.

There were other reasons for the success and popularity of these hymnal saints. Unlike the Brahmanas who propagated Hinduism through theories and the use of Sanskrit, the hymnal saints sang in easily understood forms using only the popular language, Tamil. Their Bhakti was not a reverence for a transcendent deity, but ecstatic love for an imminent one. Being unable to stand before the force of this Bhakti wave which also attracted royal support, Jainism and Buddhism had to retreat from the South.

Protest and Reform in the Bhakti Movement of the South and Later Transformation of the Bhakti Movement

Whereas the Brahmanas were obsessed with caste regulations, the Bhakti movement not only ignored caste but also included men and women of all castes. Among the Nayanar 'Karaikkal, Amrnai was a woman and Nandanar was a member of the depressed class. Among the Alvars, Andal was a woman and Timppan was a hymnist from a "low caste". Thus the whole movement carried elements of protest and reform. However, it soon became part of the establishment, lost its early character and got engulfed by brahrnanical orthodoxy.

The Bhakti movement grew first under the Pallavas and then under the cholas, Pandyas and the Cheras. Many rock temples were cut and structural temples were built for Siva and Vishnu throughout the Tamil land by almost all the reigning monarchs.

These temples were endowed with vast landed property, often tax-free. Extensive areas of land were donated to the Brahmanas as is evident from the thousands of inscriptions on the walls of the south Indian temples. A prince-priest axis soon emerged. The monarchs fervently welcomed the rich temple-centered bhakti (or unflinching loyalty) as it suited the monarchical ideology. The Brahmanas welcomed this as it enabled Brahmanism, with its institutional base in the temple centred agrarian settlements, to emerge as the most dynamic force in south India.

Everywhere the local temple was the nucleus of religious life and a new social formation. In these temples the two arms of the brahmanical religion-the ritualistic Vedic cult and the theistic devotional cult-could meet. The temple-centred Bhakti enabled the all-embracing caste system to attract all the origional tribes of south India within its fold and place them in the hierarchical caste order.

This order fixed the ritual and social status of the mbes with the Brahrnana as the fixed point of reference. The ideology of Bhakti could bring together kings, priests and the common people within a network of understandable social relations. With the increasing patronage of kings and landed magnates, the Bhakti movement soon became part of the establishment. Thus all trances of dissent, protest and reform were obliterated in the tenth century A.D. The Alvars and the Nayanars do not appear any more.

Their place was taken by Vaishnava acharyas, all of whom were Brahmanas or the Saivite acharyas who all came from the rich landed Vellala caste.

Poigai Alvar

Poigai Alvar was one of the twelve Alvars and was a Hindu saint. He belonged to the Vaishnava (worshiper of Vishnu) denomination of Hinduism. Poigai Alvar was born in a village near Kanchipuram in the seventh century CE. Poigai (pond in Tamil) was found as a baby near a pond of a Vishnu temple. Some Vaishnavas consider him to be an incarnation of *Panchajanyam*, the divine conch of Vishnu. Poigai Alvar's 100 hymns form the beginning of the Naalayira Divyap Prabhandham. Poigai Alwar's hymns start with the words *Vaiyam Tagaliya, Varkadale Neyyaaga* (I am singing these garland of verses(pAsurams) and dedicating to Him, whose vision I had is the light of the lamp of the earth, and oil being the seas, the sun being the source of the light).

Bhoothathalvar

Bhoothathalvar was one of the twelve Alvars and was a Hindu saint. He belonged to the Vaishnavite (worshiper of Vishnu) faith.

Bhoothathalvar was born in the Pallava country near Mamallapuram in the seventh century CE. Bhoothathalvar's 100 hymns form the second part of the Naalayira Divyap Prabhandham. Bhoothathalvar's hymns start with the words *Anbe Tagaliya, Aarvame Neyyaaga* (with love as the lamp and devotion as the oil). He is considered an incarnation of Vishnu's mace, Kaumodaki.

Anbe Thagliyaa Aarvame Neyyaaga
Inburugu Chintai Idu Thiriyaa
Nanpurugi Gnaana Chudar Vilakku Etrinen
Naaranarku Gnaana Thamizh Purindha Naan.

"I who wrote this song that bestows wisdom, with love as the lamp, endearing involvement as the lubricant ghee, and knowledge as the wick of the burning torch, dedicated myself to the service of the Lord"

Peyalvar

Payalvar was one of the twelve Alvars and was a Hindu saint. He belonged to the Vaishnavite (worshiper of Vishnu) faith.

Payalvar was born in Tirumayilai (Mylapore, now part of he city of Chennai om the seventh century CE. Vaishnavite traditions states that Peyalvar was found on a lily flower in the pond of the Adi Kesava Perumal Temple in Mylapore. They also believe that he was an incarnation of the sacred sword of Vishnu, Nandaki. Payalvar's 100 hymns in the Naalayira Divyap Prabhandham are the third 100 and start with the words *Tiruk Kanden, Pon Meni Kanden* ('I found the glorious, golden form of the Lord').

Tiruk Kanden Pon Meni Kanden-Thigazhum

Arukkan Ani Niramum Kanden-Seruk Kilarum

Pon Aazhi Kanden Puri Sangam Kai Kanden

En Aazhi Vannan Paal Inru.

"On witnessing the glorious vision in which the entire universe was the very body of Lord Narayana, the Alwar proceeds to describe all that he had seen."

Peyalvar's hymns are of the *Anthathi* style, in which the last word of the previous hymn is used as the first work in the next hymn.

Thirumalisai Alvar

Thirumalisai Alvar is a tamil mendicant-saint revered in the Sri Vaishnavism school of south india between the 4th to 9th century CE in Tondai Nadu [now called Kanchipuram and Tiruvallur districts]. There are only little historical records of this alvars. The legend of this saint devotees of Sri Vaishnavism say that he was the incarnation of vishnu's disc, Sudarshana. He belonged to Paraiyar caste, he proclaimed that he was "not of the 4 castes" (Brahmin, Kshatriya, Vaishya & Shudṛa) in one of his couplets as he was considered (Avarna) untouchable and casteless person.

He had the access and resources to learn about various religions because in one of his couplets he says "After my futile efforts to know the supreme principle through Jainism, and Buddhism I am blessed by sriman Narayana to take refuge at the Lotus feet of Sri Devi and have escaped all problems and misfortunes since then".

There is also evidence in his couplets that show that he was discriminated against by brahmins and asked God to help reveal their ignorance to them. Legend also says that when he displeased the pallava king and was banished, he asked the God from the temple, Yathotkari, to leave with him. Vishnu is said to have rolled up the snake Sesha like a matress and left with him. There are 216 of his paasurams in the 4000 Divya Prabhandham.

Nammalvar

Nammalvar (also Nammazhwar,Nammaazhvaar, Nammazhvar, Nammaalvaar, Nammalwar) was one of the twelve Alvars, well-known for his many hymns on devotion to Vishnu. Tradition gives him the date 3102 B.C. (i.e., the beginning of the kali yuga), but scholars give him a date 880–930 A.D which is more realistic based on the events recorded. He was born in the asterism Visakham, in what is now Alvartirunakari (also known as Tirukkurugur), Tamil Nadu. His name means "our own Alvar" (Alvar means "one immersed in God"). He was also known as Maran and Sadagopan.

Child Prodigy Discovered

He must have been born fully enlightened because as a baby he never cried or suckled and never opened his eyes. According to tradition, as a child he responded to no external stimuli and his parents left him at the feet of the statue of Vishnu. The child then got up and climbed into a hole in a tamarind, sat in the lotus position, and began to meditate.

It appears he was in this state for as long as sixteen years when a Tamil poet and scholar in North India named Madhurakavi Alvar saw a bright light shining to the south, and followed it until he reached Nammalvar's tree. Unable to elict any reaction from the child, he asked him a riddle: " If the small is born in a dead's body (or stomach), what will it eat and where will it stay?" meaning, if the subtle soul is embodied in the gross body, what are its actions and thoughts? Nammalvar broke his lifelong silence and responded, "That it will eat, and there it will rest!" meaning that if the soul identifies with the body, it will be the body but if it serves the divine, it will stay in vaikunta and eat(think) of God. Madhura-kavi realized the divinity of this child.

First Disciple

Madhura-kavi was himself a great devotee, when he asked Nammalvar the "right" question and made him speak. Immediately he took him for his Acharya (Teacher, Guru). Nammalvar consented to being his guru, instructed him in the confidential doctrines of

Vaishnavism and thereafter glorified Lord Vishnu. He composed on the spot a thousand hymns praising Vishnu, each one starting with the last word of the previous poem. We owe it to Madhurakavi for setting them to music. Madhurakavi became the Alvar's student and went on to compose poems about his prodigal master.

The following is an interesting episode regarding the way the two of them met. *MadhuraKavi Alwar was on a pilgrimage in North India, when all of a sudden, he began to observe a bright light shining forth from the southern direction. This seemed to be beckoning him and so he began to proceed in the direction of its source. His travails brought him to the scenic banks of the River tamraparani, to the Hamlet/town if Kurugoor. He observed that the light that drew him emanated from a divine being, one seemingly in his teens sitting within the hollow of a tamarind tree.*

Writings

His contribution of four works (numbering 1296 hymns) to the four thousand of the Divya Prabhandham includes the entire fourth thousand and part of the third thousand. these works are;

- Tiruv Aymozhi (1102 verses),
- Tiruviruttam (100 verses),
- Tiruv Asiriam (7 verses) and
- Periya Tiruvanthadi (87 verses).

Tiruvaymozhi describes ranganatha as a metaphor to discussing the philosophical details in;

- the nature of the paramatma
- the nature of the jeevatma
- the means for the jeevatma to attain the goal of Paramatma
- the blocks and hurdles on the way and
- the goal moksha.

The latter 2 are described in detail in the srivaishnava website. In the Srivaishnava canon these four represent in the Tamil language the four Sanskrit vedas, respectively, the Sama Veda, Rig Veda, Yajur Veda and Atharva Veda. According to tradition "He poured the cream of these vedas" into his songs and poetry that were the result of deep mystic experience. Though Nammalvar did not visit any of the 108 divyadesam temples talked about in the Vaishnava religion it appears from his works he must have had the vision of all the archa forms in the temples he had glorified in his hymns.

Acme of Devotion

The subject matter of the four works was certainly the five principles, namely, the Lord, the soul, the means, the end, and the obstacles to spirituality. Through all this ran a thread of the acme of devotion to Lord Krishna. Whatever Krishna ate, whatever He drank, whatever betel He chewed was the dearest to the saint. The supreme object of life was to be at the Lord's lotus feet and to serve him eternally in blissful love.

Therefore seek Him all your life, praise Him, surrender to Him, speak of His glories and exploits, revel in His majesty and continue the recitation of His names. This was his message to the world at large. Like the Buddha who appeared in the northernmost part of India and finally engulfed not only India but Asia and the whole world by his teachings, Nammalvar was the star of the southernmost part of India whose work engulfed the whole world of Vaishnavism.

Madhurakavi Alvar

Madhurakavi (literally meaning Poet of sweet words) was a Tamil saint/composer of the 6th to 9th century. He composed 11 couplets in praise of his guru, Nammalvar in the 4000 divya Prabhandham. He is considered one of the alvars. He is venerated as the dawn Ushas before the sun rise of nammalvar as he was born before Nammalvar. Legends say that he was a well read and well travelled Brahmin with a gift for music. He set Nammalvar's compositions to music.

Early life

Madhura Kavi aazhwar was born before Swami Nammazhwar, in a Brahmin family, in the month of Chittirai and in the chitra star in the divya desam called Thirukkolur near Aazhwar Thirunagari. The perumal in this divya desam is called Vaitha Maanidhi (Storage of great wealth).

Madhura Kavi Aazhwar learnt the Vedas and was well versed in both Tamil and Sanskrit. He used to compose poems in the praise of Bhagavan. At one stage in his life, he decided to abandon all the chains of samsara and strive towards moksham. In this pursuit he undertook a pilgrimage to the Vada naattu divya desams like Ayodhya, Mathura etc.

Meeting his Guru

When Madhura Kavi aazhwar, after long tour had reached Ayodhya and completed the mangalaasasanam of the enchanting forms of Sri Rama, Sita piratti, Lakshmana, Hanuman and others he noticed a glowing ball of fire in the sky. However much he tried, he could not understand the reason for this phenomenon. He also noticed that the ball of fire started to slowly move southwards.

He decided to follow the light which led him to Aazhwar Thirunagari and finally disappeared. Madhura Kavigal had already heard about a sixteen year old youth [Nammalvar] who had spent his life since birth under a Tamarind tree without eating anything and emitting a divine glow. Madhura kavi aazhwar proceeded straight to the Thiru puli aazhwar (seat of Swami Nammalvar) and found Swami in a trance.

Kulashekhara

Kulashekhara was an Indian King from modern day Kerala and one of the Alvars, a prominent group of Vaishnava saints. From historical estimates it is believed he lived in or around the 8th century. Born in the asterism *Punarvasu* as Kulaœekhara Varma, he was king of the Chera Dynasty and lived in Kollam in Kerala. After ruling for a few years, he gave up his throne, became a sanyasi and is revered as the 9th of the alvars (one of 12 mendicant saints venerated by South Indian Sri Vaishnavism) and wrote bhakti songs filled with yearning towards God called paasurams which are an important part of Carnatic classical music repertory.

A great devotee of Rama, he considered the painful experiences of Lord Rama to be his own. He is therefore also known as 'Perum-al', meaning 'The Great' – which is usually the epithet for the Lord. His devotion was so intense that he worshipped the devotees of the Lord as the Lord Himself. He lived in Srirangam and was serving the deity Ranganatha in the temple there.

Much of the details of Kulashekhara's personal life have been lost. He was an exceptional poet of devotional hymns and songs (including the famous Mukundamala-stotra). He wrote a set of ten exquisite poems in Tamil, and the work is called "Perumal

Tirumoli". His poems are devotional in nature, being dedicated to the most prominent avatar's of Vishnu (Rama and Krishna).

The rock band Kula Shaker is named after King Kulashekhara as is their music company, Alvar Music.

Periyalvar

One of the alvars, he was born into a Brahmin family in Srivilliputhur, near Madurai in the 6th or 9th century (conflicting reports) CE and was named Vishnuchittar meaning "one who has Vishnu in his mind". Legend says he rejected the vedic philosophical debates of his upbringing to focus on Bhakti, especially on doing simple tasks for God. He would make garlands of flowers for the deity of the temple. One day the Pallava king of the land had a competition between scholars to find one who would explain philosophical principles.

Vishnuchittar won the competition by explaining that the path to moksha is by service to God. Legend goes that the king honoured Vishnuchittar and God himself came down to earth to see this. Vishnuchittar composed a couplet called out of respect) translating to "Long live for many years, Long live for many years for Hundreds of thousands of years!" to God. This is a very important prayer in Srivaishnava liturgy today. Vishnuchittar composed some pasurams in the 4000 Divya Prabhandham called Perialvar Tirumozhi where he explores a devotee's love for God through the metaphor of Yashoda's motherly love for Krishna. He was the adopted father of Kodhai or Andal, the only woman Alvar.

Aandaal

Aandaal is an 8th century (or earlier) Tamil saint and one of the twelve Alvars (saints) and the only woman Alvar of Vaishnavism. She is credited with the great Tamil works of Thirupavai and Nachiar Tirumozhi that are still recited by devotees during the Winter festival season of Margazhi. Aandaal is known for her unwavering devotion to Lord Vishnu. The Srivilliputhoor Temple is dedicated to her and marks her birth place. Adopted by her father, the famous saint Periyalvar who found her as a baby, Aandaal avoided earthly marriage, the normal and expected path for women of her culture, to "marry" Lord Vishnu, both spiritually and physically. In many places in India, particularly in Tamilnadu, Aandaal is treated more than a saint and as a form of God herself.

Early Life

Aandaal is believed to have been discovered under a Tulsi (Basil) plant in the temple garden of Srivilliputtur, by a person named Vishnucitta who later became one of the most revered saints in Hinduism, Periyalvar. The child was named Kodhai (meaning, a beautiful garland, in Tamil) and she was raised by Vishnucitta. Goda (Sanskrit version of Kodhai) grew up in an atmosphere of love and devotion. Vishnucitta doted on her in every respect, singing songs to her about Lord Krishna; teaching her all the stories and philosophy he knew; and sharing with her his love for Tamil poetry. As Goda grew into a beautiful maiden, her love and devotion for the Lord grew to the extent that she decided to marry none but the Lord Himself. As days progressed, her resolve strengthened and she started to live in a dream world with her beloved Lord and was constantly fantasizing about marrying Him.

Vishnucitta had the responsibility of delivering flower garlands to the Lord's temple, everyday. Goda made these garlands and sent it to her beloved Lord through her father. Eventually she started acting unusual by wearing the flower garland which was meant to be offered to the Lord. This is generally considered sacrilege in Hinduism because the scriptures teach the devotees not to offer to the Lord, a thing that has already been used by a human being.

However, Goda felt she should test to see how the garland suited her and only if it did, she should offer it to the Lord. One day, she was caught red-handed by her father in this strange act, and as an orthodox devotee he was extremely upset. He rebuked her and told her not to repeat the sacrilegious act in the future. Frightened and apologetic, Goda made a new garland for the offering that day. Legend says that that very night the Lord appeared to Vishnucitta in his dream and asked him why he had discarded Goda's garland instead of offering it to Him.

The Lord is believed to have told Vishnucitta that He had whole-heartedly accepted Goda's offering all this time. This moved Vishnucitta so much even as he started to realize the Divine Love that existed between the Lord and his daughter. From this day on, Goda is believed to have been respected by the devotees and came to be known as "Aandaal", the girl who "ruled" over the Lord.

She is also known by a phrase "Soodi kodutha Sudarkodi" which means "The bright creeper-like woman who gave her garlands after wearing them".

Marrying the Lord

As Aandaal blossomed into a fifteen-year-old beautiful young woman of marriageable age (girls were married at a much younger age in those days), her father prepared to get her married to a suitable groom. Aandaal, however, was stubborn and insisted that she would marry only the Lord at Srirangam. This perplexed and worried her father. Legend has it that he had a vision give by the Lord, once again, and was instructed to send Aandaal to Srirangam; the lord simultaneously commanded the priests at Srirangam, in their dreams, to prepare for the wedding. Aandaal who was anxious to reach Srirangam was unable to control herself in her urgency to meet her beloved Lord. She ran into the sanctum sanctorum of the Lord and is believed to have merged with Him completely at that point.

Literary Works

Aandaal composed two works in her short life of fifteen years. Both these works are in Tamil verse form and are exceptional in their literary, philosophical, religious, and aesthetic content. Her contribution is even more remarkable considering that she was a girl of fifteen when she composed these verses and her prodigiousness amazes readers till date.

Her first work is the Thiruppavai, a collection of thirty verses in which Aandaal imagines herself to be a Gopi or cowherd girl during the incarnation of Lord Krishna. She yearns to serve Him and achieve happiness not just in this birth, but for all eternity, and describes the religious vows (pavai) that she and her fellow cowherd girls will observe for this purpose.

The second is the Nachiar Tirumozhi, a poem of 143 verses. Tirumozhi, literally meaning "Sacred Sayings", is a Tamil poetic style. "Nachiar" means Goddess, so the title means "Sacred Sayings of the Goddess." This poem fully reveals Aandaal's intense longing for Vishnu, the Divine Beloved. Utilizing classical Tamil poetic conventions and interspersing stories from the Sanskrit Vedas and Puranas, Aandaal creates imagery that is possibly unparalleled in the whole gamut of Indian religious literature. However, conservative Vaishnavite institutions do not encourage the propagation of Nachiar Tirumozhi as much as they encourage Tiruppavai. This is because Nachiar Tirumozhi is belongs to an erotic genre of spirituality that is similar to Jayadeva's Gita Govinda.

The impact of these works on the daily religious life of the South Indian has been tremendous. Just like the Ramayana and the Mahabharata, the Thiruppavai is recited with great religious fervor by women, men, and children of all ages, particularly in Tamil Nadu. The daily services in most Vaishnava temples and households include this recitation. Both of these works, particularly the Thiruppavai, has been studied extensively by innumerable scholars. It has also been translated into a number of languages over the centuries.

Status in the Society

Aandaal is now one of the best-loved poet-saints of the Tamils. Pious tradition reckons her to be the veritable descent of Bhumi Devi (Mother Earth) in bodily form to show humanity the way to His lotus feet. She is present in all Sri Vaishnava temples, in India and elsewhere, next to her Lord, as she always desired. During the month of Margazhi, discourses on the Tiruppavai in Tamil, Telugu, Kannada, Hindi and English take place all over India.

Thondaradippodi Alvar

Thondaradippodi Alvar was a Vaishnava Saint who is also named as "Vipra Narayanar" led his life in devotion to Lord Narayana and worked for the Perumal (Lord) by dedicating him with Garlands. He is one of the 12 Alvars.

Birth and Early Life

Thondaradippodi Alvar was born in a small village by name 'Thiru mandaggudi' in Prabhava year, Margazhi month, Krishna chaturthi, Tuesday in Kettai (Jyestha) Nakshatram (star). His father 'Veda Visaradhar' belonged to "Kudumi Sozhiyap Brahmanar" community also called as "Vipra" people, whose routine work is to praise about Sri Vishnu.

On the 12th day after his birth, he was named as "Vipra Narayanar". From an early age, bhakti towards Sri Vishnu was taught to him. He grew up with a well rounded personality. It is said that in spite of being good and beautiful and dedicated to Sri Vishnu bhakti, he had no conceit and treated all the aged persons and persons who are younger to him in the same way and gave proper respect to them.

Reaching Srirangam

As per lore, Viswakshenan, who was the commander-in-chief of Sri Vishnu's troop, once descended to earth and revealed to Vipranarayanar, why he was born in this mighty world and what are the things that he should follow to attain Moksham.

On hearing the truth of his birth, he showed much love, affection and bhakti towards Sriman Narayanan. As an extension to it, he started thinking what should be the next step to be taken to explore his bhakti. He thought of travelling to all of the temples where the Emperumaan is giving his seva. But, he had a question that from which sthalam he should start with. After a long thinking, he finally decided that he should start from the greatest of all of the Vishnu sthalams, the Srirangam, which is located on the banks of cauvery river should be the starting sthalam he should worship and started travelling towards it.

After reaching the temple, he went inside the moolavar sannadhi and was very happy to see the perumal on the Aadhiseshan (the snake) who is found in sleeping posture. After seeing the beauty of Sri Ranganathar, he did not want to see any of the things around and thought his bhakti and the remaining life should be spent completely for Aranganathan. He thought in what way he can express his bhakti towards the emperumaan and finally he thought he can offer him with the Garland daily to the perumal.

Soon after this thought, he constructed a big Nandhavanam (flower park) in Srirangam, where various beautiful and fragrance flower plants are grown. He built a small hut in the midst of the park. Daily, in the morning, as a daily work, he dedicated the Garland to Sri Ranganathar and only then did his routine jobs. Since, he thought, only Sri Aranganathar is the beautiest thing in this world, he didn't turn up towards any of the women around him.

Because of this, all the people thought he doesn't have any feelings towards the people around him. On seeing these kinds of scenes from Sri Vaikundam, thirumagal, Sri Lakshmi questioned

Sriman Narayanan that because of having the affection towards him (Sri Ranganathar) and in spite of being a male, he doesn't know how the love should be expressed towards a women and continued that which women can show her love towards a person like Vipra Narayanan? Knowing the future and what is going to happen, Sri Vishnu casually answered Sri Lakshmi that she is going to see what is going to happen for him.

Devi and Devadevi

In thirukkarambanoor, there lived two Daasis (Women who dances in front of the king to earn money) by named Devi, who is the elder sister and Devadevi, who is the younger sister. They wanted to dance to the Urayoor king and to get prize from him. Then both of them went to Sri Rangam temple to worship Aranganathar.

When they were going to the temple, they had the chance to see the Nandhavanam, which belonged to Vipra Narayanar. Devadevi wanted to see him and they both went to the small hut. Devadevi, on seeing him, was very much attracted towards him and started loving at the first sight. She expressed her love in words and continued with his work. She did service to convert him towards her side. Soon she completely turned Vipra Narayanar towards her and they both started to live together.

One day, Devadevi said to Vipra Narayanar that she wanted to see her parents and her sister. Vipra Narayanar said that he would too come along with her, since he could not live without leaving her for a second. But her mother did not want him to be in the house and asked Vipra Narayanar to get out of the house for he did not have any wealth. Since, Vipra Narayanar is helpless, he came out of the house and entered a Nandavanam and being so tired, he slept for a while. On seeing this, the Emperumaan wanted him to get of the Maya and wanted him to get along with the right path, which leads to the Thiruvadi of Him (Sri Vishnu).

He changed himself as a Student of Vipra Narayanar and went straight to Devadevi's house and gave him a big silver vessel as given by his Guru to Devadevi.

On getting that her mother thanked him and asked his Guru, Vipra Narayanar to return back to her house. On hearing this, Vipra Naryanar walked fast to the house and hugged Devadevi.

The Next morning, the archakar entered into the Sri Ranganathar sannadhi and found one Vattal (Vessel which is used to do the daily pooja) was missing and complained to the king about this. The king ordered his servants to go in search of the Vattal and they found that in Devadevi's house.

Vipra Narayanar was jailed for one night. On that night, Vipra Narayanar cried and asked the Emperumaan why like this has happened to him and prayed towards him. On the same night, the Emperumaan arise in the dream of the king and explained him what had happened and asked him to free Vipra Narayanar. The king explained that this is a small thiru Vilayaadal (game) of Sri Emperumaan.

Knowing the real truth why he came to the world, he went to Sri Ranganathar temple and praised the Lord. Then, he worshipped all the bhaktas of Sri Vishnu and put the podi (Small tiny dust particles), which is found under the feet of them in his head and sang songs in praise of Sri Ranganathar.

From then, he was called as "Thondaradipodi Alwar". Finally he realised for what he came for to the earth and went to all the Vishnu temples to praise him.

Thiruppaan Alvar

Thiruppaan Alvar is one of the 12 Alvars. He was born in an untouchable community, but as a result of his devotion towards Sriman Narayanan, he was listed among the great twelve Alvars. Paan Alvar has done Mangalasasanam on Srirangam divya desam with 10 paasuram of amalanAdhipirAn.

Birth in Baanar Community

Thiruppaan Alvar was born in Purthurmadhi year, Kaarthigai month, Wednesday in Rohini Natshatram in a small village of "Alagapuri" near Srirangam in 8th or 9th century C.E. He was born in "Baanar Cheri". Baanar are musicians who are capable of arresting the minds of all people and even the Devas and Rishis. But these baanars are kept as a separate categorized peoples and who were treated as untouchables.

It is said that Alvar is the hamsam of the small mole, called as "Srivatsam" which is found in the chest of Sriman Narayanan. Having a veena in his hand, he always sang on Sri Vishnu and his fame and spread his capabilities and the love he offers to his bhaktas, in his songs. Because of this, he is also named as "Paan perumal".

The untouchable people were ordered not to keep their feet on Cauvery river. Because of this and to obey the order, Paan Alvar did not touch the Kaveri river, but stood along the banks of the river facing Thiruvaragam temple and sung various songs, praising the Lord.

Reaching Srirangam

Legend is that Emperumaan wanted to explain the greatness and Bhakthi of Thiruppaan Alwar towards Him and as an action to it, he started to play a small drama.

The Cauvery water is used for the Thirumanjanam for Sri Ranganadhar. Loga Saaranga Maha Muneetharar, a devoted bhakta of Sri Ranganathar, would daily bring the Cauvery water for Thriumanjanam. One day, when he was sleeping, he had a dream in which the Aranganadar explained about Paan Perumal and he should be taken on the shoulders of Loga Saaranga muni, without having the mind that he is an untouchable person.

Loga Saarangamuni, who being the strong follower of Sri Vishnu, got up early next morning and went to the other side of Cauvery river and met Thiruppaan Alwar. On seeing him, he explained about the dream he had last night and asked him to climb on his shoulders, so that he can be taken to the other side of the Cauvery river, where Sri Ranganathar is giving his seva.

Thirupaan Alwar could not convince him otherwise and finally he sat on on his shoulders. Saranga Muni started walking towards him Sri Arangathan through the Cauvery river. Everyone was surprised to see this scene and stood in silence. After reaching the temple, Thiruppan Alwar could not believe his eyes because he was seeing Perumal whom he thought that he could not see him in his life. He raised his hands above his head and started to sing slokas on Sri Aranganathan.

Ten Paasurams

The first pasuram sung by Alvar is on Arangan's feet. On seeing the Thiruvadi(lotus feet)of Aranganathan he sang:

Neel madhil Arangathamman thrukkamalpadham vandhu en Kanninullana okkinrathe.

He then started to see the whole thirumeni (body) of Emperumaan and he sung a total of ten paasurams which explain the beauty of Sri Ranganathar from his thiruvadi (foot) to thirumudi(head).

He explains in his ten paasuram about the clean saffron cloth which is worn on the body of Ranganathar, his jewels the thiru vayiru (stomach) from where Lord Brahma originated, the broad chest, the red lips and finally on explaining the beauty of the two broad eyes, he fell down.

After some time, Thiruppaan Alwar was not found and he went in to the body of Thiruvaranganathan. Like Andal, whose thought was always on Aranganathan, who was captured by the love of the Perumal, Thiruppaan Alwar was also captured by the love and he went towards the Aranganathan.

Thiruppaan Alwar has sung only ten paasurams, where he has explained about how a human should be. He explains in that ten paasurams that Perumal is the leader and our aim should be to reach Him and to get the complete Saranagathi (total surrender) in His thiruvadi, and that is the final place, where all of us has to reach.

Thirumangai Alvar

Thirumangai Alvar or Tirumangai Alvar or Tirumankai Alvar or Thirumangai Mannan (8th century AD) is the last of the 12 Alvar saints of south India, who are known for their affiliation to Vaishnava tradition of Hinduism. He is considered one of the most learned Alvar and the most superior Alvar in the context of composition of verses. He holds the title *Narkavi Perumal,* the mark of an excellent poet, and *Parakala* (Beyond Time). Though he is respected as a Vaishnava saint-poet, he, initially, worked as a military commander, a chieftain and then a robber. After his conversion to Vaishnavism, he confronted practitioners of rival Hindu sect of Shaivism as well as Buddhism and Jainism.

K. C. Varadachari, author of *Alvars of South India* describes Thirumangai as:

He was a petty cheiftain. He in many respects a dynamic figure, ardent in love, spectacular in his deeds, a rebel and a social reformer, even a kind of Robin Hood, and above all an exquisite lyricist.

Dating and Hagiography

The traditional date attributed to Thirumangai is year 399 of Kaliyuga, that is 2702 BC, making him traditionally the last of the Alvar saints. Modern scholars have placed the Alvars in between 5th to 9th centuries based on few historical evidence. Dr. N. Subba Reddiar summarizes their views and arrives at the date 776 AD for Thirumangai, making him chronologically the eighth Alvar, though even these dates are disputed.

The hagiographies detailing the life of Thirumangai and other Alvars are Divya charitam (11th century) and Guruparampara-prabhavam-arayirappadi (13th century) and Guruparampara-prabhavam-muvayirappadi (14th century). Other Vaishnava scholars have written hagiographics based on the above works later.

Early Life

Thirumangai was born in Thirukuraiyular, a small village in Tamil Nadu, in a non-Brahmin, tribal family. Thirumangai's real name was Kaliyan or Kalikanti. Thirumangai's father was Nilam, a general under the Chola empire. He was skilled in archery and worked as a military commander himself for the Chola king. In recognition of his valour, he was conferred upon the title *Parakala* and rewarded a small terrority called Ali Nadu to govern, for his military services. Its capital was Thirumangai. He earned the title *Thirumangai Mannan* or chief of Thirumangai, a name he maintained even when he became a saint.

According to the traditional account, he married Kumudavalli, a Vaishnava doctor's adopted daughter and became a Vaishnava, devotee of the Hindu god Vishnu, under her influence. She also got him to promise that he would feed a 1008 Vaishnavas every day for a year. Unable to bear the heavy expense of feeding a thousand people, Thirumangai resorted to highway robbery. One day, Thirumangai tried to remove rings from the toes of a bride but could not do so.

Then he realized the bride was none other than goddess Lakshmi, the consort of god Vishnu. God Vishnu (Narayana) revealed himself to Thirumangai and transformed him by teaching the *Narayana mantra* or *Ashatara* (the eight syllabled)-"namo narayanaya", turning the robber into a saint.

The first ten verses of Thirumangai's poem *Periya Tirumoli* sing of his transformation, after receiving the spiritual knowledge from Vishnu. He sings about his transformation thus:

I became a thief deceitful and dishonest

I wandered hither and thither yet light dawned upon me-

I reached Your feet and instantly your grace fell upon me with melting heart and choked voice your praises I sing bathed in streaming tears I repeat day and night the sacred name of Narayana (Vishnu)

As a Vaishnava Saint

Transformed by his encounter with God, Thirumangai gave up his chieftainship and became a devout Vaishnava, dedicated to god Vishnu. To atone for his sins, he visited 88 of the Divya Desams, a group of 108 Vishnu shrines primarily in south India. He spread the poems of older Alvars in his wandering. He was also well versed in earlier Tamil literature like Naaladiyar, Thirrukkurai, Sangam literature and Jain literature.

Thirumangai preached against penance and advocated bhakti (devotion) as way to attain salvation. He composed 6 poems in Tamil, together acoounting for 1361 verses. In the book Divya Prabandham, 1361 verses of Thirumangai are included, making them the most composed by any Alvar. Tamil Vaishnavas consider them as the six Tamil *Vedangas* or *Angas* of the 4 poems of Nammalvar, which are considered as Vedas. His most important work is *Periya Tirumoli*, composed of 1084 hymns. The others are: *Tirunedunthandakam* (30 verses), *Tirukuruthandakam* (20 verses), *Tiruvelukkutirukkai* (a single long poem of 47 lines), *Siriya Tirumadal* (155 lines) and *Periya Tirumadal* (297 lines).

A late ninth century text, Tamilalangaram by Dandapani Swanigal describes him of having the rare privilege of biting god Vishnu's toes and being pardoned for all his sins, as he wrote in Tamil. Vaishnavas consider him as a divine incarnation of Sharanga, Vishnu's bow.

Works

Periya Tirumoli is the composition of hymns illustrating the greatness of Vaishnava shrines and their presiding deity as well as God's numerous attributes. His songs extol the largest number of shrines-over 40 forms of Vishnu, from Badrinath in North India to Tirukkurungudi in the extreme South. Thirumangai also discusses causes of human suffering and ways to overcome it to achieve salvation. Vedanta Desika praises the work as "a deep insight in spiritual knowledge".

The word *thandakam* in *Tiru-nedun-thandakam* and *Tiru-kuru-thandakam* refers to the staff used for support for climbing a hill, this refers to God as the support for sustence of the soul in context of the poems. The words *nedu* and *kuru* signify the length of the compositions and its poetic meter. In *Tirunedunthandakam*, Thirumangai speaks as a *nayaki* (nayaki is the consort of the Lord), who separated from her beloved God (Nayaka). *Tirukuruthandakam* speaks dependency of the soul on God and its way to escape suffering being God, who is the sole supporter.

Tiruvelukkutirukkai deals with the concept of surrender to God to attain freedom from suffering, the nature of God and the means of attaining Him.

Periya Tirumadal and *Siriya Tirumadal* use the *madal*, an ancient Tamil custom which is practiced by a rejected lover to win back his love, though it is prohibited for women. The custom evolves singing about his love in love, devoid of food and sleep and finally trying to commit suicide before her if all things fail. Thirumangai sings as a woman threatening Lord to finish her life if He can not reciprocate her love.

He assumes the role of a gopika (milkmaid) who threats Krishna (a form of Vishnu) with madal. He defenses the gopika's actions of performing the prohibited madal, by saying that he follows the Sanskrit literary tradition who permits madal for women, not the Tamil one. His songs are also based on *akam* love poems, and talk of employing bees and storks are messengers to God. He goes to the length of calling himself *Thirumangai Alvar*, literally "the woman Alvar", portraying himself as the nayaki, pining for the love of Vishnu.

7

Some of Famous Nayanar Saints

Amaraneedi Nayanar

Amaraneedi Nayanar was a Vaisya by caste. He was an ardent Shiva devotee. He belonged to a village named Pazhaiyaarai in the Chola Kingdom. Pazhaiyaarai was a very fertile place, surrounded on all sides by gardens and green fields. In those days this place was very famous. Amaraneedi Nayanar was a trader in gold, diamonds, silks and cotton goods. He used to import these goods from foreign countries and was selling them at reasonable prices.

He earned money honestly and became rich. Though he was engaged in worldly activities, his mind was fixed on Lord Siva. He would invite Shiva devotees to his house and worship them. He would give the Kowpeenam, money, etc., and feed them nicely and send them away happily, with other gifts. He used to visit the sacred temple of Tirunallaru during festivals and worship Lord Shiva with extreme faith and repeat Panchakshara Mantra daily.

Chandeshvara Nayanar

Chandesha or Canda or Chandeshvara is one of the 36 Nayanmars. Processional bronze images of him generally show him as a boy, with entwined locks of hair, standing with his hands in Anjali Mudra and with an axe in the crook of his arm. In the Shaiva temples of South India, his shrine is positioned within the first enclosure wall of the temple complex and to the North East of the lingam. He is there typically shown seated, with one leg dangling downwards, a hand on one thigh and an axe clasped in the other. He faces inwards towards the main temple wall. He is depicted as deeply lost in meditation, and devotees snap their fingers or clap their hands to attract his attention. Another explanation, since he is considered to be the guardian of the temple belongings, is that devotees clap their hands to show that they are leaving the temple empty-handed. It is also customary to leave even the sacred ash inside the temple itself.

His original role was probably that of recipient of *nirmalya,* that is to say of offerings of food and garlands that had originally been offered to Shiva.

Mythology

The South Indian legend, narrated, for instance, in the Periyapuranam, states that he was born into a Brahmin family. When he was a young boy, he found that cows remain uncared for, and hence he himself commenced tendering and caring for the cows. While doing so, he would pour some milk on a lingam, which he made of sand. The news of this wastage of milk reached the ear of his father, Datta; and he himself came to the field to scold his son. Chandesha was deep in meditation in front of the sand lingam, and he did not see his father. The enraged father kicked the sand lingam. At this Chnadesha's meditation was interrupted, and he struck his father's leg with a staff. The staff turned into an axe and his father's leg was severed. At this point, Shiva manifested himself, and blessed Chandesha, declared that he would become a father to Chandesha; and restored the severed leg of Datta to normal state.

In some Sanskrit works, however, Chandesha is instead said to be an incarnation of Shiva's anger. Chandesha is now often regarded as an exclusively South Indian figure, but he was once known in North India too, and probably also as far afield as Cambodia.

Ilayankudi Maranar

Maranar was born in the Tamil month of Avani at Ilayankudi of tamil nadu. He was a farmer by caste and profession. Maranar was his name and since he lived in a village called Ilayankudi, he got the name ilayankudi maranar. He is an ardent devotee of lord shiva's devotees. He took the greatest pleasure in serving them and considered that as Maheswara pooja.

On seeing a devotee of Lord Shiva, with the external marks of Vibhuti (sacred ash) and Rudraksha, he will take them as Lord Shiva himself, he will welcome them, prostrate before them, he will wash their feet (padapooja), after giving them a seat, he will worship them with flowers, Doopa, Deepa, and Naivedya, pleasing them with sweet words, thanking the Lord for this wonderful opportunity, and he will accompany the guest for some distance while sending them away. These constitute the Maheswara Pooja of Marana nayanar. This pooja also included Chariyai i.e offering food to the Lord's devotees which had purified his heart and made him a fit receptacle for the grace of God.

Nayanar was blessed with all the wealth of the world. But, he considered that the wealth belonged to the Lord, and it should be utilised only for the benefit of his devotees. Lord Shiva was delighted with His devotee. He wanted to reveal his true greatness to the world.

Years rolled by and Nayanar's wealth melted away due to his charity. His wealth had left him, but not his virtue. On the contrary, his devotion to the Lord and his devotees grew more and more deep. Nayanar sold all his property and had to sell even himself in order to be able to serve the devotees of the Lord.

One day there was a heavy downpour. Nayanar and his wife were starving for the whole day. No one came forward to help them. Finally, he bolted the door and was about to fall asleep. Just then he heard a knock at the door, and, on opening it, found a sage standing in front of the house, fully drenched with rain. Nayanar at once took the guest inside, dried his body and gave him fresh clothes to wear. He requested the sage to have dinner at his home and told his wife of to prepare some food. But both of the couple know that there was nothing to offer the devotee of the Lord. At that time Nayanar's wife suggested that he could go into the backyard and collect the grain-seeds that they had just sown that day. Nayanar accepted the idea. Because of the heavy rain, the grains were floating and it was easy for nayanar to collect them in a basket. As soon as he brought the grains, the wife fried and pound them, and with the help of some greens that grew in their own backyard, cooked a nice dinner for the guest.

Nayanar was very happy and thanked the almighty for helping him at this situation.. went to awaken the guest, but he found that the sage had disappeared. At the same time, Nayanar saw in sky, Lord Siva and Mother Parvathy blessing him and his wife. The Lord said that he was immensely pleased with their devotion to his bhaktas and both of them will very soon reach his Abode and live there for ever. Since ilayankudi maranar was born in Magha nakshatra of Avani, that day is celebrated as his day in all shiva temples.

Isaignaniyaar

Isaignaniyaar is a female poetess who lived in Tirunavalur of Tirumuraipadi. All her ancestors were ardent devotees of Lord Siva and her husband Sadaiya nayanar is too one of the 63 nayanars. She was also devoted to the Lord. Due to their virtuous deeds in their past life, a divine child was born to them. He was no other than Sundaramurthi Nayanar.

Legend

Narasinga Munaiyar, the king of that region, was attracted by the child's beauty and wanted to bring it up himself. The king approached the parents and they, without a moment's hesitation, handed the child over to him. By this action, they showed that they had no attachment at all to anything in this world.

One day the king of pandiya kingdom invited Isaignaniyaar for a singing competition. She was very talented and proved her talent over there. But the king made an injustice because his lady love is too a participant. When Isaignaniyaar came to know about this she pleaded the lord to save her. The lord by his divine voice announced that Isaignaniyaar is the winner. The king and his lover felt guilty and begged Isaignaniyaar to forgive them. Gnaniyar excused them and asked them to prostrate before lord shiva. This blessed Isaignaniyaar led the ideal Grihastha (household) life with sadaiya nayanar and finally attained the lord shiva's grace.

Iyarpagaiar

Iyarpagai Nayanar was one of the 63 nayanmar's of shaivism. He was born in Kaveripoompattinam of chola kingdom. He was born in the month of Markazhi (mid dec to mid jan) and he is Vaisya by caste. He considered Shiva Bhaktas as the living manifestations of Lord Shiva.

Lord Shiva was delighted with His devotee. He wanted to reveal his true greatness to the world. So, the Lord, in the disguise of a sage, with sacred ashes smeared all over his body, came to Nayanar's house. He welcomed the Sage with great joy, as the very sight of the holy man thrilled the Nayanar. The Sage said that he had heard about his charitable nature and he came hear for a gift. Iyarpagaiar was very happy to hear this and agreed readily. He went inside the house and informed his wife of all that had happened. She was shocked at first, but quickly regained her self-control.

According to Hinduism, to a chaste wife, her husband is God, and whatever he commands is Law and Dharma. She readily agreed to follow the Sage-guest as his wife. Iyarpagaiar came out with his wife and asked the Sage to accept the gift. The Sage feared the rage of the wife's relatives and asked Iyarpagaiar to accompany them till they were safely out of the village and out of danger. Nayanar agreed to do so and armed himself to protect the Sage. They then proceeded to go.

In the meantime the relatives of nayanar's wife came to know of the whole story and were furious. The Sage pretended to be scared. Iyarpagaiar was ready to fight them. The relatives tried to convince nayanar of the unrighteousness of the whole thing, and, when they found that they could not, they preferred to die at his hands, than submit to the shame. Iyarpagaiar at once pounced upon them and chopped off their heads.

All of them died and nayanar was actually happy because he had succeeded in keeping his vow of worshipping his devotee, preceded further with the Sage and the wife. When they reached the temple of Tiruchaikadu, the Sage asked Iyarpagaiar to leave them and return. Nayanar prostrated to the Sage and turned his steps homeward.

As he had hardly proceeded a few yards on his homeward journey, the Sage again called Nayanar by his name aloud. Thinking that there might have been another attack on the party, Iyarpagaiar hastened to where the Sage was but, to his amazement, found that the sage had disappeared and that his wife was standing alone there. At that time Lord Shiva and Mother Parvathy appeared in the sky and blessed Nayanar and his wife and said that he was immensely pleased with their devotion to his bhaktas and both of them will very soon reach his Abode. At the same time nayanar's relatives who died at his hands also attained the lotus feet of the Lord.

Since Iyarpagai nayanar was born in Uttara Phalgunî nakshatra of Markhali, that day is celebrated as his day in all shiva temples.

Kannappa Nayanar

Kannappa Nayanar or Kannappan was one of the 63 Nayanmars or holy Saivite saints, the staunch devotees of Lord Shiva. The Periyapuranam compiled by Sekkizhar and also the Tiruthhthondar Thogai by the poet-saint Sundarar enlists the 63 Nayanars.

Birth and Life

Aliases:

- Boya Tinnadu
- Thinnappan
- Tinnappan
- Thinnan
- Kannappan
- Kannappa Nayanar or Nayanmar
- Kannan
- Bhakta Kannappan
- Boya Kannappa
- Bedara Kannappa
- Dheeran
- Kannabeswara.

Kannappa Nayanar was born in a tribal family in and around the temple town of Sri Kalahasti, in present day Andhra Pradesh. He was named Thinnan or Dheeran or Boya Tinnadu by his parents.

He hunted in the forest around Sri Kalahasti and the hills-Sripuram and Mummidicholapuram.

Legends

Thinnan's devotion: Thinnan was a staunch devotee of the *Vayu linga* of Sri Kalahasti which he found in the forest while hunting. Being an illiterate and of a low-caste birth, he did not know how to properly worship Lord Shiva.

It is said that he poured water from his mouth on the Shiva lingam which he brought from the nearby river Swarnamukhi. He also offered the Lord whatever animal he hunted, including swine flesh. But the Lord accepted his offerings since Thinnan was pure at heart and his devotion was true.

Dheeran

One day, Lord Shiva tested the unshakable devotion of Thinnan. With his divine power, He created a tremor and the roof-tops of the temple began to fall. All the sages ran away from the scene except for Thinnan who covered the linga with his body to prevent it from any damage. Hence he was named thereafter as Dheeran.

Kannappan

In another incident (*thiru vilayadal* of Lord Shiva), one day Thinnan or Dheeran noticed that one of the eyes of the Shiva linga was oozing blood and tears. Sensing that the Lord's eye had been injured, Dheeran proceeded to pluck his one eye out with one of his arrows and placed it in the spot of the bleeding eye of the Shiva linga. This stopped the bleeding in that eye of the linga.

But to complicate matters further, he noticed that the other eye of the linga has also started oozing blood. So Thinnan thought that if he were to pluck his other eye too, he would become blind to exactly know the spot where he has to place his own second eye over the bleeding second eye of the lingam. So he placed his great toe on the linga to mark the spot of the bleeding second eye and proceeded to pluck out his other and only eye.

Moved by his extreme devotion, Shiva appeared before Thinnan and restored both his eyes.

"Nillu Kannappa" ("Stop Kannappan!")

He made Thinnan as one of the Nayanmars and henceforth he would be called as Kannappan or Kannappa Nayanar.

Kannabeswara

On the southern hill of the Kalahasti Temple, there is the shrine of Kannabeswara in his memory (*Kannappa* = Thinnan, *eswara* = Shiva which means "Kannappa, the devotee of Shiva").

Reincarnation of Arjun

Some Saivite traditions believe that Kannappa was the reincarnation of the Pandava-Arjuna. Arjuna worshipped Siva for seeking the Pasupatha Astra (a divine weapon) and failed to recognize Shiva when He appeared before Arjuna in the form of a hunter. Thus, due to this reason, Arjuna had to be born as Thinnan/Kannappa, the hunter and adore the Lord before attaining final liberation. This belief is not adopted by all Hindus though.

Karaikkal Ammeiyar

Karaikkal Ammaiyar one of the few females amongst the sixty three Nayanmars, is one of the greatest figures of early Tamil literature. Her birth name was *Punithavathi*, born at Karaikkal, South India, and lived during the 6th century. She was a great devotee of Lord Shiva.

Divine Life

Punithavathy was born in Karaikkal, a maritime trading city in Chola nadu to *Danathathan*, a famous merchant. From childhood Punithavathy grew up in a religious atmosphere and worshipped Lord Siva diligently. She enchanted the five letter mantra *Namasivaya* and also attended to the needs of Shaiva devotees.

When she grew up as a charming young girl she was wedded to *Paramathathan*, the son of a rich merchant in Nagapattinam. Even after marriage she continued her chosen religious life. Shaiva devotees who visited her home were lavishly fed and were given clothes and jewels according to their needs.

Divine Miracle

A Hungry Shaiva devotee came to her residence one day. As the luncheon was not ready at that time, she gave the devotee one of the two mangoes that her husband (Paramathathan) had sent home, earlier that day, to be kept for him. Later, when her husband came home she served him the one left mango that she had. The mango was very delicious and hence her husband requested for the other mango also to be served. Punithavathy was in a dilemma now. She prayed to Lord Siva and astonishingly by God's grace a mango appeared in her palm which she served to her husband.

As this fruit was divinely sweet and was infinitely delicious compared to the previous one, her husband inquired as to how she obtained this mango. When punithavathy told the truth — that she received the second Mango by god's grace, her husband could not believe. So he asked her to produce another mango with divine help. She entreated to Lord Siva, obtained another similar mango and gave it to her husband. On receiving the mango, the husband was shocked to find it disappear, realising the divine nature of the wife and his arrogance. Paramathathan shivered in fear understanding now that she is worthy of worship and unworthy he is of her. Hence he deserted her unannounced.

Mother of South Indian Music

Irrefutable evidences adduced clearly establish that Karaikkal Ammaiyar has a distinctive place of eminence by any criteria, be it antiquity of time, elegance of composition, depth of meaning, spread of philosophy or inspirer of new excellence. Compared to great musical exponents who had been given appropriate titles as "Sangeetha Mummoorthigal", "Aadhi Mummoorthigal", "Sirpy of Padams", "Sangeethaa Pithamagar", "Chanthap paavala peruman" and "Thevaara Moovar" and are being remembered today, Karaikal Ammaiyar is the sole exception who has not been given adequate and meaningful recognition. Judged by the criterion of time, Karaikal Ammaiyar is by far the oldest in this great galaxy of musical exponents and can therefore rightly lay claim as the "Mother of South Indian Music"

Karaikkal Ammaiyar in Art

In 1954 A.L. Basham published in his *The Wonder that was India* a photograph depicting an ascetic or demonic female figure that he called "Kali as Demoness playing Cymbals" and in 1955 also Heinrich Zimmer called this female character "Kali". One year later this similar type of figure was not called Kali anymore, but the Tamil nayanar Karaikkal Ammaiyar by Jean Filliozat in Karavelane's *Kareikkalammeiyar avers editees et traduites*. In 1956 Karavelane and Jean Filliozat presented a publication that included the first complete translation (in French) of the verses ascribed to the South Indian (Tamil) poet nayanar Karaikkal Ammaiyar probably to be dated to the 7th century.

The publication pointed out that the figure described in the verses, Karaikkal, (perhaps) was depicted in South Indian art from the 11th century onwards. In the publication several plates depicting the female nayanar, in bronze, stone or as being a part of a templestructure, are published. Most interesting is perhaps the dancing Siva on the Vimana's south wall of the Brhadesvara temple at Gangaikondacolapuram (c. AD 1025).

On Siva Nataraja's left side, below, an emaciated female figure is depicted playing the cymbals and displaying ascetic or demonic features: she has wild flaring out hair, has pointed shrivelled breasts and a fierceful facial expression. Filliozat identified this figure as being Kareikkalammeiyar. This similar depiction of the squatting female figure was published by Hermann Kulke in 1970 in his excellent analysis of the religious and historical background of Cidambaram in Tamilnadu based on the Cidambaramahatmya. In this he also calls the figure Kareikkalammeiyar and states that this emaciated figure strongly resembles the seventh mothergoddess Camunda (Kulke 1970:123).

In 1976 Mireille Benisti published an article in which she states that the figure of Karaikkal is depicted not only in South Indian art, but also in Khmer art, especially in Cambodia. On a lintel from Vat Baset in Cambodia she found a figure that she, on the basis of a comparison of Kareikkalammeiyar's verses and South Indian and Khmer arthistorical sources, interpreted as being the emaciated Tamil-nayanar Kareikkalammeiyar. From this time onwards some other publications on this subject came out, based on Khmer-material found before Pol Pot's genocidal Khmer Rouge regime from 1975 to 1979, and the presence of Kareikkalammeiyar in Khmer-art was accepted.

After the horrible Khmer Rouge regime no more intensive research on this subject has been done. As stated above, the presence of Kareikkalammeiyar in Khmer-art was accepted and therefore perhaps of little interests anymore.

After new research in 2007 Peter de Bruijn published *Kareikkalammeiyar, Part 1: An iconographical and textual study, Part 2: Poems for Siva* in which he clearly pointed out that on the basis of arthistorical and literary sources Karaikkal Ammaiyar is not tea be found in countries outside India.

Cheraman Perumal (Nayanar)

Rajasekhara Varma known as a 'Cheraman Perumal (Great man of the Cheras) was a Nayanar regal saint from the ancient Chera country (Kongu Nadu). He is said to have ruled from the seat of Cheras, Karuvur vanchi (modern Karur) located on the shores of Anporunai (modern Amaravati River). He also ruled the Koduntamizh regions of Kuttanadu, Venadu and Tenpandinadu, the first two north and south modern Kerala and the third, the southern tail end districts of Tamil Nadu from his seat at Karur.

Kochengat Chola

Kochengat Chola Nayanar is a chola king. He was one of the 63 nayanars of shaivism. He was born in the Shatabhisha nakshatra of the tamil month Masi(Mâci).

Mythology

In Chandra Tirtha, a village in the Chola kingdom there was a thick grove. In that grove under a Jambu tree there was a Shiva Lingam. A white elephant used to come there daily and do puja for the Lingam. A spider which was also devoted to the lord, noticed some dry leaves falling on the shiva lingam. In order to prevent this, the spider wove a web above the Lingam. The next day when the elephant came to worship, he found the web, and thought that someone had polluted the place.

So the elephant tore the web, offered his worship and went away. The spider came upon the scene and felt sorry that his web had been destroyed. So he woven another web and went away. The next day, as the elephant was pulling the web away, the spider which was already present there, gave him a sting. The elephant died on the spot due to the poison. The spider too, was caught in the elephant's trunk, and perished. Due to the almighties grace, the spider was born as the son of Suba Devan, the Chola king.

History

Suba Devan and his dutiful wife Kamalavati went to Chidambaram and eagerly prayed to the Lord Nataraja(a form of Shiva) for a son. The Lord granted their wish. Soon the queen conceived and the day of delivery arrived. Astrologers foretold that if the child could be delivered a few minutes later, it would rule the three worlds. Hearing this the queen asked that she should be tied to the roof of the room upside down, with a tight bandage around her waist. When the auspicious time came, she was released and the child was born.

This was the spider reborn, The child had red eyes as he had remained in his mother's womb a little longer. The mother, looking into the babies red eyes and said Kochengkannano, which literally means king with red eyes, and expired. Thus, he was named Kochengat Cholan. When he reached the proper age, his father enthroned him king, retired from the world and, after severe penance, reached the Lord's Abode.

Legend

Kochengat Cholan promoted Shaivism. In Tiruanaika he built a beautiful temple and installed the Siva Lingam under the same Jambu tree. In Chola Nadu he built many shrines and mansions for the use of shiva's devotees. He provided houses and agri lands to the three thousand Brahmins of Tillai for regular worship at the Chidambaram temple. Finally he reached the Lord's Abode. His glories were sung by the famous Tamil poet Poygayar in his Kalavazhi Narpathu.

Manakkanychaara Nayanar

Manakkanychaara Nayanar was one of the 63 Nayanmars of the Saivite faith of South India. He lived in the village of Kancharur in the Chola kingdom during the eighth century CE. He belonged to the Vellala cast and was a heriditory commander in the Chola Military of Chola Raajym to day refferd as Tamilnadu.

Legend

Manakkanychaara had no children for a long time. He and his wife worshipped Siva for a child and they soon had a daughter. Nayanar celebrated the birth of this child donating generously to charity. When the daughter attained the marriageable age, Manakkanychaara arranged her wedding with Eyarkon Kalikamar who was also an earnest and sincere devotee of Siva.

Meanwhile, an ascetic appeared before Manakkanychaara who received him with great delightand asked his daughter to bow to the ascetic and receive his blessings. The ascetic saw her flowing hair, and said: 'Oh Manakkanychaara, I am delighted to see her hair. This can be conveniently made into a Panchavati (the thread that adorns my chest).' At once, Nayanar took a knife and, without thinking for a moment, cut the hair off his daughter's head and handed it to the ascetic. In his extreme devotion to the Siva Yogi, he did not even consider the fact that he was disfiguring his only daughter, and that the bridegroom might refuse to accept her. Lord Siva in the form of the ascetic immediately disappeared and blessed Manakkanychaara and his family and restored the hair on the girl's head.

Meiporul Nayanar

Meiporul Nayanar was a pious king. He is one of the 63

nayanmar's of shaivism. He ruled over the hill tribes of Sethi. He was chivalrous and brave. He fought many battles and was always victorious.

To him Siva and his devotees, adorned Rudraksha and sacred ashes represented only truth, absolute Truth, and all the rest of the world was straw. He saw everything as Sivamayam. Nayanar's fame soon spread far and wide. This evoked the jealousy of Muthanathan, the king of the neighbouring state. He collected a big army and attacked Nayanar several times, but he was repeatedly defeated. So, Muthanathan resorted to foul-play. One day, he disguised himself as a Siva Yogi and entered the palace at night.

The gate-keepers did not question him because their king ordered them to allow shiva devotees into the palace at any time. But the soldiers conveyed this to their Minister Dathan, who rushed to the Kings bed room. But before he reach the kings room, the fraudulent sage had killed the king. Dathan jumped to dehead the sage, but nayanar ordered to save muthanathan since he was disguised like a shiva devotee. Dathan did the same and Meiporul nayanar spelled the name of shiva and lost his breath.

Lord shiva suddenly appeared there with mother parvathy and said he was immensely pleased with the cosmic love and unquestioning devotion to his devotees. He said even in a murderer the king saw shiva. Thus he blessed him with the Highest Abode which even the Devas cannot hope to reach. With these words the Lord disappeared and Maiporul Nayanar also attained his Abode.

Since Meiporul nayanar was born in the Tamil month of Karthigai, in Uthiram Nakshatra, that day was celebrated as his day in all shiva temples.

Nesa Nayanar

Nesa Nayanar was the native of village called Kampili. He was a weaver by profession and was highly devoted to Lord Shiva and his devotees. His mind was well fixed on the lotus feet of the Lord. His lips always uttered the Panchakshara Mantra. His hands were ever busy in the service of Shiva's devotees. These three virtues gained the Lord's grace for him. Lord Siva who had pleased with his immense service, came with Mother Parvathy and showered their blessings on him. They raised Nesa nayanar to his holy Abode and nayanar lived there for ever.

Since he was born in the star Rohinî of tamil month Phalguna, that day is celebrated in all shiva temples as his day.

Pusalar

Pusalar was a Brahmin of Tiruninravur in Thondai Mandalam. He believed in the mental worship of the Lord shiva because mental worship is thousands of times better than external ritualistic worship. Mental worship soon leads to samadhi (superconscious state) and Self-realisation.

Legend

Pusalar strongly desired to build a temple for Lord Shiva, but he did not have the money for it. So, he decided to construct a temple in his heart for lord shiva. Mentally he gathered the necessary materials for the purpose. He laid the foundation stone on an auspicious day. He raised the temple and had even fixed an auspicious day for the pradishta (installation) of the deity in it.

The Kadava king who was also a great devotee of Lord Siva had built a magnificent temple in kanjeevaram. By chance he had also fixed the date which Pusalar had mentally chosen, for the installation of the Lord in his temple. The Lord wanted to show the king the superiority of Pusalar's great devotion. So, the Lord appeared in the king's dream and asked him to postpone the installation ceremony in his temple. He said he is going to the temple constructed by his devotee at Tiruninravur. The king woke up from sleep and was intensely eager to have the darshan of the devotee mentioned by the Lord and also have a look at the great temple he had built, which he thought would be far superior than his temple.

The king came to Tiruninravur and searched all over the place for the temple but he could not find any. Then the king enquired about Pusalar. He found out Pusalar's house and approached him. Pusalar was stunned when he heard of the king's dream. Soon, he recovered and was filled with joy. He thought how kind and merciful the Lord is because he had accepted his mental shrine as his Abode. He told the king that that temple was only in his mind. The king was greatly surprised to hear this. Admired by Pulasar's devotion, the king fell at his feet and worshipped him. The king then promised pusalar to construct a temple for shiva in Tiruninravur. He constructed a temple and installed the deity first for pusalar and then he installed the deity in his own temple at kanjeevaram.

Pusalar was very happy and he praised the king. He did the pujas in the temple everyday and continued to worship shiva till he attained his abode.

Pugazh Thunai Nayanar

Pugazh Thunai Nayanar was a pious Adi Shaiva of Srivilliputhur. He was an ardent Siva Bhakta. He was a

Pujari (priest) in the temple. His daily duty was to do the Puja in the temple, according to the Siva Agama's.

Legend

Once a famine swept over the land and he had no money to buy food. People started to migrate from the village. Nayanar loved Shiva and his daily duty in the temple so much. So he did not like to leave the place in spite of the starvation. He stuck to that place and continued the Pooja. His body was emaciated. One day, in spite of his weakness, he fetched water for the Lord's Bath (Abhishekam) in a pot and went into the shrine when he was pouring the water on the Lingam, the water-pot slipped from his hand and fell on the shiva lingam.

Nayanar was shocked. He forgot himself in sheer exhaustion and fainted away. The Lord appeared in his dream and said that he will leave one gold coin in the temple every day till the famine was over so that he could procure the necessary food for his family with that money. Nayanar woke up and found a gold coin and came to know that the dream was true. The Lord thus made his devotee to get over the famine. He continued his daily Pooja in the temple with sincerity and finally reached the Lord's Abode.

Sadaiya Nayanar

Sadaiya Nayanar is an Adi Saivite saint who is one of the 63 nayanars. He lived in Tirunavalur in Tirumuraipadi. All his ancestors were ardent devotees of Lord Siva. He was also pious and devoted. Isaijnaniyar was his dutiful wife. She was also devoted to the Lord and one of the 63 nayanars too. Due to their honourable deeds in their past life, a heavenly child was born who was no other than Sundarar.

He is too a Nayanar. In the history of all the nayanars, these three nayanars got a credit that they all belongs to a same family. Both sadaiya nayanar and his wife led the ideal Grihastha (household) life and finally attained the lords abode.

Since he was born in the star thiruvadhirai (Ardra) of tamil month Market, that day is celebrated in all shiva temples as his day.

Cuntarar

Cuntarar (8th C.C.E.), whose name is also rendered Sundara, Sundaramurti Nayanar etc., was one of the most prominent among the Nayanars, the Shaiva bhakti (devotional) poets of Tamil Nadu. The *Periya Puranam,* which collects the legends of the Nayanars, starts and ends with him. The hymns of seventh volume of the *Tirumurai,* the twelve-volume compendium of the poetry of Tamil Shaiva Siddhanta, were composed by him.

Life

Cuntarar is unique among the Nayanars in that both of his parents are also recognised as Nayanars. He was born Nambi Arurar to an Adi Shaiva brahmin couple, Sadayanar and Isaignani, in the village of Tirunavalur (Adi Saivas are temple priests). The ruler of the local kingdom (Thirumunaipadi-Nadu), Narasingamunaiarayar, adopted him and brought up as his own son, attracted by the beauty of the child he saw playing in the street.

Legend states that while the Cuntarar was being married, the service was interrupted by an old ascetic who asked for Cuntarar as his servant and follower. Speaking as Shiva, the figure told him: "you will be known as Vanthondarm the argumentative devotee. Did you not call me a mad man just a short while ago? Begin your hymn addressing me 'O mad man!'".

Subsequently, Cuntarar moved around Tamil Nadu, visiting several Shiva Temples of Tamilnadu. In Tiruvarur, in the Thanjavur district, he fell in love with a girl named Paravayar, of the Rudra Kanyakayar caste of female ascetics, and married her. In Thiruvottriyur, a sea-side suburb of Madras, he prayed at the Padampakkanathar/Thyagarajar/Vadivudaiamman Temple, where he saw a farmer's girl, Sangiliyar, who was preparing flower garlands and married her, promising never to leave.

It is said that his only purpose in incarnating was his desire for these two, that Shiva intervened to pacify Paravayar's jealousy and also that he was temporarily struck blind when he broke his promise never to leave Sangiliyar. The poet himself mentions his two children; Vanapakai and Cinkati.

The legend states that at Tiruvarur he recited the names of all sixty-three future Nayanars: this recitation is called *Tiruttondar-Tokai*. His fame reached the ears of Cheraman Perumal, the king of Kerala, who came to Tiruvarur. Both embarked on a pilgrimage. But Cuntarar became tired of life and was taken up to heaven by a white elephant. The king followed him on his horse. This occurred in "Swathi Nakshtra" in the Tamil month of "Aadi".

Temples reputedly visited by Cuntarar:

1. Tiruvarutturai Temple at Tiruvenai Nallur.
2. Tirunaavaleswarar Temple at Tirunavalur.
3. Turaiyurppesurar Temple at Trurhuraiyur (Tirutarur).
4. Nataraja Temple at Thillai (Cidambaram).
5. Tiruvadhigai Veerattaanam Temple at Tiruvadhigai.
6. Manikkamenivaradhar Temple at Tirumanikusi (Thirumaandakuzhi).
7. Tirundheeswarar Temple at Tirurinainagar (Teerthanagiri).
8. Brahmapuresar Temple at Sirgasi.
9. Saptapreswarar Temple at Tirukolaka.
10. Shivaloganaathar Temple at Tirupungur.
11. Mayooranaathar Temple at Mayiladuturai (Maayooram).
12. Tiruvambar Maakaalam Temple at Tiruvambar (Ambal).
13. Agnipuriswarar Temple at Tirupugalur.
14. Tyageapruman Temple at Tiruvarur.
15. Kolilinathar Temple at Tirukkolili (Tirukuvalai).
16. Karinateswarar Temple at Tirunatiyathankudi.
17. Manatunainatar temple at Tiruvalivalam.
18. Cuntareswarar Temple at Tirupanaiyur.
19. Prakasheswarar Temple at Tirunanilam (nannilam).
20. Vizhiyasagar Temple at Tiruvisimasalai.
21. Vanjaligeswarar Temple at Tiruvanjiyam.
22. Swarnapuresar Temple at Trikaduvaikarai Putur.

23. Cuntarareswarar Temple at Tirunaraiyur.
24. Padikalitta Eeswarar Temple at Arisirkarai Putur (Azhagar Puthur).
25. Masilamaiyisar Temple at Tiruvavaduthurai.
26. Marudappar Temple at Tiruvidaimarudur.
27. Shenbagaranyeswarar Temple at Tirunageswaram.
28. Brahmapuri Nayagar Temple at Tiruchivapuram.
29. Amirdhakalayeswarar Temple at Torukalayanalur (Saakkottai).
30. Kumeswarar Temple at Tirukudamuku (Kumbakonam).
31. Sithisar Temple at Tiruvalanjusi.
32. Periyandeswarar Temple at Tirunallur.
33. Tolayacelvesar Temple at Tiruchotruturai.
34. Virataneswarar Temple at Tirukkandiyur.
35. Panchanadhiswarar Temple at Tiruvaiyaru.
36. Pushpavananadheswarar Temple at Tirupundhuruti.
37. Atmanadeswarar Temple at Tiruvalamposil.
38. Vajranadeswara Temple at Tirumasabadi.

Tirumular

Tirumular (also spelt Thirumoolar etc., originally known as Sundaranatha) was a Tamil Shaivite mystic and writer, considered one of the sixty-three Nayanars and one of the 18 Siddhars. His main work, the *Tirumantiram* (also sometimes written *Tirumanthiram, Tirumandhiram,* etc.), which consists of over 3000 verses, forms a part of the key text of the Tamil Shaiva Siddhanta, the *Tirumurai.*

Tirumantiram contains a synthesis of knowledge drawn from the Upanishads, Siddhayoga and the devotional (Bhakti) revival, yet criticises ritualistic idolatry and the external gymnastics of occult practice. It is deep, simple, cryptic and polyvalent.

Legend has it that Tirumular was a travelling Shaiva saint and scholar from Kailash who used his yoga powers to transmigrate into the body of a southern cowherd, Mulan. He woke up from his yogic trance once a year and composed one verse until he attained salvation. The dates of Tirumular's life are hotly contested and, because his work makes reference to so many currents of religious thought, the dates that different scholars assign are often appealed to for anchoring the relative chronology of other religious literature in Tamil and Sanskrit. The first known reference to Tirumular that specifies that he was the author of a work called the *Tirumantiram* appears to be that of Sekkizhar in his *Periyapura Gam*, a work that was composed in the twelfth century A.D. Verse 74 of the *Tirumantiram* makes the claim that Tirumular lived for 7 aeons (*yuga*) before composing the *Tirumantiram*.

Some are therefore inclined to place his composition well before the Common Era. The scholar and lexicographer S. Vaiyapuripillai, however, suggested that he probably belonged to the beginning of the eighth-century AD, pointing out that Tirumular could not very well be placed earlier given that he appears to refer to the *Tevaram* hymns of Sambandar, Appar and Sundarar, that he used 'very late words' and that he made mention of the weekdays. Others wish to push the date still later.

Dominic Goodall, for instance, appears to suggest, on the grounds of religious notions that appear in the work with Sanskrit labels for which a certain historical development can be traced in other datable works, that the *Tirumantiram* cannot be placed before the eleventh or twelfth century AD. Yet another view, alluded to for instance by Vaiyapuripillai (*ibid.*), is that the text may contain an ancient core, but with "a good number of interpolated stanzas" of later date. Whatever the case, allusions to works and ideas in the *Tirumantiram* cannot, at least for the moment, be used as useful indicators of their chronology.

Nandanar

Nandanar was a Nayanar saint born in South India who became a great devotee of Lord Shiva.

Nandanar was born in a village called Adhanur in a poor family. He was born at the cruel time where untouchability was being practised, as he belonged to Paraiyar community, which was considered as a untouchable Avarna.

He worked as a Naatamaikar under a Brahmin who owned around 240 acres (0.97 km^2) of land. He had the love of the Brahmin who believed that Nandanar had a midas touch and that he is very loyal and sincere in his duty. But nothing was explicitly shown by the landlord towards the poor Nandan who served him devotedly. Though Nandanar's deity was Karuppanasami, the protector lord of villages, He was a great devotee of Lord Shiva. He visits the Thirupangur Shiva Temple where the Bull (Nandikeshwar or Nandi) hides the Lord from His vision. Untouchability and caste-curse being very dominant at that time, the poor Nandanar could not enter the temple to have darshan.

But without losing hope, Nandanar prays to the Lord and the Nandi moves aside, letting Him have the darshan of the Lord thus proving even gods practised untouchability those days,matter of fact it was he who moved the nandhi reason why if the god inside moved that he would have been let in. who knows the god himself may be afraid of the caste hindus. He sings the glory of the Great God (Mahadeva) and returns back, only to lose his job since the Brahmin was told that Nandan went to the temple ignoring the work that was pending.

While on His way back, He hears that the Lord who dwells also in Chidambaram must be seen at least once in a lifetime. Thus, the desire to visit Chidambaram grew in Nandanar to a great extent that he started pestering the Brahmin to grant him permission to visit Chidambaram at least once. Nandanar is named Thiru Naalai Povar since he tells everyone that he will be going to Chidambaram tomorrow (naalai).

The Brahmin refuses to grant him permission and also ridicules Him of His desire to see the Lord of Chidambaram in spite of being born in a so called low-caste. But upon Nandanar's constant requests, he agrees but in one condition. It is that Nandanar can visit Chidambaram after all the 240 acres (0.97 km^2) of land is cultivated and harvested.

Nandanar knew that it is a task next to impossibility. He cried to Lord Shiva in despair and Lord Shiva orders his Ganas to do all the work in a single night. The Brahmin gets astonished with the devotion of Nandanar, falls down in His feet and requests him to pardon him for his ignorance. Nandanar happily sets forth to Chidambaram and there too, he faces the same problem of being a low-caste born. He sits there in the entrance of the city, filled with anguish to see the Lord.

Lord Shiva appears in the dream of the 3000 saints of Thillai and instructs them to receive Nandanar with due respect after he purify himself with fire.

Here the story turns controversial where some say that when Nandanar was asked to enter fire to prove his purity he came out of fire unhurt and He got merged with the Lord. Some say that the Brahmins cleverly burnt him and covered the story as he got merged with the Lord. Nevertheless, Saint Nandanar is a great example of true devotion.

Tirunavukkarasar

Tirunavukkarasar, (meaning King of the Tongue or Lord of Language), also known as Appar ("Father"), birth-name Marulnikkiyar, was a seventh century Saivite poet-saint of Tamil Nadu, one of the most prominent of the sixty-three Nayanars.

Cuntarar states in his *Tiruttondartokai* that Appar composed 4900 hymns of ten verses each: this is repeated by Nambiyandar Nambi and Sekkizhar but only 313 have survived. These are collected into the Tirumurai, along with the compositions of Cuntarar and Campantar, where Appar has his own volumes, called Tevaram.

Life

Details of Appar's life are found in own hymns, Sekkizhar's *Periya Puranam* (the last book of the *Tirumurai,* yo travelled to nearby Patalipura to join a Jain monastery. He was given the name Dharmasena by his Jain teachers. Nambiyandar Nambi described this event: "seeing the transcient, ephemeral world he decided to probe into truth through renunciation."

After a while, afflicted by a painful illness, Dharmasena returned home. At the Siva temple where his sister served he prayed for relief and was cured. He sang his first hymn *Kootrayinavaru Vilakkaghileer....* His reconversion prompted the Pallava king Mahendravarman I to subject Appar to a number of ordeals and punishments. He overcame all of these apparently miraculously and converted the king himself.

Navukkarasar is supposed to have stayed many years at Atikai with his sister then he began visiting other Siva temples to sing in praise of Siva. He heard of Campantar and went to Sirkali to meet him. Campantar respectfully addressed Navukkarasar as *Appar* (father) and he and Appar travelled together singing hymns. Appar is said to have travelled to about a hundred and twenty-five temples in different cities or villages in Tamil Nadu. He died in "Sadya Nakshtra" in the Tamil month of "Chithirai" at Pukalur at the age of 81.

Appar's Tevaram

Appar's Tevaram hymns are grouped into three books, forming the fourth, fifth and sixth volumes of the *Tirumurai,* the Tamil poetic canon of Shaiva Siddhanta. The compilation of these books is generally ascribed to Nambiyandar Nambi (tenth CCE). Some of Appar's hymns set to various *Panns,* the melodic modes of Ancient Tamil music-the rest are set to *Tirunerisai* and *Viruttam* metres

Viralminda Nayanar

Viralminda Nayanar was born in Sengundru, a hilly place. He was a Vellala by caste. To him worship of Shiva devotees was equal, if not even superior to the worship of Lord Shiva Himself. He felt that no one could get Shiva's grace without first worshipping his devotees. Daily he used to visit the templeand before worshipping the Lord, he used to worship the Shiva devotees who might be found there.

One day he left Sengundru on a pilgrimage and came to Thiruvarur when he was worshipping the Lord in a shiva temple, Sundaramurthi nayanar (Sundarar) came to the temple. Sundarar by-passed all the devotees who were waiting for the prayer in the temple and went into the shrine to worship the Lord. This made Viralmindar irritated. He could not tolerate this insult to His Devotees. He started to shout at sundarar that he had insulted the Shiva Devotees by this act and he said sundarar is unfit to remain in the holy circle of Shiva Devotees.

No one can control viralmindar and he was very furious. Sundarar immediately understood Viralmindar's inner feelings towards the Devotees as well as towards Lord Shiva, and prostrated before him. He then sang a Padigam (poem) praising him. The Padigam (poem) melted Viralmindar's heart so much that he greeted Sundarar and praised him for his service to shiva and Shiva Devotees.

Lord Shiva was greatly pleased with Viralmindar's great steadfastness in his devotion to Shiva Devotees. Viralminda nayanar was blessed and then elevated to the sacred plane of the Shiva Ganas where the Lord made him leader of the Ganas.

Periya Puranam

Periya Puranam (the *great purana* or epic), sometimes also called *Tiruttontarpuranam* (the purana of the holy devotees) is a Tamil poetic account depicting the legendary lives of the sixty-three Nayanars, the canonical poets of Tamil Shaivism. It was compiled during the 12th century by Sekkizhar. It provides evidence of trade with West Asia The *Periya Puranam* is part of the corpus of Shaiva canonical works.

Sekkizhar compiled and wrote the *Periya Puranam* or the *Great Purana,* (the life stories of the sixty-three Shaiva Nayanars, poets of the God Shiva) who composed the liturgical poems of the Tirumurai, and was later himself canonised and the work became part of the sacred canon. Among all the hagiographic *Puranas* in Tamil, Sekkizhar's *Tiruttondar Puranam* or *Periyapuranam,* composed during the rule of Kullottonga Chola II(1133-1150) stands first.

Background

Sekkizhar was a poet and the chief minister in the court of the Chola King Kulothunga Chola II. Kullottonga Chola II was a staunch devotee of Lord Siva Natraja at Chidambaram. He continued the reconstruction of the center of Tamil Shaivism that was begun by his ancestors. However, Kullottonga II was also enchanted by the Jain epic, *Jivaka Cintamani.*

Jivaka Cintamani, is a courtly epic that consisted of erotic flavour called *Srngara Rasa.* In brief, the hero of the epic is Jivaka who combines heroics and erotics to marry seven damsels and gains a kingdom. In the end he realises the transiency of possessions and renounces his kingship and finally attains Nirvana by prolonged *tapas* or meditation.

In to order to wean Kullonttonga Chola II away from a heretical work such as *Jivaka Cintamani,* Sekkizhar undertook the task of writing the *Periyapuranam.*

Periyapuranam

The study of *Jivaka Cintamani* by Kullottonga Chola II, deeply affected Sekkizhar who was very religious in nature. He exhorted the king to abandon the pursuit of impious erotic literature and turn instead to the life of the Shaiva saints celebrated by Sundaramurti Nayanar and Nambi Andar Nambi. The king thereupon invited Sekkizhar to expound the lives of the Shaiva saints in a great poem. As a minister of the state Sekkizhar had access to the lives of the saints and after he collected the data, he wrote the poem in the *Thousand Pillared Hall* of the Chidambaram temple.

This work is considered the most important initiative of Kullottonga Chola II's reign. Although, it is only a literary embellishment of earlier hagiographies of the Shaiva saints composed by Sundarar and Nampi Antar Nambi, it came to be seen as the epitome of high standards of the Chola culture, because of the highest order of the literary style. The *Periyapuranam* is considered as a veritable fifth Veda in Tamil and immediately took its place as the twelfth and the last book in the Shaiva canon. It is considered as one of the masterpieces of the Tamil literature and worthily commemorates the Golden age of the Cholas.

Significance

All the saints mentioned in this epic poem are historical persons and not mythical. Therefore, this is a recorded history of the 63 Shaiva saints called as Nayanmars (devotees of Lord Siva), who attain salvation by their unflinching devotion to Siva. The Nayanmars that he talks about belonged to different castes, different occupations and lived in different times.

Nambiyandar Nambi

Tirunarayur Nambiyandar Nambi was an eleventh-century Shaiva scholar of Tamil Nadu in South India who compiled the hymns of Campantar, Appar and Cuntarar and was himself one of the authors of the eleventh volume of the canon of the Tamil liturgical poetry of Shiva, the Tirumurai.

Nambiyandar was born in the town of Tirunaraiyur into the tradition of the Adi Shaivites, brahmin priests in the temples of Lord Shiva. The great Chola emperor Rajaraja requested him to collect the hymns of the three great poet-saints Campantar, Appar and Cuntarar. Nambi managed to get palm-leaf manuscripts of the hymns, though some had been eaten away by termites.

They were able to recover around ten percent of the entire set of hymns. Nambi also wrote a memoir of the lives of the sixty-three great devotees mentioned by Cuntarar; the *Tiruttondar Tiruvandhadhi*. His hymns in praise of Campantar and Appar provide some biography of those saints

Tirumurai

The word Tirumurai literally means the *sacred book*. It is a compendium of songs or hymns in the praise of Shiva in the Tamil language.

In South India, Shaivites have the Tirumurai as their religious text while Vaishnavas have the Nalayira Divyaprabandham as their sacred work.

History and background

The Pallava period in the history of the Tamil land is a period of religious revival of Hinduism by the Shaivite Nayanars who by their Bhakti hymns captured the hearts of the people.

They made a tremendous impression on the people by singing the praise of Lord Shiva in soul-stirring devotional hymns.

Brief Overview

The Shaiva Tirumurais are twelve in number. The first seven Tirumurais are the hymns of the three great Shaivite saints, Sambanthar, Appar and Sundarar.

These hymns were the best musical compositions of their age:

- The first three Tirumurais are the extempore compositions of Campantar
- The fourth, the fifth and the sixth Tirumurais are those of Appar
- The seventh Tirumurai consists of saint suntarar's hymns
- The eighth Tirumurai consists of saint Manikkavasagar's hymns
- The ninth Tirumurai has been composed by Tirumalikaittever, Centanar, Karuvurttevar, Nampikatava Nampi, Kantaratittar, Venattatikal, Tiruvaliyamutanar, Purutottama Nampi and Cetirayar
- The tenth Tirumurai has been composed by Tirumular
- The eleventh Tirumurai has been composed by Karaikkal Ammaiyar, Ceraman Perumal, Pattinattu p-pillaiyar, Nakkiratevar, Kapilateva, Tiruvalavaiyudaiyar, Nampiyantarnampi, Iyyadigal katavarkon, Kalladateva, Paranateva, Ellamperuman Adigal and Athirava Adigal
- The twelfth Tirumurai has been composed by Sekkizhar.

Manikkavacakar

Manikkavavakar was a Tamil poet who wrote Tiruvacakam, a book of Shaiva hymns. Manikkavacakar was one of the Nayanar poets of the Hindu bhakti revival: his work forms one volume of the Tirumurai, the key religious text of Tamil Shaiva Siddhanta. A minister to the Pandya king Varagunavarman II (c. 862 C.E. – 885 C.E.), he lived in Madurai. His work is a poetic expression of the joy of God-experience, the anguish of being separated from God.

Life and Works

Manikkavacakar is said to have been born in Vadhavoor, seven miles from Madurai on the banks of river Vaigai.

According to legend the king entrusted him with a large amount of money to purchase horses. On his way he met an ascetic devotee of Siva, who in fact was Siva himself. Manikkavacakar was given enlightenment, realised material things are transitory and built the temple of Siva in Tirupperunturai with the money.

Thereafter Manikkavacakar moved from one place to other, singing and composing devotional songs. Finally, he settled in Chidambaram. His Tiruvacakam is placed near the image of Shiva there.

Manikkavacakar's work has several parts. The Tiruvembavai, a collection of twenty hymns om which he has imagined himself as a woman following the Paavai Nonbu and praising Shiva. The twenty songs of Tiruvembavai and ten songs of Tiruppalliezhuchi on the Tirupperunturai Lord are sung all over Tamil Nadu in the holy month of Margazhi (The 9th month of the Tamil calendar, December and January).

His feast is celebrated in the Tamil month of Aani. Manikkavacakar's hagiography is found in the *Tiruvilaiyatar Puranam* (16th century AD). Sculptures illustrating the myth are found in the Minakshi-Sundaresvara temple at Madurai.

8

Kalhana

Kalhana, a Kashmiri Brahmin, was the author of *Rajatarangini,* an account of the history of Kashmir. He wrote *Rajatarangini* in Sanskrit during 1147-1149 CE.

Rajatarangini is regarded as one of the most valuable sources of the history of India.

Rajatarangini

The Rajatarangigi is a metrical chronicle of the kings of Kashmir from earliest time written in Sanskrit by Kalhaga. It is believed that the book was written sometime during 1147-1149 CE. The work generally records the heritage of Kashmir, but 120 verses of Rajatarangigi describe the misrule prevailing in Kashmir during the reign of King Kalash, son of King Ananta Deva of Kashmir.

Although the earlier books are far from accurate in their chronology, they still provide an invaluable source of information about early Kashmir and its neighbors, and are widely referenced by later historians and ethnographers.

Context

The broad valley of Kashmir, also spelled Cashmere is almost completely surrounded by the Great Himalayas and the Pir Panjal range. Kalhana states that the valley of Kashmir was formerly a lake. This was drained by the great rishi or sage, Kashyapa, son of Marichi, son of Brahma, by cutting the gap in the hills at Baramulla Vraha (in Sanskrit Boar), Mulla (in Sanskrit Molar).

With a fertile soil and temperate climate, the valley is rich in rice, vegetables and fruits of all kinds, and famous for the quality of its wool. Kashmir has been inhabited since prehistoric times, sometimes independent but at times subjugated by invaders from Bactria, Tartary, Tibet and other mountainous regions to the North, and from the Indus valley and the Ganges valley to the South.

At different times the dominant religion has been Hindu, Buddhist, Animist and (after the period of the history) Muslim.

Kalhana: The Author & his Philosophy

Kalhana a Kashmiri Brahmin was the author of Rajatarangini, and is regarded as Kashmir's first historian. In fact, his translator Aurel Stein expressed the view that his was the only true Sanskrit history. Little is known about him except from what he tells us about himself in the opening verses of his book. His father Champaka (of Champa) was the minister in Harsha of Kashmir's court.

Kalhana in his opening Taranga of Rajatarangini presents his views on how history ought to be written.

From Stein's translation:

- Verse 7. Fairness: That noble-minded author is alone worthy of praise whose word, like that of a judge, keeps free from love or hatred in relating the facts of the past.
- Verse 11. Cite earlier authors: The oldest extensive works containing the royal chronicles [of Kashmir] have become fragmentary in consequence of [the appearance of] Suvrata's composition, who condensed them in order that (their substance) might be easily remembered.
- Verse 12. Suvrata's poem, though it has obtained celebrity, does not show dexterity in the exposition of the subject-matter, as it is rendered troublesome [reading] by misplaced learning.
- Verse 13. Owing to a certain want of care, there is not a single part in Ksemendra's "List of Kings" (Nrpavali) free from mistakes, though it is the work of a poet.
- Verse 14. Eleven works of former scholars containing the chronicles of the kings, I have inspected, as well as the [Purana containing the] opinions of the sage Nila.

- Verse 15. By looking at the inscriptions recording the consecretations of temples and grants by former kings, at laudatory inscriptions and at written works, the trouble arising from many errors has been overcome.

Despite these stated principles, and despite the value that historians have placed on Kalhana's work, it must be accepted that his history was far from accurate. In the first three books, there is little evidence of authenticity and serious inconsistencies. For example, Ranaditya is given a reign of 300 years. Toromanu is clearly the Huna king of that name, but his father Mihirakula is given a date 700 years earlier. It is known, however, that Mihirakula was the son of Toramana. The chronicles only start to align with other evidence by book IV,

Structure of Rajatarangini Chronicle

The author of the Rajatarangini history chronicles the rulers of the valley from earliest times, from the epic period of the Mahabharata to the the reign of Sangrama Deva (c.1006 CE), before the Muslim era. The list of kings goes back to the 19th century BCE. Some of the kings and dynasties can be identified with inscriptions and the histories of the empires that periodically included the Kashmir valley, but for long periods the Rajatarangini is the only source.

This work consists of 7826 verses, which are divided into eight books called *Tarangas* (waves).

Kalhaga's account of Kashmir begins with the legendary reign of Gonarda, who was contemporary to Yudhisthira of the Mahabharata, but the recorded history of Kashmir, as retold by Kalhaga begins from the period of the Mauryas. Kalhaga's account also states that the city of Srinagar was founded by the Mauryan emperor, Ashoka, and that Buddhism reached the Kashmir valley during this period. From there, Buddhism spread to several other adjoining regions including Central Asia, Tibet and China.

The Dynasties

The kings of Kashmir described in the Rajatarangigi can be roughly grouped into dynasties as in the table below.

Notes in parentheses refer to a book and verse. Thus (IV.678) is Book IV verse 678.

Gonanda I	The Rajatarangini (I.59) lists Gonanda I as the first king of Kashmir, a relative of Jarasasamdha of Magadh.
Lost and Unknown kings	Skipping over "lost kings" we come to Lava of an unknown family. After his family, Godhara of another family ruled (I.95).
Mauryas	The Maurya Empire was a geographically extensive and powerful political and military empire in ancient India, founded by Chandragupta Maurya in 322 BCE. His grandson Ashoka the Great (273-232 BCE) built many stupas in Kashmir, and was succeeded by his son Jalauka.
Kushanas	After a Damodara ("of Asoka's kula or another"), we have Hushka, Jushka and Kanishka (127–147 CE) of the Bactrian Kushan Empire. (Note the confusion of dates in this and the following sections. Kalhana appears to made little attempt to determine the actual dates and sequence of rule of the kings and dynasties he recorded)
Gonandiya	After an Abhimanyu, we come to the main Gonandiya dynasty, founded by Gonanda III. He was (I.191) the first of his race. Nothing is known about his origin. His family ruled for many generations.
Some others	Eventually a Pratapaditya, a relative of Vikrmaditya (not the Shakari) became king (II.6). After a couple of generations a Vijaya from another family took the throne (II.62). His son Jayendra was followed by Sandhimat-Aryaraja (34 BCE-17 CE) who had the soul of Jayendra's minister Sandhimati. Kalhana says that Samdhimat Aryaraja used to spend "the most delightful Kashmir summer" in worshiping a lingam formed of snow/ice "in the regions above the forests" (II.138). This too appears to be a reference to the ice lingam at Amarnath.

Contd....

Huna	Kalhana describes the rules of Toramana and Mihirakula (510-542 CE), but does not mention that these were Huna people: this is known from other sources.
Gonandiya again	After the Huna, Meghavahana of the Gonandiya family was brought back from Gandhara. His family ruled for a few generations. Meghavahana was a devout Buddhist and prohibited animal slaughter in his domain.
Karkota dynasty (625-1003 CE)	Gonandiya Baladitya made his officer in charge of fodder, Durlabhavardhana (III.489) his son-in-law because he was handsome. Lalitaditya Muktapida (724-760 CE) of this dynasty created an empire based on Kashmir and covering most of Northern India and Central Asia. (With his account of the Karkota dynasty, relatively recent at the time he wrote his chronicles, Kalhana's information becomes more consistent with other sources.) Kalhana relates that Laliditya Muktapida invaded the tribes of the north and after defeating the Kambojas, he immediately faced the Tusharas. The Tusharas did not give a fight but fled to the mountain ranges leaving their horses in the battle field. Then Lalitaditiya meets the Bhauttas in Baltistan in western Tibet north of Kashmir, then the Dardas in Karakoram/ Himalaya, the Valukambudhi and then he encounters Strirajya, the Uttarakurus and the Pragjyotisha respectively (IV.165-175).
Utpala	In the Karkota family, Lalitapida had a concubine, a daughter of a Kalyapala (IV.678). Her son was Chippatajayapida. The young Chippatajayapida was advised by his maternal uncle Utpalaka or Utpala (IV.679). Eventually the Karkota dynasty ended and a grandson of Utpala became king.

Contd....

Kutumbi	After the Utpala dynasty, a Yashaskara became king (V.469). He was a great-grandson of a Viradeva, a Kutumbi (V.469). Here maybe Kutumbi = kunabi (as in kurmis of UP and Kunbi of Gujarat/Maharastra). He was the son of a treasurer of Karkota Shamkaravarman. Kalhana describes Shamkaravarman (883–902) thus (Stein's trans.): "This [king], who did not speak the language of the gods but used vulgar speech fit for drunkards, showed that he was descended from a family of spirit-distillers". This refers to the fact that the power had passed to the brothers of a queen, who was born in a family of spirit-distillers.
Divira	After a young son of Yashaskara, Pravaragupta, a Divira (clerk), became king. His son Kshemagupta married Didda, daughter of Simharaja of Lohara. After ruling indirectly and directly, Didda (980-1003 CE) placed Samgramaraja, son of her brother on the throne, starting the Lohara dynasty.
Lohara	The Lohara family was founded by a Nara of Darvabhisara (IV.712). He was a vyavahari (perhaps merchant) who along with others who owned villages like him had set up little kingdoms during the last days of Karkotas. The Loharas ruled for many generations. The author Kalhana was a son of a minister of Harsha of this family.

Kalhana: The Chronicler

Chronicle-writing is not foreign to the imagination of the Kashmiri Brahmins. A host of histories Charitas and Mahatmyas amply testify to this assertion. However, the history as it is taken in the modern parlance, is absent in Sanskrit literature. History is not an account of rise and fall of kings but should embrace in its ambit the political, social and religious attainments and aspirations of the people at large. To glean such fool-proof material. from Kalhana's Raja Tarangini (River of Kings) will only mean love's labour lost. In the first instance in his time such a conception of history-writing was not at all known; Even the earlier Greek memoirs cannot be deemed free from this defect. I before accusing Kalhana of inefficient handling of the subject-matter, it is to be borne in mind that he holds brief only for the "Rajas" i. e. Kings, and does not dabble in any other literary or historical pastime concerning people. He has very faithfully and aptly captioned his chronicle as "The River of Kings". Hence he limits his poetic description to the kings for and about whom he has written this Kavya. Thus it can safely be stated that Dr. Mecdonnel's remarks about the non-existence of truly historical material in Raja-Tarangini is only partly true. Among the galaxy of such writers of Historical Kavyas Kalhana shines the brightest. He is the only Kashmiri author who has I taken his assignment seriously. He is the first and the best in the line.

Obviouly enough the name Kalhana is non Sanskritic but may have had some meaning in the local dialect at that time; this is not even now intelligible to Kashmiri people.

Kashmiri writers have shown a preference for coining their names in local dialect instead of Sanskrit over which their command was praise-worthy. So names as, Bilhana, Mammatta, Kayatta etc are striking examples of this trend.

However, Dr. Stein in his masterly introdution to Raja Tarangini has taken pains in establishing the affinity of "Kalyan", as given in the Srikanthacaritam of Mankha, with "Kalhana" of RajaTarangiDi:

Moreover, the commentator of Sri Kantlia Caritam, jonaraja has said that "Alakadatta was actually the "Sandhi-Vigrahaka" or the minister of war and peace." He further says that the stories (Kathas) in which "Kalyan" is said to be proficient are the stories from Mahabharata and other epics. But being himself a man of letters and having taken up the thread of chronicle-writing from Kalhana has also given his local name and has not cared to identify it with "Kalyan." Even though phonetically "Kalyan" can be rendered into 'Kalhana" Apabhramsa, yet we have to rely on the verdict of Dr. Keith who seems to take this conclusion with a grain of salt.

Kalhana is silent about his pedigree or the sort of life he lived. His name only appears on the colophons of his work including the direct reference to him by jona-Raja who wrote some three centuries after him. This establishes beyond doubt that inspite of his being shy about self-introduction unlike "Bilhana"' the tradition had not forgotten him and his merit. Some scholars have tried to identify certain names in the text of the Raja Tarangini as the relations of the Chronicler e.g. "Canpaka" as his father and "Kamaka" probably his uncle. It is true that this name occurs frequently and with evident respect also:

> *"When Canpaka who was stationed as incharge of the 'gate' was ready to go in for that assignment under the orders of the king, Vataganda (Ananda) endeavoured to stop him.'*

Unless this surmise is corroborated by any other, evidence contemporary or later, we are constrained to dismiss it as extraneous. Fortunately for us Kalhana has not left us into guessing the date of his composition. He explicitly says that he began the writing of his chronicle in year 4224 of the Laukika era i.e. 1148-49 AD. and finished it in the year following.

Kalhana does not brag about the originality of his Kavya but instead very humbly says:

> *"If I again narrate the subject matter of tales which have been related by others earlier, still the virtuous ought not turn their faces from me without hearing my purpose".*

He very frankly admits that the tradition of chronicle-writing was very popular even before his advent, but to his dismay these chronicles no longer existed in a complete state in his time. He further says that the loss of such chronicles was due to the fact that one "Suvrata" condensed all these chronicles into one book, hence nobody bothered for the originals; having fallen into disuse, these in course of time, were consigned to the forgotten niches of the houses. Before embarking on his task of writing the chronicle, Kalhana very rightly wants to be dispassionate in narrating the events. He would like to sit on the fence recording the events in a most judicious and unprejudiced manner; He believes that:

> *"That talented one is alone praiseworthy whose intellect devoid of love or hatred relates the past anecdotes like an umpire."*

The chronicler acknowledges the debt of Eleven works of former scholars containing "the chronicles of Kings" including the Nilamata Purana. Out of these eleven chronicle only three are named by him and about other eight he is silent. The first title he refers to as his source, is Ksemendra's Nrpavali or List of Kings. However, this useful book is now lost along with the works of "Padam Mihira" and "Helaraja" who had also composed a List of Kings (Parthivavali)." In view of his giving a direct quotation from "Chavillakara's" uncaptioned work which furnished him with the name of Ashoka and five other ancient kings it can be safely inferred that this work was extant at that time but subsequently could not stand the ravages of time, hence was lost.

Besides this, he made ample use of inscriptions and edicts for building the chronicle uptodate. He could not also ignore the popular tradition which has occupied a sizable portion of his chronicle. However, on even a cursory perusal of the chronicle we can very safely infer that he had studied the "Vikramanka Deva Caritam" of Bilhana, a fellow-poet of his. He has not at times refrained from quoting his phraseology and style even. Another earlier work which he must have consulted is Bana's "Harsacarita". It is a well-known fact that this historical record of King Harsa Vardhana of Kanauj enjoved popularity in Kashmir as Mammatta in his Kavya Prakasa has quoted a passage from it. It cannot also be gainsaid that Kalhana was very well conversant with the epics-Ramayana and Mahabharta. In this connection copious examples can be culled from the Raja Tarangini. Having armed himself with all this material, he took up his assignment in all seriousness and tried to overcome "the difficulties arising from any errors".

The oldest manuscript (in Sarada characters) of 'Raja' is in the possession of Govt. Research Library, Srinagar. There is another manuscript of this chronicle prepared by one Pt. Gana Kak, with explanatory notes by Pt. Saheb Ram.

Kalhana originally wrote in Sarada and subsequently it was transcribed into Devanagri. However, it is to be borne in mind that the scribes (lipikaras) engaged for this purpose seem not to have mastery either over, the lanouage or the script. Hence many errors crept into it. Moreover, Sarada is a very intricate script and the resemblance of several words with each other could only be detected by scholars of profound learning. Unfortunately the lack of command of the transcribers over the language has corrupted and even ruined the text at places. This is mainly responsible for the defects inherent in the Calcutta edition of the "Raja". Confusing 'Rilhana' with 'Bilhana' is a glaring example of such neglect. This edition was so corrupt that the translation of this gave rise to many controversies.

Taking cue from Dr. Buhler, who first of all pointed out the defects of the Calcutta edition, the search for a more authentic manuscript was continued by the subsequent indologists. The efforts of Dr. Stein were crowned with success, when he could find access to the "zealously guarded Codex Archetypus (date of composition from 1648. A. D. to 1685 A. D.) of Rajanaka Ratnakantha by his successors," through the good offices of Pandit Suraj Kaul, member of the Kashmir State Council and his son Pandit Hari Krishen Koul.

This genuine Kashmiri recension of Raja Tarangini solved many mysteries and a trustworthy text of this great chronicle, in the hands of Rajanaka Ratanakantha, was unearthed in 1890 A D. Moreover, Dr. Stein could also lay his hands on the Lahore edition of Raja Tarangini in 1895; it was in the possession of a Kashmiri Brahmin named Pandit Jagmohan Lal Hundu, who had migrated to Lahore from Srinagar. These two valuable finds were instrumental in dispelling doubts regarding the authenticity or genuine-character of Raja Tarangini. Earlier, Dr. Buhler had also been able to procure a manuscript of Raja Tarangini, in Sarada, from one Pt. Keshava Raina in Srinagar. This MS according to the learned scholar, was only hundred or hundred and fifty years old.

However, the credit of introducing this Kashmiri chronicle to the world goes to Professor Wilson. In 1825 A.D he compiled an essay on the first six cantos (tarangas) of Rajatarangini and published it in Asiatic Researches. Thereafter the text was published also from Calcutta in 1835 by the Asiatic Society and later on Mr. Troyer undertook the stupendous task of translating all the eight cantos in 1840 and completed these in 1852.

His knowledge of Sanskrit being faulty, he made the confusion arising out of the Calcutta edition, worse confounded. Then onwards, in addition to this, many other European scholars have made references to this chronicle and have gleaned much useful data from it. Prof. Lassen, in his Encyclopedia of Indian Antiquities, has given a complete analysis of this work. General Cunningham treated its chronology in an admirable article in the 'Numismatic chronicle of 1918. Inspite of all this, Prof.

Wilson had to concede that a close translation of these cantos in such a pretty mess with regard to linguistic inaccuracies, would have been impractiable. It is noteworthy to mention here that no of these scholars had seen the MS in Sarada characters. They based all their conjectures on Devanagri manuscripts. Professor Wilson, in particular had seen the sent by Mr.Moorcraft from Kashmir and two copies in Devanagri gifted to the India House Library Lond by Mr. Colebkooke. Dr. E. Hultzsch also utilized the material brought to light by the above mention scholars for many of his thought-provoking articles. Among the Indian scholars Shri Yogeshchander Dutt's English version and R.S. Pandit's translation also deserve mention. Both these works are based on Calcutta edition. Before we proceed, it is desirable to allude to a controversy raised by Mr. Troyer. He contends in his introduction to the translation of Raja Tarangini that the last two cantos of this chronicle have not been written by Kalhana but are the composition of some other poet.

To substantiate his theory he argues:

i) He (Kalhana) allots to the last two hundred and fifty years double the number of verses of what he devotes to the preceding three thousand and odd years.

ii) The references and resumes given in the VII and VIII do not tally with those of the first six.

iii) Canto VIII relates events which occurred after 1148 A. D.

Prof. Lassen also notes the difference in style between the first six and last two cantos.

In meeting his arguments it useful to bear in mind that:

i) Last two cantos can roughly be called the contemporary history delineated by the chronicler. It definitely deserved more space, because Kalhana was sure about the ground under his feet. The first six cantos are based on different sources coupled with tradition; so Kalhana wanted to skip through these. The matter he was treating was more or less not so authentic from his view-point and so was given lesser space.

ii) The so-called varying references are mainly, due to the bad and faulty MS; and to crown all, his incorrect translation. No such contradictions have been detected by, subsequent scholars, more recently by Dr. Stein because of the correct text. Mr. Troyer's hold on Sanskrit was not so good. He has translated Mukhtapida and Lalitaditya as two different personalities while actually they are one and the same person. With regard to this Dr. Buhler has to say "He (Troyer) undertook a task very much beyond his strength for which he was qualified neither by learning nor by natural talent;

iii) With regard to the third argument it may safely be said that he began to write his chronicle in Saptrsi Samvat 24 which works out at 4224 (Saptrsi Samvat) i e. 1148-49 A.D. It contained thousands of slokas, hence could not be completed in the same year by any stretch of imagination. If he mentioned events happening nine years later (VIII book) in Saptrsi Samvat 33, it only proves that the poem was not completed until after that year.

iv) The so called difference in style referred to by Prof Lassen is not at all detectable.

The most unassailable evidence regarding the authenticity of the last two cantos of 'Raja' is furnished by Jona Raja when he took up the thread from Kalhana (nearly three centuries afier him) and completed his Raja Tarangini. He explicitly mentions that Kalhana finished the "Account of Kings" with the reign of Jaya Simha. One fact should not be lost sight of that canto VI, ends abruptly which can never be termed as the conclusion.

Hence it has been made sufficiently clear that, all the eight cantos are from the fertile pen of one and the same author and that is Kalhana. However, it is to be conceded (with all that is said and done) that Kalhana's text of 'Raja', as it is available to us at present, does suffer from some shortcomings. After making due allowance for the corruptions which might have crept into the text by careless transcription and, at times, deliberate interpolation's, yet some unpardonable oversights have been made by the 'renowned' chronicler. Kalhana's mastery over the language is also at times doubtful when he repeats the Alankaras word by word particularly in the Canto VIII.

At times consistency with the anecdotes related earlier is not maintained and it seems that he was either in hurry in completing the assignment or treated the subject-matter towards the conculsion in a slip-shod manner. In view of his accurate detailing and exactness, it can only be surmised that he did not care to revise his manuscript for one reason or nother, or he could not find time to do so.

As regards the over-sights, he has made a glaring error: while describing King " Sacinara" in Book I he extolls him like " Sacipati"; Indra, or the husband of saci (queen), but in Book VIII while giving the resume of the reigns of different kings he mentions "Sacinara" as the "son of Saci" (queen Mother):

"Thereafter his son (Janakas's) the illustrious Sacinara like an Indra on the globe protected the earth. He was forbearing and his commands could not be disobeyed."

The latter's son (Suvarna's) was janaka, whose son was Sacinara born of Saci (queen mother).

Even if we may contend that Kalhana has play on the word Saci, yet it is not in good taste to describe "Saci" as the wife and the mother at the same time in respect to one and the same perso Moreover in Book VIII he has altogether forgotten to mention King Nara I whom he has treated at length in the Book I. Also while giving the names of the lovers of Srilekha queen of Samgrama Raja in Book VII he has not mentioned Vyaddasuha who plundered the treasures of the King and courted his consort as given in the Book VIII. To crown all, at some places we are confronted with bad Sanskrit and even wrong metres employed.

Besides this, he has been so much influenced by Bilhana's Vikramankdeva-caritam and Bana's Harsacaritam that he has not refrained from borrowing their words and even phraseology. From epics also he has enriched his vocabulary and has not resisted the temptation of quoting Verbatum from these. Kalidasa's Reghuvamsa has been also used by him for his treatise and even the thought and diction have been borrowed from it:

"(He King Kalasa) had approached the woman (daughter in-law of Jindu Raja of licentious Character), having sent in advance the noselessman (His vita). That very inauspicious man because of his disfigurement was responsible for the frustration of his amors". Evidently the books which have attracted Kalhana to borrow do come also under the purview of chronicles, e.g. Ramayana, Mahabharata, Raghuvamsa etc,. hence he could not but get acquainted with these so as to make his own composition more authentic and traditionally accurate. The point to be emphasized here is his freedom with which he has drawn upon these and has even quoted the words, vocabulary and to crown all imitated the style.

But such lapses are few and far between, and do not, in any way, tarnish his image as a chronicle-writer. Out of a compendium of some 8000 Slokas such defects are quite natural when, the canvas is very wide before the chronicler.

In his introduction to his 'Raja' Kalhana very clearly indicates that he would prefer to be a poet because:-

"Who else but the poets resembling Prajapati in (creative power) and able to bring forth lovely productions, can place the past times before the eyes of men."

He thinks that transformation of the past into the present can be attained by the deft pen of a poet only. A Kavya has been defined as a composition in prescribed metres, being devoid or blemishes (Dosa) having meaningful words containing Rasa (sentiment), Guna (quality) and embellishments. Such and other ingredients of Kavya presuppose a thorough study of Rhetorics, poetics and embellishments. Kalhana has not cared to give any account of his literary attainments. To whatever poetic horizon be reaches is to be gleaned from this chronicle. Therefore, we may assert that he is a poet by intuition and a historian by profession. Primarily his concern was to put into words the hierarchy of Kings which ruled Kashmir; poetry was used by him only as a convenient vehicle. Having read other Kavyas, Raghuvamsa and Vikramankadevacaritam and the epics about which we are sure very thoroughly, he must have gained proficiency in the art of Kavya-writing and there can be no surprise, in noticing that at times he rises to the heights of poetic prowess also:

"Having come out of the grove off lowery creepers, (a young Brahmin visakha) saw before him two virgins donning blue robes and having very sweet eyes. The corners of their eyes were very attractive and were smeared with a very thin line of collyrium, as if this was the stalk of the red ruby-like lotuses used by these as ear-ornaments. To their two shoulders were pinned their faces, as it were like flags, the ends of which in the shape of their captivating eyes were fluttering in the gentle wind."

The similies used in these stanzas are not only very beautiful but also homely. In his benedictory tribute to Siva and his consort Parvati in book III, the dialogue between the two, reminds us of the same situation in Kalidasa's Kumar Sambhavam. Herein Kalhana has most poetically justified the otherwise ugly demeanour of Lord Siva:

"May Siva protect you who in his form composed of two halves (male and female, Ardhanarisvara) gives these replies (to Parvati's queries):

"Leave away this elephant-skin". "In the inner recesses of the frontal globe on his fore-head are pearls which can effortlessly

adorn the tips of your breasts." "Why this fire on your forehead." "From these you may take the collyrium for your eyes" and who even, if objection were raised by his beloved to the Snake, would suffer such an answer."

In the Stanzas below the use of Alankaras (poetic, embellishments) has been made dexterously

While describing the burning of the Cakradhara temple in the reign of Sussala 1121 A. D. to 1128 A. D. the poet in Kalhana weaves a graphic panorama of words and images:

1. "The sky was densely screened by huge columns of smoke from which shone moving flames resembling the bushy and tawny red-hair and beards of goblins.
2. The tongues of the flames emanating from the fire the smoke of which was spent-up, gave the impression of waves of gold coming out of a golden cloud which had been, as it were, melted by the excessive beat.
3. The columns of fire strewn on the sky looked like the red headgear fallen from the crests of gods fleeing in scare before the conflagration."

Even if Kalhana tries to live up to the norms of a Kavya as enjoined by the Alankarashastra, yet his 'forte' being chronicle-writing, he has therefore conveniently ignored many of the tenets laid therein. Even though he employs a variety of metres yet his mastery over these is deficient. Some scholars are forced to label it as "versified prose." In view of what has been shown to illustrate his poetic prowess earlier, this verdict seems unjust. Many such examples can be copiously quoted from the 'Raja' to show that Kalhana is no poet of mean order, even if he cannot catchup with his fellow country-man Bilhana.

The didactic import of his work is also distinctly pronounced. In this branch of his poetic fancy he has amply drawn from the epics, Dharamasastras and Nitishastras;

The diamond can be held as proof against all metals and stone-dykes against the waters, but nothing (is proof against) the false." His mastery over the pun can be sufficiently illustrated by the following stanza:

There Gauri though she has assumed the form of Vitasta still keeps her wonted inclination. (For in her river-shape) she turns her face towards the ravine (Guha), just as (in her godlike form) she turns it towards (her son) Kumara, (Guha) (in her river shape) the mouths of the Nagas (Naga Mukha) drink her abundant water (Apita bhuri Paya) just as (in her god like form) elephant faced (son Ganesha Naga Mukha) drank her abundant milk (Apita bhuri Paya).

Alankara Shastras also lay it down that every poetic composition should have a Rasa (sentiment) permeating throughout. the length and breadth of the Kavya. To live up to this tenet Kalhana says:

> *"Suddenly coming to life of living beings and their transitory nature is to be seriously thought over; sothe Santa (indifference to worldly objects and pleasures) sentiment will reign supreme here-in in this book)."*

This Santa Rasa is very much pronounced in Mahabharta. While defining Santa Rasa Vishva Nath Kaviraja has to say: Wherein there is no Sorrow or joy, nor fear, as neither apathy nor attachment and no desire. The great munies have called such a state of mind as shanta, where in all sentiments and their consequent expression are equal in measure.

One point needs clarification here. Raja Tarangini is composed of thousands of anecdotes in which individual "Rasa" in view of its subject matter, should naturally run. So in the description of war vira is there; in the details giving amors of various queens "Srinagar" is present. The intrigue and court conspircacies arouse "Jugupsa" and the sad end of some kings excites "Shoka". These sentiments are all subservient to the motif of the chronicle i.e. "Santa". Perhaps this is the reason that Kalhana ends four out of eight Tarangas of his chronicle with the description of such kings who gave up their thrones by acts of pious resignation and renunciation. He has emphasized off and on that despite regal glory and affluence, every king, one after another, had to renounce this by the everlasting natural law that nothing is permanent in this world.

What is born is to die definitely." Hence every one should take a lesson from this and try to remain resigned and cultivate in himself an attitude which remains unruffled in pleasure or paid, plenty or penury; herein the patent influence of Mahabharata is clearly seen on the chronicler.

Without mincing words we are alive to the fact that Kalhana's poetical prowess was limited by his assignment of chronicle-writing. He wants to be a poet and a chronicler at the same time. Kalidasa did combine poetic acumen with history in his "Raghuvamsa" but therein also his talents and unparalleled skill have suffered a jolt-especially towards the closing chapters of his Kavya. Kalhana has also tried to emulate his example. Let us now discuss how far he has been successful in making a happy compromise between the two. Perhaps sensing some such insinuations Kalhana has very succinctly made a confession:

> *"Though in view of the length of the narrative, diversity could not be secured by means of amplification, still there may be found something in it that will please the rightminded."*

Hence the chronicler is aware of the fact that his treatise cannot boast of diversity by elaborate events, because that would lengthen his narrative and as such he has to be brief and factual. This axe of brevity is to be employed even though the chronicler may not have liked it. Important events need to be emphasized and minor ones skipped over. This very fact goes a long way in proving that Kalhana even though wanting to retain the poet in himself does actually make it subordinate to his skill of chronicle-writing. Not only this he has also set a norm for his chronicle-recording:

> *"Only that person of merit is worthy of praise who while relating the past does keep himself away from partiality or otherwise like an Umpire."*

So, it is abundantly clear that Kalhana would not like to indulge in fanciful hyperbole or otherwise like a poet, but would like to record the facts as these took place, in an unattached bent of feeling. The vehicle for this he has chosen is the poetry, otherwise his motive is to write a chronicle uptodate which had become fragmentary. The inference that Kalhana is a chronicler first and a poet afterwards, can very safely be made from the preceding stanzas. Poetry to him was only a means to an end, the end being pure and simple-chronicle-writing. The soul of a chronicle is art of narration. Hence Kalhana's merit as a chronicler can be measured by his deftness in narrating events. Narration 'does not mean only flow of events but events should also admit of impartiality of the narrator. Secondly, the individuality of characters and their personal traits have also to be taken into consideration. Thirdly, historicity of the narrative is the touchstone on which the merit or otherwise of the chronicler is to be tested. About the impartiality and independence of judgment as depicted by Kalhana we have earlier shown his attitude to his assignment. However, as practice is better than precept we have to see the veracity of his professing an "Umpire-like attitude."

Happily for us, Kalhana has lived upto this maxim. He has been a close witness of the rise and fall of kings from Sussala to jayasimha of whom he was a contemporary. In narrating the events of the reign of Jaya-Simha he has not hesitated to bring into relief his defects also. He has not been a panegryist. He has very emphatically critisized the conduct of high-ups in his own times, the omissions and faulty judgment of the king under whom he wrote. At times we feel that such trenchant criticism could not have been publicised at that time for fear of punishment.

About the exploitation of their subjects, Kalhana records: The riches which the kings amass by tormenting people go to the rivals or enemies or are consumed by fire." Ill gotten wealth does not last long. In order to illustrate his point he says:

> *"The treasures of King Kalasa which he had contrived to get through malpractices were very soon squandered by his son on unworthy persons and by his wife on lovers."*

Ordinarily like all other Kavya-writers even in his own land Kalhana should have followed a policy of safety first and painted the kings only in white splendour; but like a true chronicler he does not hesitate from using black paint whenever occasion arises. In this connection he has placed a host of rulers in the dock.

In this respect we should remember this fact that Kalhana was alive and a close witness of events of Sussala's and his son's Jayasimha's reign. About Sussala, the father of the reigning king, be has not a single 'kind word and even for Jayasimha he does not ignore to pen down his bad points. This needs high order of courage and that also at that time when political murders and diplomatic reprisals were a common feature. He also gives a graphic account of Sycophants, parasites and flatterer of the kin, Jaysimha who definitely held high office in his government. He is not at all afraid of their revenge and very faithfully paints their detestable figures. The ruling king also does not escape his chastisement:

> *"Uneven, indeed are the features also in his (Jayasimha's) character. Not perceiving the excellence of their (aggregate) result, the people have concluded that-these were faults."*

Now we come to the moot point of historicity in Kalhana's chronicle. He has given us the eyewitness account of at least three kings-Harsa, Sussala and Jayasimha. Herein his historical acumen is at its highest. However in the first six books he has relied on the sources which he has described at length in the begining of his chronicle. He has also taken help from tradition which he could not ignore at any price. In this way if the events are treated in a very loose and general way in the first six books, it is the fault not of the chronicler but of the sources at his disposal. He has tried his best to weave into one the scattered threads of history.

The first king of Kashmir has been named as Gonanda I by him and he has been shown a contemporary of Yudishthira of Mahabharta. The date of accession to throne by Yudishthira is given as 653rd year of Kali era. Kalhana has given this very date as the start of Gonanda's rule or Kashmir-history on the authority of Nilamata Purana. However, from Gonanda III he gives the length of reigns regularly. For this he supplies a cogent reason in as much as " fifty two lost kings" he has not been able to identify or locate. Among the fifty two lost kings he has given us names of seventeen perhaps on the basis of the tradition.

Still there is a veritable gap of thirty five kings between Gonanda I and Gonanda III which he has not succeeded in filling. Out of these seventeen kings whom he has retrieved, he has given us the name of Ashoka (B.C. 300)- the great Buddhist monarch of Pataliputra who had also annexed Kashmir. Kalhana's record about Ashoka is corroborated by his inscriptions and by the chinese travellers. One of the famous deeds of this monarch was to found the city of Srinagar which was called "Srinagari" at that time:

> *"That illustrious king (Ashoka) founded the important city of Srinagari with ninety six lakhs of houses full of wealth".*

The Turkish incursions into Kashmir have been amply dealt with by Kalhana while mentioning the names of great Kushan ruler Kanishka and other two Huska and Juska, while describing these foreign, kings Kalhana has shown extreme sense of catholicity. They bad embraced Buddhism and as such this religion-a virtual reaction against Brahmanism-also was popular in Kashmir, for which Kalhana a staunch Shaiva has no regrets; instead he praises this religion and its founder.

These kings founded the towns Huskapura, Juskpura, and Kaniskapura now known as "Vushkur, Zokur, and Kanispur r^espectively, the first and last are in the vicinity of Baramulla (Varahmula) and "Zokur" near the famous Naseem Bagh. The chronicler also refers to famous Buddhist philosopher "Nagarjuna" having lived here at Sadarhadvana (the first of six Arhats-Buddhist mendicants). This place has been indentified as the present "Harwan" where on the hillocks remains of the Buddhist monasteries are still visible.

Another alien king who retired to Kashmir as narrated by Kalhana, is the white Hun Mihir Kula whom he refers as "Trikotihan"-killer of three crores. After perpetrating countless atrocities, he embraced Shaivism here and later out of penitence consigned himself to flames. Out of the indigenous kings Kalhana has given us illuminating accounts of the following. These illustrious kings are very renowned in Kashmir:

Pravarsena II (A.D. 580 roughly): This king has been portrayed as a valiant warrior; when he was invited to occupy the throne, he was leading an expedition in Trigarta (modern Kangra) to recover the kingdom of his fore-fathers. He is said to have built his capital named Pravarapura, (Pravarasenapura) perhaps on the same site on which modern Srinagar stands. However, on further scrutiny and reading through the lines, it can be safely established that the new city was founded on the outskirts of Sharika parvat or Hari parvat in Kashmir. In Kalhana's own words this hill was situated in the centre of the new city.

Lalitaditya Mukhtapida (A.D. 750) has been painted in very profuse colours and also at length by Kalhana. Here-in the evidence of foreign notices and monuments is so striking that Kalhana's account does not seem only credible but also accurate, Lalitaditya was a great conqueror and inflicted crushing defeats on Yasovarman, the king of central India, Tokharians (Dwellars of upper oxus or more precisely Badakhshan of the Muslim Historians) from where he brought a very astute person Cankuna by name and made him his minister, and also some Turks who lived in the upper Indus.

Not only this, he invaded Baltistan and Tibet with Chinese connivance and subjugated Dard tribes. He has also been portrayed as having crossed the sand-ocean perhaps in central Asia. In this way we are told thrt the whole of his life was spent in wars and he perished while with anexpedition to distant North in the excessive snow. Not only this he made the king of Bengal his vassal. Even though his hands were full with waging wars, he did find some time to build some famous buildings in Kashmir. One of these is the sun-temple at Martanda which the king constructed at the site of the Tirtha of the same name. Its massive walls of stones with a lofty enclosure have been clearly mentioned. He also founded the city of Parihasapura which served as the royal residence also. He also built a cluster of temples around it.

This city had been built by the king for merrymaking (parihasa) as a respite after strenuous wars. "The karewas of Paraspor and Diwar are situated at a distance of fourteen miles from Srinagar on the Baramulla road." Another two towns namely " Lalitpura" and "Lokapunya", "Lalitpur" an abbreviation of Lalitadityapura can be identified easily. It is called "Letapor" now, but no remains are seen there above ground. May be these lie buried under the saffron-growing udars.

The "Loka Punya" is the "Lookabhavan" of today; the former town did not find favour with the king as it had been designed and built by his architect in his absences. This great king also made elaborate arrangements for the irrigation of villages by water-wheels drawing water from the Vitasta.

The reign of Avantivarman (A. D. 855-883) has been rightly called the period of consolidation for the country. Even though the suzeranity of Kashmir was not extended beyond its frontiers as in the time of Lalitaditya, but the king gave ample attention to the internal problems of the country, which had become more pronounced during the reign of weak successors of Lalitaditya.

The king founded the town of "Avantipur" situated at a distance of some seventeen miles from Srinagar on Srinagar Jammu Highway. The fame of Avantipur is still preserved by the huge temples he built there, which are still erect though in dilapidated condition. Among these ruins the most valuable are a series of sculptures which have been placed in the Srinagar Museum. His very astute and wise Minister Sura was also as pious as the king. He also founded a town after his name Surapura called Hurpora at present.

The landmark of his reign is the dredging of the Vitasta undertaken by Engineer Suyya. By his ingenous methods he regulated the course of Vitasta and the scare of famine looming large every year by excessive floods was warded off for ever. New land was also reclaimed and on one of these tracts Sayya built a township named "Suyyapur," Sopore of today. King Avanti Varman died of an affliction at Jyeshtheshvara shrine overlooking the "Dal" lake where he had retired earlier. This shrine is called "Zeethayar" at present near the Chismashi spring. In his court there were such luminaries as Muktakana, Sivaswami, Ananda Vardhana and Ratnakara.

Among the most powerful women who changed the course of the history of Kashmir by their irresistible personality "Dida" deserves full mention. Actually being the consort of "Khemagupta" (A. D. 950-958) she wielded the real regal power, as her consort was a weakling given to licentious habits. She was the daughter of "Simha Raja" the king of Lohara. She tried to give clean administration to the people by getting rid of corrupt ministers and even the prime-minister Phalguna. Many rebellions raised their head but were quelled by Dida as she did not show any mercy.

After the death of her husband she ruled the country as a regent for minor Abhimanyu. However, Abhimanyu died prematurely and his son Nandi Gupta was installed on the throne by Dida his grandmother. He ruled for one year only and died of "witch craft" employed by her grandmother. Her other grand sons Tribhuvaha and Bhima Gupta were also despatched to other world in the same way and path became clear for the queen to ascend the throne herself. She had a love affair with Tunga a cowhered boy from Poonch and made him the prime-minister.

After annointing her brother's son "Samgrama Raja" as the Yuva Raja she died in A.D. 1003 121 after having ruled for 53 long years both as a regent and a monarch in a most ruthless way. After the assasination of Sussala (A.D. 1123), Jayasimha ascended the throne in the face of conspiracies, intrigues and famine. This is the last king of Kashmir as narrated by Kalhana.

His reign was marked by the revolt of Damaras an in the end the king had to make a compromise with them so that the troubles in the land would end. In this way the chronocler had described the reins of 109 kings from Gonanda I to Jayasimha spreading over a period of 1182 B. C. to 1149 A.D. As has been said earlier, Kalhana has given the tenure of reigns of each king from Gonanda III and prior to him the dates have been given in a hyperbolic manner; these have not been consequently added to the span of years given above. The exact number of verses he has employed to condense this account is 7126. Kalliana is at his best when he gives an exact topographical account of ancient Kashmir. The veracity of his interest in this field can be very conveniently established even now after such a lapse of time. It seems probable that he had visited each and every place before describing it in words. The exactness of their position and accurate description are a feather to his cap. By even a cursory perusal of the chronicle the geography of Kashmir can be built with precise dexterity. Copious examples can easily be gleaned from the chronicle to illustrate this point. About the sanctity of the soil of his land he does not exaggerate when he says:

> *"(Where in my county) Keshava (Visnu) and Isana (Siva) shine like Chakrabrt and Vijayesa and also in other forms, there is not space even as a fraction of sesamum seed without having a Tirtha."*

To this day, the whole valley is strewn with holy places, springs and temples and even every pebble of this land has been deified.

The names of towns and villages have Nagara, Pura, Bhoga, Dhama, and Grama, as endings respectively, but in Kashmiri pronounced as Nagra, Pora, Bug, Homa, Gama, respectively; Srinagar e. g. Lyatapora, Shalabug, Danyahoma, and Chandigama. Perhaps the best tribute we can pay to the the precision with which Kalhana has penned down topography is the route of vitasta with its serpentine flow. The names of places through which it flows have been faithfully recorded. The Kashmiri Buga is evidently derived from Bhoga meaning property.

Even though Kashmir valley is hemmed in between continuous chains of mountains, yet. Kalhana has given us a lucid description of the 'Dvaras' or gateways to Kashmir. Through these 'dvaras' invasions took place as also the traffic on both sides was maintained to and fro.

At the eastern corner of the Pir Panjal range Banasala has been mentioned. A castle had been built there perhaps as a watch-tower also. This pass be easily identified as Banihal nowadays. Anantvarman's Minister Sura built a town Surapura, modern Hurpor which has been also mentioned as an entrance to the valley. Herein also a watch-tower was built. This route connected RajaPuri, (Rajouri) with the valley. This road was also known as "Salt road," as alluded to by Ksemendra, as the salt has been all along an imported commodity into Kashmir.

The other route, which connected Kashmir with Lohara (modern Lohrin) and Parantosa (Poonch) passing through the Tosamaidan was very well known at that time. The ancient name of this route was Karkota Dranga.

Even though the village Dranga situated at the foot of the hill still bears that name, yet Dranga in Kalhana's time was an equivalent of watch station. The mountain-ridge known nowadays as Kakudar (Kashmiri) is a corrupt form of KaraKota dhara. Tosa maidan of present day is made up of "Tausi" the plain of "Tohi" as known in Poonch and the persian 'maidan' (a plain).

The frontiers of ancient Kashmir as narrated by Kalhana should also deserve mention here. The actual territory on which the monarch at Srinagar ruled can be ascertained by the reference to chiefs and independent Rajas bordering on the outskirts of the valley beyond mountains.

On the southeast Kashtavata (modern Kishtwar) and Bhadravakasa (modern Badarwah) were ruled by the local Hindu rajas. The Rajas of Chamba (ancient Champa) often had matrimonial alliances with the Lohara Kings which reigned over Kashmir. To the west of Champa and south of Bhadravakasa was situated Vallapura the Billavar of today in Jammu district. The chieftains of this territory were independent and have been described by Kalhana often.

To the south west and west of Kashmir lay the hill-states of Darvabhisara. Actually it is combination of Darvas and Abhisaras finding mention in Mahabharta also. The prominent principality of this region was Rajapuri known as Rajouri today. Owing to its strategic position of being on the route to plains, the rulers of Kashmir always tried to subjugate it. To the North-west of Rajapuri was the territory of Lohara-the moden Lorin (now in Poonch district). The chiefs of this family ruled Kashmir also for some time. In those times Parantosa, (Poonch) was included in Lohara.

On the North west of Parantosa the valley of Kashmir was situated. Vitasta flowed in between the valley and further to the west lay the Kingdom of Urasa, district Hazara of today to which many expeditions by kings of Kashmir were led.

The tract of land now known as Keran or Karnaha bore the old name of Karnaha, though under local rule, paid tribute to Kashmir kings. The valley of Kishenganga was known as Drava derived from Duranda as given by Kalhana. This was a feudatory state of Kashmir and one of the most sacred Tirthas of Kashmir 'Sarada' is situated therein. This is now under the unauthorised rule of Pakistan.

At the other end of this valley the territory of Dards (Dard-Desa) is located. It was a separate kingdom though small in extent. This is, therefore, in nutshell the political topography as given by Kalhana about the Kashmir of his times.

As has been said earlier, Kalhna is concerned only with the rise and fall of kings and people at large have been left untouched by him directly. However, the mercurial fate of kings which at times smiled at them and at times frowned also, has afforded sufficient opportunites to him to study the behaviour and character of his people.

The most noteworthy trait of Kashmiri character is its tolerance and catholicity. There are numerous examples in his chronicle to show that Buddhist viharas and stupas were built side by side with Visnu and Siva temples. The great conqueror Lalita Ditya though himself a Vaisnava erected a massive Buddhist vihara at his newly built capital Parihasapura.

Even though the king professed a certain faith, his ministers or people could subscribe freely to a any other faith. King Avanti Varman was a Vaishnava but his minister Sura was a Shaiva and there was no tension between the two on this score. Even the Kashmir rulers did not hesitate to appoint ministers of foreign descent and foreign faith. Cankuna the Turk was the minister of Lalitaditya 'Sarada' Mukhtapida. The secular out look towards life was ever present in Kashmir even in those hoary days.

The foreigners like Khasas, Bombas, Turuskas, Dards and Bhatitiyas etc were free to practise their own faith and if they felt impressed by Hindu or Buddhist out-look on life and embraced one of these, there was no compulsion in this behalf. Not a single communal trouble is mentioned by Kalhana in his chronicle. The holicity of a Kashmiri can very faithfully be proved the existence of Turuska-Raja Bhairava, a Siva shrine at the new colony Narsinghgarh, Srinagar.

As the name conclusively suggests that a foreign Turk has been made into a Bhairava and is being propitiated even now regularly. The foreign kings like Huska, Juska, and Kanishka ruled over the country and have left the annals of Kashmir history by founding cities after their names.

Kashmiris according to him are also fatalists of the highest order. They ascribe all their woes and otherwise to the unseen and unknown fate, perhaps this trait in their character has to a large extent deprived them of their initiative but at the same time has also afforded them calm composure at the changes which so frequently took place at that time:

> *"He (Guru Isana) was amazed and thought how this would come about. Pondering for long he said (to himself) that the power of fate is unpredictable." The people of Kashmir were so much enthralled by this unseen power of fate that Kalhana says that "fate is the mine of all miracles."*

The firm belief in what is ordained already can be illustrated eloquently by this:

> *"The lightening of good fortune, the crane of fame, the thunder of bravery, and the rainbow of glory come in the wake of the cloud of fate."*

As a natural corollary to the above trait, Kashmiri character has firm belief in Divine retribution. Evil doer can in no way reap a harvest of virtue. Only good actions can be rewarded and bad deeds will receive punishment sooner or later. There is no escape from this:

> *"Cursed by the oppressed subjects, the king's (Shankar Varman's) who was taking to evil path, some twenty or thirty sons died without being ill (suddenly)."*

The Kasbmiri subjects being powerless before tyrants invoked the Divine wrath over them and felt gratified to see that such despots fleecing their subjects did lose family, life, name, and even glory.

Since good deeds are rewarded, hence the Kashmiris have all along been charitible-this being a good deed, helping the needy. The importance ot charity has been extolled and consequently practised. Alms giving has been stressed in Niti Shastras as well as in the Mahabharta also, and is an inalienable ingredient of Hindu culture. Kalhana says that even if wealth may be got through fraud but becomes righteous if given in charity.

As a matter of fact, a peoples' revolt has never taken place in Kashmir as narrated by Kalhana.

The kings often squeezed blood from their subjects who were already groaing under the weight of their abject poverty. Moreover the favourites of kings exploited them to their fill. Perhaps they drew satisfaction from the Fatalism and the Divine retribution present in their character. Indigenous rule at times changed hands with foreign domination. Intrigue, treason and lust reigned supreme in royal courts.

To all this, Kashmiris reacted in a most stoical way. Whenever counter-conspiracies are hatched, it is not the Kashmiri but a foreigner finding favour with the king. Sometimes revolutions of far-reaching consequences rocked their native land but they sat with fingers crossed. This clearly shows that they did not feel any sense of partipation or belonging with high-ups above them. Hence Kalhana very faithfully draws the picture of idle and indifferent crowds in the bazars:

> *"The indifferent crowds without any feelings whatssoever, looked at their king fighing with his contenders at the bridge, as if it was a horse-show on the first day of Asvin Month."*

In view of such a pacifist and indifferent attitude to life, Kashmiri character has obviously been nonmilitant. Inflicting injury on others could not be their blood as they believed in Divine retribution, Violence in any form cannot be termed as a noble act, being essentially an evil action, the Kaslimiris refrain from indulging in such actions. Absence of militant traits in their character has given ample opportunities to Kalhana to jeer at his own countrymen:

> *"Canga etc who were the confidants and advisers of Tonga became dumb-founded with terror like women, though being armed."*

Consequently Kashmiri soldier was undenendable and the kings had to employ mercenaries from fighting clans in the adjoining areas. The pepole detested war and when a foreign army came to invade them, they felt despondent. They could never think of giving it a fight:

> *"At the sight of a hostile army the people felt their bodies aching as if paralysed by the sudden appearance of untimely clouds, and their energy began to give way."*

A Kashmiri could never be a spendthrift in as much as he had to provide for the rainy day. Such "rainy days" were legion in his time in the shape of famines seiges, and invasions. So, he is calculating in expenditure and does not waste his hard-earned money. Even the kings learnt the utility of such wise-spending:

> *"(The king Uccala) a Kashmiri as he was, did not invest his riches in building and dismantling palaces time and again; or purchasing horses only to make these apart of the dust or the robbers (respectively)."*

These pages have most succinctly brought into bold relief the claims of Kalhana as a chronicler. Since he is the first to initiate this form of literary-writing yet, as has been shown, he is humble and does not brag about his prowess in this field. He may not touch the high water-mark of historical attitude of mind, but is very careful about his shortcomings also. All the criticism that is levelled against him does not ruffle him.

No better tribute could be paid to the denizens of this land of "learning, palacial houses, saffron, icy water and grapes difficult to find in heaven even," for their piety and spiritual attainments:

> *"The inhabitants of this land can be conquered only by spiritual force and never by brute-force of arms, hence they have the fear of the other world only."*

9

Hindu Temple Architecture

A small Hindu temple consists of an inner sanctum, the *garbha griha* or womb-chamber, in which the image is housed, often circumambulation, a congregation hall, and possibly an antechamber and porch. The sanctum is crowned by a tower-like *shikara*. At the turn of the first millennium CE two major types of temples existed, the northern or Nagara style and the southern or Dravida type of temple. They are distinguishable by the shape and decoration of their shikharas (Dehejia 1997).

- Nagara style: The tower is beehive shaped.
- Dravida: The tower consists of progressively smaller storeys of pavilions.

The earliest Nagar temples are in Karnataka (e.g. Galaganath at Pattadakal) and some very early Dravida-style temples (e.g. Teli-ka-Mandir at Gwalior) are actually in North India. A complex style termed Vesara was once common in Karnataka which combined the two styles.

This may be seen in the classic Hindu temples of India and Southeast Asia, such as Angkor Wat, Brihadisvara Temple, Khajuraho, Mukteshvara, and Prambanan.

Design and History

The temple is a representation of the macrocosm (the universe) as well as the microcosm (the inner space).

The Magadha empire rose with the Shishunaga dynasty in around 650 BC. The Ashtadhyayi of Panini, the great grammarian of the 5th century BC speaks of images that were used in Hindu temple worship. The ordinary images were called pratikriti and the images for worship were called archa. Patanjali, the 2nd century BC author of the Mahabhashya commentary on the Ashtadhyayi, tells us more about the images. Deity images for sale were called Shivaka etc., but an archa of Shiva was just called Shiva. Patanjali mentions Shiva and Skanda deities. There is also mention of the worship of Vasudeva (Krishna). We are also told that some images could be moved and some were immoveable. Panini also says that an archa was not to be sold and that there were people (priests) who obtained their livelihood by taking care of it.

Panini and Patanjali mention temples which were called prasadas. The earlier Shatapatha Brahmana of the period of the Vedas, informs us of an image in the shape of Purusha which was placed within the altar.

The Vedic books describe the plan of the temple to be square. This plan is divided into 64 or 81 smaller square, where each of these represent a specific divinity.

Amongst the foremost interpreters of Indian art and architecture are Stella Kramrisch, Vidya Dehija, M.A. Dhaky, Lokesh Chandra and Kapila Vatsyayan. The greatest living traditional temple architect is Dr. V. Ganapati Sthapati (Chennai) the only living Shilpi Guru. He is followed by his grand nephew Santhanam Krishna Sthapati of Chennai. Both are associated with The American University of Mayonic Science and Technology.

Badami Chalukya Architecture

The *Chalukya style* originated during A.D. 450 in Aihole and perfected in Pattadakal and Badami.

The period of Badami Chalukyas was a glorious era in the history of Indian architecture. The capital of the Chalukyas, Vatapi (Badami, in Bagalkot district, North Karnataka in Karnataka) is situated at the mouth of a ravine between two rocky hills. Between 500 and 757 AD, Badami Chalukyas established the foundations of cave temple architecture, on the banks of the Malaprabha River. Those styles mainly include Aihole, Pattadakal and Badami, The sites were built out of sand-stone cut into enormous blocks from the outcrops in the chains of the *Kaladgi hills*.

At Badami, Chalukyas carved some of the finest cave temples. Mahakuta, the large trees under which the shrine nestles.

In Aihole, known as the "Cradle of Indian architecture", there are over 150 temples scattered around the village. The Ladkhan temple is the oldest. The Durga Temple is notable for its semi-circular apse, elevated plinth and the gallery that encircles the sanctum sanctorum. A sculpture of Vishnu sitting atop a large cobra is at *Hutchimali Temple*. The Ravalphadi cave temple celebrates the many forms of Shiva. Other temples include the *Konthi temple complex* and the *Meguti Jain temple.*

Pattadakal is a (World Heritage Site), where one finds the *Virupaksha temple*; it is the biggest temple, having carved scenes from the Ramayana and the Mahabharata. Other temples at Pattadakal are Mallikarjuna, Kashivishwanatha, Galaganatha and Papanath.

Gadag Architecture Style

The *Gadag style of Architecture* is also called Western Chalukya architecture. The style flourished for 150 years (1050 to 1200 CE); in this period, about 50 temples were built. Some examples are The *Saraswati temple* in the Trikuteshwara temple complex at Gadag, the Doddabasappa Temple at Dambal, the Kasivisvesvara Temple at Lakkundi, and the Amriteshwara temple at Annigeri. which is marked by ornate pillars with intricate sculpture. This style originated during the period of the Kalyani Chalukyas, (also known as Western Chalukya) Someswara I.

Tripartite Struggle

The Tripartite struggle was a struggle for power and control over the central Gangetic valley among three major empires in India during the 8th Century. These three empires were the Pratiharas, the Rastrakutas and the Palas. The Pratiharas were settled in western India in the Avanti-Jalaor region. The Rastrakutas who were essentially from the Deccan region were interested in Kannauj due to the fact that it formed an important center for trade and commerce. The Palas occupied the eastern parts of India (present day Bengal) and were very strong contenders in this struggle.

The Pratihara ruler named Vatsaraja had a dire ambition to take control over the region of Kannauj. At the same time, the Pala ruler Dharmapala also had an eye over the same region. This brought the two rulers into a conflict. During this time the Rastrakuta king Dhruva attacked the two of them and claimed to have won. This is what led to the Tripartite Struggle. Dharmapala however somehow gained control over the territory and set his nominee on the throne. The Rastrakutas were busy with their own problems in their kingdom in south.

During the end of the 8th Century, the successor of Pratihara ruler Vatsaraja named Nagabhata II attacked Kannauj and established his rule, though it was short lived. In the beginning of the 9th Century he was defeated by the Rastrakuta ruler Govinda III. However, he was kept busy in internal politics by an alliance of different kingdoms in the south. The struggle for Kannauj became serious after the Pratiharas exercised control over it.

During the rule of Krishna III, there was successful campaign against the Cholas. The Rastrakutas also formed a matrimonial relationship with the Gangas and defeated the kingdom of Vengi. By the end of the 9th Century the power of the Rastrakutas started to decline along with the Palas. This was seen as an ideal opportunity by the feudal king Taila II who defeated the Rastrakuta ruler and declared his kingdom there. This came to be known the Later Chalukya dynasty. Their kingdom included the states of Karnataka, Konkan and northern Godavari. By the end of the tripartite struggle, the Pratiharas emerged victorious and established themselves as the rulers of central India.

Rashtrakuta Dynasty

The Rashtrakuta Empire was a royal Indian dynasty ruling large parts of southern, central and northern India between the sixth and the tenth centuries. During this period they ruled as several closely related, but individual clans. The earliest known Rashtrakuta inscription is a seventh century copper plate grant that mentions their rule from Manpur in the Malwa region of modern Madhya Pradesh. Other ruling Rashtrakuta clans from the same period mentioned in inscriptions were the kings of Achalapur which is modern Elichpur in Maharashtra and the rulers of Kannauj. Several controversies exist regarding the origin of these early Rashtrakutas, their native home and their language.

The clan that ruled from Elichpur was a feudatory of the Badami Chalukyas and during the rule of Dantidurga, it overthrew Chalukya Kirtivarman II and went on to build an impressive empire with the Gulbarga region in modern Karnataka as its base. This clan came to be known as the Rashtrakutas of Manyakheta, rising to power in South India in 753. At the same time the Pala dynasty of Bengal and the Prathihara dynasty of Malwa were gaining force in eastern and northwestern India respectively.

This period, between the eight and the tenth centuries, saw a tripartite struggle for the resources of the rich Gangetic plains, each of these three empires annexing the seat of power at Kannauj for short periods of time. At their peak the Rashtrakutas of Manyakheta ruled a vast empire stretching from the Ganga River and Yamuna River doab in the north to Cape Comorin in the south, a fruitful time of political expansion, architectural achievements and famous literary contributions. The early kings of this dynasty were Hindu but the later kings were strongly influenced by Jainism.

During their rule, Jain mathematicians and scholars contributed important works in Kannada and Sanskrit. Amoghavarsha I was the most famous king of this dynasty and wrote *Kavirajamarga,* a landmark literary work in the Kannada language. Architecture reached a milestone in the Dravidian style, the finest example of which is seen in the Kailasanath Temple at Ellora. Other important contributions are the sculptures of Elephanta Caves in modern Maharashtra as well as the Kashivishvanatha temple and the Jain Narayana temple at Pattadakal in modern Karnataka, all of which are UNESCO World Heritage Sites.

History

The origin of Rashtrakuta dynasty has been a controversial topic. These issues pertain to the origins of the earliest ancestors of the Rashtrakutas during the time of Emperor Ashoka in the second century BCE, and the connection between the several Rashtrakuta dynasties that ruled small kingdoms in northern and central India and the Deccan between the sixth and seventh centuries. The relationship of these medieval Rashtrakutas to the most famous later dynasty, the Rashtrakutas of Manyakheta (present day Malkhed in the Gulbarga district, Karnataka state), who ruled between the eighth and tenth centuries has also been debated.

The sources of Rashtrakuta history include medieval inscriptions, ancient literature in the Pali language, contemporaneous literature in Sanskrit and Kannada and the notes of the Arab travellers. Theories about the dynastic lineage (*Surya*

Vamsa—Solar line and *Chandra Vamsa*—Lunar line), the native region and the ancestral home have been proposed, based on information gleaned from inscriptions, royal emblems, the ancient clan names such as "Rashtrika", epithets (*Ratta, Rashtrakuta, Lattalura Puravaradhiswara*), the names of dynasty princes and princesses, and clues from relics such as coins. Scholars debate over which of the many ethnic groups the early Rashtrakutas belonged, the north western ethnic groups of India, the Kannadiga, Reddi, the Maratha, or the ethnic tribes from the Punjab region.

Scholars however concur that the kings of the imperial dynasty in the eighth to tenth century made the Kannada language as important as Sanskrit. Rashtrakuta inscriptions are in the two languages of Kannada and Sanskrit (historians Sheldon Pollock and Jan Houben claim they are mostly in Kannada), and the kings encouraged literature in both languages. The earliest existing Kannada literary writings are credited to their court poets and royalty. Though these Rashtrakutas were Kannadigas, they were conversant in a northern Deccan language as well.

The heart of the Rashtrakutas empire included nearly all of Karnataka, Maharashtra and parts of Andhra Pradesh, an area which the Rastrakutas ruled for over two centuries. The Samangadh copper plate grant (753) confirms that the feudatory King Dantidurga, who probably ruled from Achalapura in Berar (modern Elichpur in Maharashtra), defeated the great Karnatic army (referring to the army of the Badami Chalukyas) of Kirtivarman II of Badami in 753 and took control of the northern regions of the Chalukya empire. He then helped his father-in-law, Pallava King Nandivarman regain Kanchi from the Chalukyas and defeated the Gurjaras of Malwa, and the kings of Kalinga, Kosala and Srisailam.

Dantidurga's successor Krishna I brought major portions of present day Karnataka and Konkan under his control. During the rule of Dhruva Dharavarsha who took control in 780, the kingdom expanded into an empire that encompassed all of the territory between the Kaveri River and Central India. He led successful expeditions to Kannauj, the seat of northern Indian power where he defeated the Gurjara Pratiharas and the Palas of Bengal, gaining him fame and vast booty but not more territory. He also brought the Eastern Chalukyas and Gangas of Talakad under his control. According to a historian, the Rashtrakutas became a pan-India power during his rule. The ascent of Dhruva Dharavarsha's third son, Govinda III, to the throne heralded an era of success like never before. There is uncertainty about the location of the early capital of the Rashtrakutas at this time. During his rule there was a three way conflict between the Rashtrakutas, the Palas and the Pratiharas for control over the Gangetic plains. Describing his victories over the Pratihara King Nagabhatta II and the Pala King Dharmapala, the Sanjan inscription states the horses of Govinda III drank from the icy waters of the Himalayan streams and his war elephants tasted the sacred waters of the Ganga.

His military exploits have been compared to those of Alexander the Great and Pandava Arjuna of Mahabharata. Having conquered Kannauj, he travelled south, took firm hold over Gujarat, Kosala (Kaushal), Gangavadi, humbled the Pallavas of Kanchi, installed a ruler of his choice in Vengi and received two statues as an act of submission from the king of Ceylon (one statue of the king and another of his minister). The Cholas, the Pandyas and the Keralas all paid him tribute. As one historian puts it, the drums of the Deccan were heard from the Himalayan caves to the shores of the Malabar. The Rashtrakutas empire now spread over the areas from Cape Comorin to Kannauj and from Banaras to Broach.

The successor of Govinda III, Amoghavarsha I made Manyakheta his capital and ruled a large empire. Manyakheta remained the Rashtrakutas regal capital until the end of the empire. He came to the throne in 814 but it was not until 821 that he had suppressed revolts from feudatories and ministers. Amoghavarsha I made peace with the Gangas by giving them his two daughters in marriage, and then defeated the invading Eastern Chalukyas at Vingavalli and assumed the title *Viranarayana*. His rule was not as militant as that of Govinda III as he preferred to maintain friendly relations with his neighbours, the Gangas, the Eastern Chalukyas and the Pallavas with whom he also cultivated marital ties.

His era was an enriching one for the arts, literature and religion. Widely seen as the most famous of the Rashtrakuta kings, Amoghavarsha I was an accomplished scholar in Kannada and Sanskrit. His *Kavirajamarga* is considered an important landmark in Kannada poetics and *Prashnottara Ratnamalika* in Sanskrit is a writing of high merit and was later translated into the Tibetan language. Because of his religious temperament, his interest in the arts and literature and his peace-loving nature, he has been compared to the emperor Ashoka and called "Ashoka of the South". During the rule of Krishna II, the empire faced a revolt from the Eastern Chalukyas and its size decreased to the area including most of the Western Deccan and Gujarat. Krishna II ended the independent status of the Gujarat branch and brought it under direct control from Manyakheta. Indra III recovered the dynasty's fortunes in central India by defeating the Paramara and then invaded the doab region of the Ganges and Jamuna rivers. He also defeated the dynasty's traditional enemies, the Pratiharas and the Palas, while maintaining his influence over Vengi.

The effect of his victories in Kannauj lasted several years according to the 930 copper plate inscription of King Govinda IV. After a succession of weak kings during whose reigns the empire lost control of territories in the north and east, Krishna III the last great king consolidated the empire so that it stretched from the Narmada River to Kaveri River and included the northern Tamil country (Tondaimandalam) while levying tribute on the king of Ceylon.

During the rule of Khottiga Amoghavarsha, the Paramara King Siyaka Harsha attacked the empire and plundered Manyakheta, the capital of Rastrakutas. This seriously undermined the reputation of the Rastrakuta Empire and consequently led to its downfall. The final decline was sudden as Tailapa II, a feudatory of the Rashtrakuta ruling from Tardavadi province in modern Bijapur district, declared himself independent by taking advantage of this defeat. Indra IV, the last king, committed Sallekhana (fasting unto death practised by Jain monks) at Shravanabelagola. With the fall of the Rashtrakutas, their feudatories and related clans in the Deccan and northern India declared independence.

The Western Chalukyas annexed Manyakheta and made it their capital until 1015 and built an impressive empire in the Rashtrakuta heartland during the eleventh century. The focus of dominance shifted to the Krishna River-Godavari River doab called Vengi. The former feudatories of the Rashtrakutas in western Deccan were brought under control of the Chalukyas and the hitherto suppressed Cholas of Tanjore became their arch enemies in the south.

In conclusion, the rise of Rashtrakutas of Manyakheta had a great impact on India, even on India's north. Sulaiman (851), Al Masudi (944) and Ibn Khurdadba (912) wrote that their empire was the largest in contemporary India and Sulaiman further called it one among the four great contemporary empires of the world. Some historians have called these times an "Age of Imperial Kannauj".

Since the Rashtrakutas successfully captured Kannauj, levied tribute on its rulers and presented themselves as masters of North India, the era could also be called the "Age of Imperial Karnataka". During their political expansion into central and northern India in the eighth to the tenth centuries, the Rashtrakutas or their relatives created several kingdoms that either ruled during the reign of the parent empire or continued to rule for centuries after the its fall or came to power much later. Well known among these were the Rashtrakutas of Gujarat (757–888), the Rattas of Saundatti (875–1230) in modern Karnataka, the Gahadavalas of Kannauj (1068–1223), the Rashtrakutas of Rajasthan (known as Rajputana) and ruling from Hastikundi or Hathundi (893–996), Dahal (near Jabalpur), Mandore (near Jodhpur), the Rathores of Dhanop, Rashtraudha dynasty of Mayuragiri in modern Maharashtra and Rashtrakutas of Kannauj.

Administration

Rashtrakuta Kings (753-982)	
Dantidurga	(735-756)
Krishna I	(756-774)
Govinda II	(774-780)
Dhruva Dharavarsha	(780-793)
Govinda III	(793-814)
Amoghavarsha I	(814-878)
Krishna II	(878-914)
Indra III	(914-929)
Amoghavarsha II	(929-930)
Govinda IV	(930 – 936)
Amoghavarsha III	(936 – 939)
Krishna III	(939 – 967)
Khottiga Amoghavarsha	(967 – 972)
Karka II	(972 – 973)
Indra IV	(973 – 982)
Tailapa II (*Western Chalukyas*)	(973-997)

Inscriptions and other literary records show the Rashtrakutas selected the crown prince based on heredity. The crown did not always pass on to the eldest son. Abilities were considered more important than age and chronology of birth, as exemplified by the crowning of Govinda III who was the third son of king Dhruva Dharavarsha. The most important position under the king was the Chief Minister (*Mahasandhivigrahi*) whose position came with five insignia commensurate with his position namely, a flag, a conch, a fan, a white umbrella, a large drum and five musical instruments called *Panchamahashabdas*.

Under him was the commander (*Dandanayaka*), the foreign minister (*Mahakshapataladhikrita*) and a prime minister (*Mahamatya* or *Purnamathya*), all of whom were usually associated with one of the feudatory kings and must have held a position in government equivalent to a premier. A *Mahasamantha* was a feudatory or higher ranking regal officer. All cabinet ministers were well versed in political science (*Rajneeti*) and possessed military training. There were cases where woman supervised significant areas as when Revakanimaddi, daughter of Amoghavarsha I, administered Edathore *Vishaya*.

The kingdom was divided into *Mandala* or *Rashtras* (provinces). A *Rashtra* was ruled by a Rashtrapathi who on occasion was the emperor himself. Amoghavarsha I's empire had sixteen *Rashtras*. Under a *Rashtra* was a *Vishaya* (district) overseen by a Vishayapathi. Trusted ministers sometimes ruled more than a *Rashtra*. For example, Bankesha, a commander of Amoghavarsha I headed Banavasi-12000, Belvola-300, Puligere-300, Kunduru-500 and Kundarge-70, the suffix designating the number of villages in that territory. Below the *Vishaya* was the *Nadu* looked after by the Nadugowda or Nadugavunda; sometimes there were two such officials, one assuming the position through heredity and another appointed centrally. The lowest division was a *Grama* or village administered by a *Gramapathi* or *Prabhu Gavunda*.

The Rashtrakuta army consisted of a large infantry, numerous horseman, and many elephants. A standing army was always ready for war in a cantonment (*Sthirabhuta Kataka*) in the regal capital of Manyakheta. Large armies were also maintained by the feudatory kings who were expected to contribute to the defense of the empire in case of war. Chieftains and all the officials also served as commanders whose postings were transferable if the need arose.

The Rashtrakutas issued coins (minted in an *Akkashale*) such as *Suvarna, Drammas* in silver and gold weighing 65 grains, *Kalanju* weighing 48 grains, *Gadyanaka* weighing 96 grains, *Kasu* weighing 15 grains, *Manjati* with 2.5 grains and *Akkam* of 1.25 grain.

Economy

The Rashtrakuta economy was sustained by its natural and agricultural produce, its manufacturing revenues and moneys gained from its conquests. Cotton was the chief crop of the regions of southern Gujarat, Khandesh and Berar. Minnagar, Gujarat, Ujjain, Paithan and Tagara were important centres of textile industry. Muslin cloth were manufactured in Paithan and Warangal.

The cotton yarn and cloth was exported from Bharoch. White calicos were manufactured in Burhanpur and Berar and exported to Persia, Turkey, Poland, Arabia and Cairo. The Konkan region, ruled by the feudatory Silharas, produced large quantities of betel leaves, coconut and rice while the lush forests of Mysore, ruled by the feudatory Gangas, produced such woods as sandal, timber, teak and ebony. Incense and perfumes were exported from the ports of Thana and Saimur.

The Deccan soil, though not as fertile as that of the Gangetic plains, was rich in minerals. The copper mines of Cudappah, Bellary, Chanda, Buldhana, Narsingpur, Ahmadnagar, Bijapur and Dharwar were an important source of income and played an important role in the economy. Diamonds were mined in Cudappah, Bellary, Kurnool and Golconda; the capital Manyakheta and Devagiri were important diamond and jewellery trading centres. The leather industry and tanning flourished in Gujarat and some regions of northern Maharashtra. Mysore with its vast elephant herds was important for the ivory industry.

The Rashtrakuta empire controlled most of the western sea board of the subcontinent which facilitated its maritime trade. The Gujarat branch of the empire earned a significant income from the port of Bharoch, one of the most prominent ports in the world at that time. The empire's chief exports were cotton yarn, cotton cloth, muslins, hides, mats, indigo, incense, perfumes, betel nuts, coconuts, sandal, teak, timber, sesame oil and ivory.

Its major imports were pearls, gold, dates from Arabia, slaves, Italian wines, tin, lead, topaz, storax, sweet clover, flint glass, antimony, gold and silver coins, singing boys and girls (for the entertainment of the royalty) from other lands. Trading in horses was an important and profitable business, monopolised by the Arabs and some local merchants. The Rashtrakuta government levied a shipping tax of one golden *Gadyanaka* on all foreign vessels embarking to any other ports and a fee of one silver *Ctharna* (a coin) on vessels travelling locally.

Artists and craftsman operated as corporations (guilds) rather than as individual business. Inscriptions mention guilds of weavers, oilmen, artisans, basket and mat makers and fruit sellers. A Saundatti inscription refers to an assemblage of all the people of a district headed by the guilds of the region. Some guilds were considered superior to others, just as some corporations were, and received royal charters determining their powers and privileges. Inscriptions suggest these guilds had their own militia to protect goods in transit and, like village assemblies, they operated banks that lent money to traders and businesses.

The government's income came from five principal sources: regular taxes, occasional taxes, fines, income taxes, miscellaneous taxes and tributes from feudatories. An emergency tax was imposed occasionally and were applicable when the kingdom was under duress, such as when it faced natural calamities, or was preparing for war or overcoming war's ravages. Income tax included taxes on crown land, wasteland, specific types of trees considered valuable to economy, mines, salt, treasures unearthed by prospectors. Additionally, customary presents were give to the king or royal officers on such festive occasions as marriage or the birth of a son.

The king determined the tax levels based on need and circumstances in the kingdom while ensuring that an undue burden was not placed on the peasants. The land owner or tenant paid a variety of taxes, including land taxes, produce taxes and payment of the overhead for maintenance of the Gavunda (village head). Land taxes were varied, based on type of land, its produce and situation and ranged from 8% to 16%.

A Banavasi inscription of 941 mentions reassessment of land tax due to the drying up of an old irrigation canal in the region.

The land tax may have been as high as 20% to pay for expenses of a military frequently at war. In most of the kingdom, land taxes were paid in goods and services and rarely was cash accepted. A portion of all taxes earned by the government (usually 15%) was returned to the villages for maintenance.

Taxes were levied on artisans such as potters, sheep herders, weavers, oilmen, shopkeepers, stall owners, brewers and gardeners. Taxes on perishable items such as fish, meat, honey, medicine, fruits and essentials like fuel was as high as 16%. Taxes on salt and minerals were mandatory although the empire did not claim sole ownership of mines, implying that private mineral prospecting and the quarrying business may have been active. The state claimed all such properties whose deceased legal owner had no immediate family to make an inheritance claim. Under miscellaneous taxes were ferry and house taxes. Only Brahmins and their temple institutions were taxed at a lower rate.

Culture

Religion: The Rashtrakutas kings supported the popular religions of the day in the traditional spirit of religious tolerance. Scholars have offered various arguments regarding which specific religion the Rashtrakutas favoured, basing their evidence on inscriptions, coins and contemporary literature. Some claim the Rashtrakutas were inclined towards Jainism since many of the scholars who flourished in their courts and wrote in Sanskrit, Kannada and a few in Apabhramsha and Prakrit were Jains.

The Rashtrakutas built well known Jain temples at locations such as Lokapura in Bagalkot district and their loyal feudatory, the Western Ganga Dynasty, built Jain monuments at Shravanabelagola and Kambadahalli. Scholars have suggested that Jainism was a principal religion at the very heart of the empire, modern Karnataka, accounting for a more than 30% of the population and dominating the culture of the region.

King Amoghavarsha I was a disciple of the Jain acharya Jinasena and wrote in his religious writing, *Prashnottara Ratnamalika,* "having bowed to Varaddhamana (Mahavira), I write Prashnottara Ratnamalika". The mathematician Mahaviracharya wrote in his *Ganita Sarasangraha,* "The subjects under Amoghavarsha are happy and the land yields plenty of grain. May the kingdom of King Nripatunga Amoghavarsha, follower of Jainism ever increase far and wide." Amoghavarsha may have taken up Jainism in his old age.

However, few of the Rashtrakuta kings were Hindus, followers of the Shaiva, Vaishnava and Shakta faiths. Almost all of their inscriptions begin with an invocation to god Vishnu or god Shiva. The Sanjan inscriptions tell of King Amoghavarsha I sacrificing a finger from his left hand at the Lakshmi temple at Kolhapur to avert a calamity in his kingdom. King Dantidurga performed the *Hiranyagarbha* (horse sacrifice) and the Sanjan and Cambay plates of King Govinda IV mention Brahmins performing such rituals as *Rajasuya*, *Vajapeya* and *Agnishtoma*. An early copper plate grant of King Dantidurga (753) shows an image of god Shiva and the coins of his successor, King Krishna I (768), bear the legend *Parama Maheshwara* (another name for Shiva).

The kings' titles such as *Veeranarayana* showed their Vaishnava leanings. Their flag had the sign of the Ganga and Yamuna rivers, perhaps copied from the Badami Chalukyas. The famous Kailasnatha temple at Ellora and other rock-cut caves attributed to them show that the Hinduism was flourishing. Their family deity was a goddess by name *Latana* (also known as *Rashtrashyena*, *Manasa Vindyavasini*) who took the form of a falcon to save the kingdom. They built temples with iconification and ornamentation that satisfied the needs of different faiths. The temple at Salotgi was meant for followers of Shiva and Vishnu and the temple at Kargudri was meant for worshipers of Shiva, Vishnu and Bhaskara (Surya, the sun god).

In short, the Rashtrakuta rule was tolerant to multiple popular religions, Jainism, Vaishnavaism and Shaivism. Buddhism too found support and was popular in places such as Dambal and Balligavi, although it had declined significantly by this time. The decline of Buddhism in South India began in the 8th century with the spread of Adi Shankara's Advaita philosophy.

Islamic contact with South India began as early as the 7th century, a result of trade between the Southern kingdoms and Arab lands. Jumma Masjids existed in the Rashtrakuta empire by the 10th century and many Muslims lived and mosques flourished on the coasts, specifically in towns such as Kayalpattanam and Nagore. Muslim settlers married local women; their children were known as Mappilas (*Moplahs*) and were actively involved in horse trading and manning shipping fleets.

Society

Chronicles mention more castes than the four commonly known castes in the Hindu social system, some as many as seven castes. One traveller's account mentions sixteen castes including the four basic castes of Brahmins, Kshatriya, Vaishya and Chandalas. The *Zakaya* or *Lahud* caste consisted of communities specialising in dance and acrobatics. People in the professions of sailing, hunting, weaving, cobblery, basket making and fishing belonged to specific castes or subcastes. The *Antyajas* caste provided many menial services to the wealthy. Brahmins enjoyed the highest status in Rashtrakuta society; only those Kshatriyas in the *Sat-Kshatriya* sub-caste (noble Kshatriyas) were higher in status.

The Jains enjoyed a very high status during this period.

The careers of Brahmins usually related to education, the judiciary, astrology, mathematics, poetry and philosophy or the occupation of hereditary administrative posts. Also Brahmins increasingly practiced non-Brahminical professions (agriculture, trade in betel nuts and martial posts). Capital punishment, although widespread, was not given to the royal Kshatriya sub-castes or to Brahmins found guilty of heinous crimes as the killing of a Brahmin in medieval Hindu India was itself considered a heinous crime. As an alternate punishment to enforce the law a Brahmin's right hand and left foot was severed, leaving that person disabled.

By the ninth century, kings from all the four castes had occupied the highest seat in the monarchical system in Hindu India. Admitting Kshatriyas to Vedic schools along with Brahmins was customary, but the children of the Vaishya and Shudra castes were not allowed. Landownership by people of all castes is recorded in inscriptions Intercaste marriages in the higher castes were only between highly placed Kshatriya girls and Brahmin boys, but was relatively frequent among other castes. Intercaste functions were rare and dining together between people of various castes was avoided.

Joint families were the norm but legal separations between brothers and even father and son have been recorded in inscriptions. Women and daughters had rights over property and land as there are inscriptions recording the sale of land by women. The arranged marriage system followed a strict policy of early marriage for women. Among Brahmins, boys married at or below 16 years of age and the brides chosen for them were 12 or younger. This age policy was not strictly followed by other castes. Sati (a custom in which a dead man's widow tended to immolate herself on her husband's funeral pyre) was practiced but the few examples noted in inscriptions were mostly in the royal families. The system of shaving the heads of widows was infrequent as epigraphs note that widows were allowed to grow their hair but decorating it was discouraged. The remarriage of a widow was rare among the upper castes and more accepted among the lower castes.

In the general population men wore two simple pieces of cloth, a loose garment on top and a garment worn like a *dhoti* for the lower part of the body. Only kings could wear turbans, a practice that spread to the masses much later. Dancing was a popular entertainment and inscriptions speak of royal women being charmed by dancers, both male and female, in the king's palace. Devadasis (girls were "married" to a deity or temple) were often present in temples. Other recreational activities included attending animal fights of the same or different species. An Atkur hero stone (*virgal*) has been found made for the favourite hound of the feudatory Western Ganga King Butuga II that died fighting a wild boar in a sport. There are records of game preserves for hunting by royalty. Astronomy and astrology were well developed as subjects of study, and there were many superstitious beliefs such as catching a snake alive proved a woman's chastity. Old persons suffering from incurable diseases preferred to end their lives by drowning in the sacred waters of a pilgrim site or by a ritual burning.

Literature

Kannada became more prominent as a literary language during the Rashtrakuta rule with its script and literature showing remarkable growth, dignity and productivity. This period effectively marked the end of the classical Prakrit and Sanskrit era. Court poets and royalty created eminent works in Kannada and Sanskrit that spanned such literary forms as prose, poetry, rhetoric, Hindu epics and life history of Jain tirthankaras. Famous scholars wrote on secular subjects such as mathematics.

Kavirajamarga (850) by King Amoghavarsha I is the earliest available book on rhetoric and poetics in Kannada, though it is evident from this book that other styles of Kannada literature and poetry had already existed in previous centuries. *Kavirajamarga* is a guide to poets (*Kavishiksha*) that aims to standardize these various styles. The book refers to early Kannada prose and poetry writers such as Durvinita, perhaps the 6th century monarch of Western Ganga Dynasty.

A jain writer named Pampa, widely regarded as one of the greatest Kannada writers, became famous for *Adipurana* (941). Written in champu (mixed prose-verse style) style, it is the life history of the first Jain tirthankara Rishabhadeva. He is called as Adikavi Pampa. Pampa's other notable work was *Vikramarjuna Vijaya* (941), the author's version of the Hindu epic, Mahabharata, with Arjuna as the hero. Also called *Pampa Bharata*, it praises the writer's patron, King Chalukya Arikeseri of Vemulavada (a Rashtrakuta feudatory), comparing the king's virtues favorably to those of Arjuna. Pampa demonstrates such a command of classical Kannada that scholars over the centuries have written many interpretations of his work.

Another great jain writer in Kannada was Sri Ponna, patronised by King Krishna III and famed for his description of the life of the 16th Jain tirthankara Shantinatha entitled *Santipurana*. He earned the title *Ubhaya Kavichakravathi* (supreme poet in two languages) for his command over both Kannada and Sanskrit. His other writings in Kannada were *Bhuvanaika-karamabhyudaya*, *Jinaksaramale* and *Gatapratiagata*. Adikavi Pampa, Sri Ponna are called "gems of Kannada literature".

Prose works in Sanskrit was prolific during this era as well. Important mathematical theories and axioms were postulated by Mahaviracharya, a native of Gulbarga, who belonged to the Karnataka mathematical tradition and was patronised by King Amoghavarsha I. His greatest contribution was *Ganitasarasangraha*, a writing in 9 chapters. Somadevasuri of 950 wrote in the court of Arikesari II, a feudatory of Rashtrakuta Krishna III in Vemulavada. He was the author of *Yasastilaka champu*, *Nitivakyamrita* and other writings. The main aim of the *champu* writing was to propagate Jain tenets and ethics. The second writing reviews the subject matter of *Arthasastra* from the standpoint of Jain morals in a clear and pithy manner.

Trivikrama was a noted scholar in the court of King Indra III. His classics were *Nalachampu* (915), the earliest in champu style in Sanskrit, *Damayanti Katha, Madalasachampu* and Begumra plates. Legend has it that Goddess Saraswati helped him in his effort to compete with a rival in the kings court. Jinasena was the spiritual preceptor and guru of Amoghavarsha I. A theologian, his contributions are *Dhavala* and *Jayadhavala* (written with another theologian Virasena). These writings are named after their patron king who was also called Athishayadhavala. Other contributions from Jinasena were *Adipurana* later completed by his disciple Gunabhadra, *Harivamsha* and *Parshvabhyudaya.*

Architecture

The Rashtrakutas contributed much to the architectural heritage of the Deccan. The Rashtrakuta contributions to art and architecture are reflected in the splendid rock-cut cave temples at Ellora and Elephanta, located in present day Maharashtra. The Ellora site was originally part of a complex of 34 Buddhist caves probably created in the first half of the sixth century in rocky areas also occupied by Jains monks whose structural details show Pandyan influence. Cave temples occupied by Hindus only became feasible later.

The Rashtrakutas renovated these Buddhist caves and re-dedicated the rock-cut shrines. Amoghavarsha I espoused Jainism and there are five Jain cave temples at Ellora ascribed to his period. The most extensive and sumptuous of the Rashtrakutas work at Ellora is their creation of the monolithic Kailasanath Temple, a splendid achievement confirming the "Balhara" status as "one among the four principle Kings of the world". The walls of the temple have marvellous sculptures from Hindu mythology including Ravana, Shiva and Parvathi while the ceilings have paintings.

The Kailasanath Temple project was commissioned by King Krishna I after the Rashtrakuta rule had spread into South India from the Deccan. The architectural style used was Dravidian. It does not contain any of the *Shikharas* common to the *Nagara* style and was built on the same lines as the Virupaksha temple at Pattadakal in Karnataka. The achievement at the Kailasanath temple is considered an architectural consummation of the monolithic rock-cut temple and deserves be considered one of the wonders of the world. As an accomplishment of art, the Kailasnatha temple is considered an unrivalled work of rock architecture, a monument that has always excited and astonished travellers.

While some scholars have claimed the architecture at Elephanta is attributable to the Kalachuri, others claim that it was built during the Rashtrakuta period. Some of the sculptures such as *Nataraja* and *Sadashiva* excel in beauty and craftmanship even that of the Ellora sculptures. Famous sculptures at Elephanta include *Ardhanarishvara* and *Maheshamurthy*. The latter, a three faced bust of Lord Shiva, is 25 feet (8 m) tall and considered one of the finest pieces of sculpture in India. It is said that, in the world of sculpture, few works of art depicting a divinity are as balanced. Other famous rock-cut temples in the Maharashtra region are the Dhumer Lena and Dashvatara cave temples in Ellora (famous for its sculptures of Vishnu and Shivaleela) and the Jogeshvari temple near Mumbai.

In Karnataka their most famous temples are the *Kashivishvanatha* temple and the Jain Narayana temple at Pattadakal, a UNESCO World Heritage site. Other well known temples are the *Parameshwara* temple at Konnur, *Brahmadeva* temple at Savadi, the *Settavva, Kontigudi II, Jadaragudi* and *Ambigeragudi* temples at Aihole, *Mallikarjuna* temple at Ron, *Andhakeshwara* temple at Huli (Hooli), *Someshwara* temple at Sogal, Jain temples at Lokapura, *Navalinga* temple at Kuknur, *Kumaraswamy* temple at Sandur, at Shirival in Gulbarga and the *Trikuteshwara* temple at Gadag which was later expanded by Kalyani Chalukyas. Archeological study of these temples show some have the stellar (multigonal) plan later to be used profusely by the Hoysalas of Belur and Halebidu. One of the richest traditions in Indian architecture took shape in the Deccan during this time and one writer calls it *Karnata dravida* style as opposed to traditional Dravida style.

Language

With the ending of the Gupta Dynasty in northern India in the early sixth century, major changes began taking place in the Deccan south of the Vindyas and in the southern regions of India. These changes were not only political but also linguistic and cultural. The royal courts of peninsular India (outside of Tamilakam) interfaced between the increasing use of the local Kannada language and the expanding Sanskritic culture. Inscriptions, including those that were bilingual, demonstrate the use of Kannada as the primary administrative language in conjunction with Sanskrit. Government archives used Kannada for recording pragmatic information relating to grants of land.

The local language formed the *desi* (popular) literature while literature in Sanskrit was more *marga* (formal). Educational institutions and places of higher learning (*ghatikas*) taught in Sanskrit, the language of the learned Brahmins, while Kannada increasingly became the speech of personal expression of devotional closeness of a worshipper to a private deity. The patronage Kannada received from rich and literate Jains eventually led to its use in the devotional movements of later centuries.

Contemporaneous literature and inscriptions show that Kannada was not only popular in the modern Karnataka region but the linguistic change had spread further north into present day southern Maharashtra and to the northern Deccan by the eighth century. Kavirajamarga, the work on poetics, refers to the entire region between the Kaveri River and the Godavari River as "Kannada country". Higher education in Sanskrit included the subjects of Veda, *Vyakarana* (grammar), *Jyotisha* (astronomy and astrology), *Sahitya* (literature), *Mimansa* (Exegesis), *Dharmashastra* (law), *Puranas* (ritual), and *Nyaya* (logic).

An examination of inscriptions from this period shows that the *Kavya* (classical) style of writing was popular. The awareness of the merits and defects in inscriptions by the archivists indicates that even they, though mediocre poets, had studied standard classical literature in Sanskrit. An inscription in Kannada by King Krishna III, written in a poetic Kanda metre, has been found as far away as Jabalpur in modern Madhya Pradesh. Kavirajamarga, a work on poetics in Kannada by Amoghavarsha I, shows that the study of poetry was popular in the Deccan during this time. Trivikrama's Sanskrit writing, *Nalachampu*, is perhaps the earliest in the *champu* style from the Deccan.

Origin of Rashtrakuta Dynasty

The origin of the Rashtrakuta Dynasty has been a controversial topic and has been debated over the past decades by historians, but it is said that the Rashtrakuat Dynasty was started when a warioir in charge named as Dantidurga defeated the Chalukya overloard. The differing opinions mostly revolve around issues such as the home of the earliest ancestors of the medieval Rashtrakutas, a possible southern migration during the early part of the first millennium and the relationship between the several Rashtrakuta dynasties that ruled small kingdoms in northern and central India and the Deccan in the 6th century-7th century. Further, the relationship of these medieval Rashtrakutas to the most important and famous dynasty, the Rashtrakutas of Manyakheta of the 8th century-10th century time period has also been debated. Also contested is whether the Rashtrakutas of Manyakheta were related by ancestry to the early Kannada, Maratha, Reddi, Rajput or Punjabi communities of the Deccan and northern India.

While the history of the early Rashtrakutas has caused much debate, the history of the Rashtrakutas of Manyakheta (in present day Gulbarga) of the 8th-10th centuries can be accurately constructed because numerous contemporaneous inscriptions and texts refer to them.

The crux of the Manyakheta empire extended from the Kaveri river in the south to the Narmada in the north. At their peak they were the only south Indian empire that conquered regions in far northern India (Kannauj) as well as the extreme south (Tamilakam). The Lata branch of the empire (in present day Gujarat) was an important dynasty belonging to the Manyakheta family line which later merged with the Manyakheta kingdom during the 9th century.

Research

The study of the history of the early Rashtrakutas and the Rashtrakutas of Manyakheta has been made possible by the availability of numerous inscriptions spread all over the Deccan, ancient literature in Pali, contemporaneous Kannada literature such as *Kavirajamarga* (850) and *Vikramarjuna Vijaya* (941), Sanskrit writings by Somadeva, Rajashekara, Gunabhadra, Jinasena and others and the notes of Arab travellers of those times such as Suleiman, Ibn Haukal, Al Masudi, Al Istakhri and others. Scholars have left no topic unstudied in an effort to accurately propose the history of the Rashtrakutas.

Theories about their lineage (*Surya Vamsa* or *Chandra Vamsa*), native region and ancestral home have been proposed using clues from inscriptions, royal emblems, ancient clan names such as "Rashtrika", epithets such as *Ratta, Rashtrakuta, Lattalura Puravaradhiswara,* names of royalty, coins and contemporaneous literature.

These theories from noted scholars have resulted in claims that the Rashtrakutas were from either Rajput, Kannadiga, Reddi, Maratha, or Punjabi origin.

Epithets

The appearance of the terms *Rathika, Ristika* (*Rashtrika*) or *Lathika* in conjunction with the terms *Kambhoja* and *Gandhara* in some Ashokan inscriptions of 2nd century BCE from Mansera and Shahbazgarhi in North Western Frontier Province (present day Pakistan), Girnar (Saurashtra) and Dhavali (Kalinga) and the use of the epithet "Ratta" in many later inscriptions has prompted a claim that the earliest Rashtrakutas were descendants of the *Arattas,* natives of the Punjab region from the time of Mahabharata who later migrated south and set up kingdoms there, while another theory points more generally to north western regions of India. Based on this theory, the Arattas may have become natives of the Deccan having arrived there during the early centuries of the first millennium.

This is counter to the argument by other scholars that the term *Rishtika* used together with *Petenika* in the Ashokan inscriptions implied they were hereditary ruling clans from modern Maharashtra region and the term "Ratta" implied *Maharatta* ruling families from modern Maharashtra region. But this has been rejected on the basis that from ancient books such as *Dipavamsha* and *Mahavamsha* in Pali language it is known the term *Maharatta* and not *Rashtrika* has been used to signify hereditary ruling clans from modern Maharashtra region and the terms *Rashtrika* and *Petenika* appear to be two different displaced ruling tribes.

It is noted by another scholar that ruling clans called *Rathis* and *Maharathis* were in power in parts of present day Karnataka as well in the early centuries of the Christian era, which is known inscriptions from the region and further proven by the discovery of lead coins from the middle of 3rd century bearing *Sadakana Kalalaya Maharathi* in the heart of modern Karnataka region near Chitradurga.

In the face of these facts it is claimed it can no longer be maintained that the *Rathi* and *Maharathi* families were confined only to present day Maharashtra. It is claimed there is sufficient inscriptional evidence that several *Maharathi* families were related to Kannadiga families by marriage and they were naga worshippers, a form of worship very popular in the Mysore region (modern Karnataka). Also, no evidence to confirm that these families were either Aryan or non-Aryan is available.

The epithet *Ratta,* it is also claimed is a Kannada word from which the word *Rashtrakuta* has been derived. The use of the word *Rattagudlu* (meaning an office) has been found in inscriptions from present day Andhra Pradesh dated prior to the 8th century indicating it was a South Indian word. From the Deoli plates and Karhad records it is argued there was a prince called Ratta and his son was called Rashtrakuta. Hence it has been argued the Rashtrakutas were of Kannada origin. It is also said the term *Rashtra* means "kingdom" and *Kuta* means "lofty" or *Rashtra* means province and *Kuta* means chieftain.

Another epithet used in inscriptions of Amoghavarsha I was *Lattalura Puravaradhiswara.* It is proposed that it refers to their original home *Lattalur,* modern day Latur in Maharashtra state, bordering Karnataka. This area it is claimed was predominantly Kannada speaking based on surviving vestiges of place names, inscriptions and cultural relics. It is explained that *Latta* is a Prakrit variation of *Ratta* and hence Rattana-ur became Lattana-ur and finally Lattalur. Another theory is that Latalurapura is modern day Ratnapur in Bilaspur district of central India.

Royal Names and Signatures

In linking possible connections between the medieval Rashtrakuta families to the imperial family of Manyakheta it has been pointed out that only the family members ruling from Elichpur (Berar or modern Amravati district, modern Maharashtra) had names that were very similar to the names of Kings of the Manyakheta dynasty. From the Tivarkhed and Multhai inscriptions it is clear that the kings of this family were Durgaraja, Govindaraja, Svamikaraja and Nannaraja. These names closely resemble the names of Manyakheta kings or their extended family, the name Govindaraja appearing multiple times among the Manyakheta line. These names also appear in the Gujarat line of Rashtrakutas whose family ties with the Manyakheta family is well known.

It has been noted that princes and princesses of the Rashtrakuta family used pure Kannada names such as Kambarasa, Asagavve, Revakka and Abbalabbe as their personal names indicating that they were native Kannadigas. It has been pointed out that princesses of family lineage belonging to Gujarat signed their royal edicts in Kannada even in their Sanskrit inscriptions. Some examples of this are the Navsari and Baroda plates of Karka I and the Baroda plates of his son Dhruva II. It has been attested by a scholar that the Gujarat Rashtrakuta princes signed their inscriptions in the language of their native home and the race they belonged to. It is well known that the Gujarat line of Rashtrakutas were from the same family as the Manyakheta line.

It is argued that if the Rashtrakutas were originally a Marathi speaking family, then the Gujarat Rashtrakutas would not have signed their inscriptions in Kannada language and that too in far away Gujarat.

The theory that under the rule of the Badami Chalukyas of Kannada country, Kannada speaking dynasties were established in the far corners of the Chalukyan empire in Gujarat, Andhra and Berar (present day Vidharba region in modern Maharashtra) and hence the ancestors of King Dantidurga, the founder of the Manyakheta empire were Kannadigas. It is further claimed there is proof that in the locality where Dantidurga lived Kannada was the spoken language.

Emblems

Several Rashtrakuta families ruled India during the 6th century-7th century period. Scholars have tried to understand their relationship with the Rashtrakutas of Manyakheta by a comparative study of the emblems.

The only Rashtrakuta family whose royal emblem is similar to that of the rulers of Manyakheta, the golden eagle or Garuda *lanchhana* (emblem) is that of the family that ruled from Amravathi district of modern Maharashtra. It has been theorised that this line may possibly have been ancestors of the Manyakheta kings. Their inscriptions (Tivarkhed and Multhai) were issued from Achalapura (modern Elichpur) which may have been their capital. Another Rashtrakuta family ruling from Manapur in Malwa region with its founder King Abhimanyu had the emblem of a lion. This makes it improbable that they were the ancestors of the Manyakheta family.

While the Garuda is normally indicative Vaishnavite leanings, it has to be observed here that earlier coins belonging to King Krishna I's period use the legend *Parama Maheshwara,* which in turn indicate staunch Shaivite leanings. This change in symbology has been used to theorise that the Rashtrakutas may have originally been Shaivites and embraced Vaishnavism later.

Vamsha (Genealogy)

With regards to their *vamsha* (whether they belonged to *Surya Vamsha* (solar lineage) or *Chandra Vamsha* (lunar lineage), Rashtrakuta inscriptions remained silent on the issue, until about 860. Some 75 inscriptions have been found thereafter in the Deccan and Gujarat which speak about their *vamsha*. Of these, only 8 lay claim that they belonged to the Yadava line. While one inscription of 860 claims that King Dantidurga was born to the *Yadava Satyaki*, 1800 coins of King Krishna I (772), his successor calls him *Parama Mahesvara* indicating his solar lineage origin and Shaiva faith.

An inscription of King Govinda III (808) mentions "by the birth of this virtuous king, the Rashtrakuta dynasty became invincible just as the Yadava dynasty by the birth of Lord Krishna". This is considered only a comparative statement. Only a few records attest to a possible Yadava connection and even the descendants of the Rashtrakutas such as the Gahadavalas of Kanauj, Rathors of Rajasthan claim to be from *Surya Vamsha* (solar lineage), a sure sign the Rashtrakutas belonged to the *Surya Vamsha*. The opinion that the Rashtrakutas did not belong to the Yadava line is supported by another scholar as well.

Language

While the linguistic leanings of the early Rashtrakutas has caused considerable debate, the history and language of the Rashtrakutas of Manyakheta has been free of such confusion. It is clear from inscriptions, coinage and prolific contemporaneous literature that the court of these Rashtrakutas was multi-lingual, used Sanskrit and Kannada as their administrative languages and encouraged literature in Sanskrit and Kannada. However this period was the very end of the classical era of literary Sanskrit and Prakrit. As such, from the Kavirajamarga of 9th century, it is known that Kannada was popular from Kaveri river up to the Godavari river, an area covering large territory in modern Maharashtra.

The Rashtrakuta inscriptions call them the vanquishers of the *Karnatabala*, a sobriquet used to refer to the near invincibility of the Chalukyas of Badami. This however it is claimed should not be construed to mean that the Rashtrakutas themselves were not Kannadigas. Their patronage and love of the Kannada language is apparent in that most of their inscriptions within modern

K. rnataka are in Kannada, while their inscriptions outside of modern Karnataka tended to be in Sanskrit. An inscription in classical Kannada of King Krishna III has also been found as far away as Jabalpur in modern Madhya Pradesh which further supports the view of their affinity to the language.

Adikavi Pampa, Sri Ponna, Shivakotiacharya and King Amoghavarsha I were among the noteworthy scholars in Kannada, the Apabhramsha poet Pushpadanta wrote several works and famous Sanskrit scholars such as Jinasena and Virasena (both of who were theologians), mathematician Mahaviracharya and poets such as Trivikrama and Gunabhadra adorned their courts.

The earliest extant Kannada literature belongs to this time. These Rashtrakuta kings married princess from Northern and Southern India and several Rashtrakuta branches emerged in Northern India during the their imperialistic expansion in the 9th century.

The argument that the Rashtrakutas were either Marathi speaking Marathas or Telugu speaking Reddies in origin has been rejected. Reddy's in that time period had not come into martial prominence even in the Telugu speaking regions of Andhra, being largely an agrarian society of cultivators who only much later (in the 14th century-15th century) came to control regions in the Krishna-Rajamundry districts. The Rashtrakuta period did not produce any Marathi inscriptions or literature (with the exception of a 981 CE Shravanabelagola inscription which some historians argue was inscribed later).

In addition very few literary works in Prakrit language are available from this period. Jainism which played such an important role in giving patronage to early Kannada literature did not flourish as much in the present day Maharashtra region which is why no Marathi literature emerged during this period. Hence Marathi as the language of the Rashtrakutas, it is claimed, is not an acceptable argument.

Rashtrakutas and Rajputs

The Rashtrakutas emerged before the term "Rajput" came to be used as a community. The emergence of Rajputs in Rajasthan and Gujarat coincides with the arrival of the Rashtrakutas and Chalukyas in the region.

Pala Empire

The Pâla Empire was a Buddhist dynasty as well as one of the major middle kingdoms of India that ruled from Bengal in the eastern region of the Indian subcontinent. The Palas were often described by opponents as the *Lords of Gauda*. The name *Pala* means *protector* and was used as an ending to the names of all Pala monarchs. The Palas were followers of the Mahayana and Tantric schools of Buddhism. Gopala was the first ruler from the dynasty. He came to power in 750 in Gaur by a democratic election.

This event is recognized as one of the first democratic elections in South Asia since the time of the Maha Janapadas. He reigned from 750-770 and consolidated his position by extending his control over all of Bengal. The Buddhist dynasty lasted for four centuries (750-1120 AD) and ushered in a period of stability and prosperity in Bengal. They created many temples and works of art as well as supported the Universities of Nalanda and Vikramashila. Somapura Mahavihara built by Dharmapala is the greatest Buddhist Vihara in the Indian Subcontinent.

The empire reached its peak under Dharmapala and Devapala. Dharmapala extended the empire into the northern parts of the Indian Subcontinent. This triggered once again the power struggle for the control of the subcontinent. Devapala, successor of Dharmapala, expanded the empire to cover much of South Asia and beyond. His empire stretched from Assam and Utkala in the east, Kamboja (modern day Afghanistan) in the north-west and Deccan in the south. According to Pala copperplate inscription Devapala exterminated the Utkalas, conquered the Pragjyotisha (Assam), shattered the pride of the Huna, and humbled the lords of Pratiharas, Gurjara and the Dravidas.

The death of Devapala ended the period of ascendancy of the Pala Empire and several independent dynasties and kingdoms emerged during this time. However, Mahipala I rejuvenated the reign of the Palas. He recovered control over all of Bengal and expanded the empire. He survived the invasions of Rajendra Chola and the Chalukyas. After Mahipala I the Pala dynasty again saw its decline until Ramapala, the last great ruler of the dynasty, managed to retrieve the position of the dynasty to some extent. He crushed the Varendra rebellion and extended his empire farther to Kamarupa, Orissa and Northern India.

The Pala Empire can be considered as the golden era of Bengal. Never had the Bengali people reached such height of power and glory to that extent. Palas were responsible for the introduction of Mahayana Buddhism in Tibet, Bhutan and Myanmar. The Palas had extensive trade as well as influence in south-east Asia. This can be seen in the sculptures and architectural style of the Sailendra Empire (present-day Malaya, Java, Sumatra). The Pala Empire eventually disintegrated in the 12th century under the attack of the Sena dynasty.

Origin of the Palas

The Ramacharitam of Sandhyakar Nandi attests that Varendra (or North Bengal) was the fatherland (*Janakabhu*) of the Palas. In the Bangarh Copperplate of Mahipala I, it has been stated that Mahipala recovered his ancestral homeland (*Rajyam Pitram*) from the usurpers (which was until that time occupied by the Kamboja-Pala Kingdom).

Caste

The caste origin of the Palas is not clearly stated in any of the numerous Pala records. The Khalimpur Plate of Dharmapala, the second Pala emperor, states that Gopala I was a son of a warrior (*Khanditarat*) named Vapyata, grandson of a highly educated man (*Saryavidyavadat*) named Dayitavishnu, and he himself was elected to the throne of Bengal, therefore he was not initially of a distinguished royal blood from the Hindu point of view.

The Kamauli Copper Plate inscription of king Vaidyadeva of Kamarupa (Assam) connects the Palas to the Kshatriyas of "*Mihirasya vamsa*" (Surya lineage).

Balla-Carita says that the "The Palas were low-born Kshatriya", a claim reiterated by the historian Taranatha in his "History of Buddhism in India" as well as Ghanarama in "Dharma Mangala" (both written in the 16th century CE). The Ramacharitam also attests the fifteenth Pala emperor, Ramapala, as a Kshatriya. As Gopala I was a Buddhist, he was also branded as a Œudra king in some sources. According to Manjuúree Mulakalpa, Gopala I was a Uudra. Arabic accounts tell us that Palas were not kings of noble origin. According to Abul-Fazl ibn Mubarak (in Ain-i-Akbari), the Palas were Kayasthas. There are even accounts that claim Gopala may have been from a Brahmin lineage.

Matsyanyaya and the Ascendancy of the Palas

After Shashanka's reign, Bengal was shrouded in obscurity and was shattered by repeated invasions. During the reign of Manava, Bengal was invaded and divided between Harshavardhana and Bhaskaravarman. In 730 CE Jayavardhana of the Shaila Dynasty from Central India invaded Bengal and killed the king of Pundra Kingdom. Yasovarman (725-752) of Kannauj killed the king of Magadha and Gauda. Later Lalitaditya Muktapida (724-760) of Kashmir who defeated Yasovarmana invaded Bengal. Sri Harsha of Kamarupa conquered Anga, Vanga, Kalinga and Odra.

The social and political structure of Bengal was devastated. According to Taranatha: Every single Brahman, every Kshatriya, every Elite became all powerful in their areas and surrounding regions. This condition has been described by him as Matsyanyam (Eating of small fish by the big fish) or the Dark Age of Bengal. Disgusted at the situation the desperate people of Bengal made a bold move which marked a glorious period in the history of the sub-continent. They elected Gopala, a popular military leader, as their king by a democratic election which was probably the only democratic election in medieval India.

Buddhism

After the Buddhist king Harsha Vardhana, Buddhism faced the possibility of extinction. The Palas emerged as the champion of Buddhism, and they patronized Mahayana Buddhism. The Palas supported the Universities of Vikramashila and Nalanda which became the premier seats of learning in Asia. The Nalanda University which is considered one of the first great universities in recorded history, reached its height under the patronage of the Palas..

The Palas were responsible for the spread of Mahayana Buddhism to Tibet, Nepal, Bhutan, Myanmar and the Malay archipelago. Bengal became famous in the Buddhist world for the cultivation of Buddhist religion, culture and other knowledge in the various centres that grew under the patronage of the Pala rulers. Buddhist scholars from the Pala empire travelled from Bengal to the Far-East and propagated Buddhism. A few outstanding individuals among them are Shantarakshit, Padmanava, Dansree, Bimalamitra, Jinamitra, Muktimitra,

Sugatasree, Dansheel, Sambhogabajra, Virachan, Manjughosh and many others.

But the most prominent was Atish Dipankar Srigyan who reformed Buddhism in Tibet after it had been destroyed by king Langdharma. Although the Palas were Vaishnavas, they had also given support to Shaiva ascetics, typically the ones associated with the Golagi-Math. Many of the Pala Dynasty's coins also bear the image of Shiva and his bull. Besides sculptures of Vaishnava deities, they had also constructed statues of Siva and Saraswati.

Main Pala Rulers:

- Gopala I (756-781)
- Dharmapala (781-821)
- Devapala (821-861)
- Mahendrapala, Shurapala I, Vigrahapala I (861-866)
- Narayanapala (866-920)
- Rajyapala (920-952)
- Gopala II (952-969)
- Vigrahapala II (969-995)
- Mahipala I (995-1043)
- Nayapala (1043–1058)
- Vigrahapala III (1058–1075)
- Mahipala II (1075–1080)
- Shurapala II (1080–1082)
- Ramapala (1082–1124)
- Kumarapala (1124–1129)
- Gopala III (1129–1143)
- Madanapala (1143–1162)
- Govindapala (1162–1174).

Peace and Expansion

Gopala united all of Bengal and brought peace and prosperity in the region. The period of anarchy ended with his election. The Pala kings devoted themselves in public welfare and social reform. The Palas adopted the policy of religious toleration and co-existence of the Buddhists and the Hindus. Pala kings won the heart of the people by welfare activities like digging tanks and establishing towns took place in many folklores in the rural areas of Bengal.

The *Mahipala Geet* (Songs of Mahipala) is still popular in the rural areas.

Palas adopted aggressive policy and began the period of expansion under Dharmapala and Devapala. At its height Dharmapala's empire covered most of northern and central region of the Indian Subcontinent. His successor Devapala extended the boundaries of the empire further to Assam in the east, Kamboja in the north-wast and the Deccan in the south. Devapala united much of South Asia under his rule, a feat only achieved before by Ashoka the Great. The successors of Devapala had to contend with the Gurjara-Pratihara and the Rashtrakutas for the supremacy of the Kannauj Triangle. After Narayanpala the Pala empire declined but was revived once more under the vigorous reigns of Mahipala and Ramapala.

Pala Administration

Pala rule was Monarchial. King or Monarch was the centre of all power. Pala kings would adopt Imperial titles like *Parameshwar, Paramvattaraka, Maharajadhiraja*. Pala kings appointed Prime Ministers. The Line of Garga served as the Prime Ministers of the Palas for 100 years. Garga I Darvapani I Someshwar I Kedarmisra I Vatt Guravmisra Pala Empire was divided into separate Vuktis (Provinces), Vuktis into Vishaya (Divisions) and Mandala Districts. Smaller units were *Khandala, Bhaga, Avritti, Chaturaka,* and Pattaka. Administration covered widespread area from the grass root level to the imperial court.

The Pala copperplates mention following administrative Posts:*Raja, Rajanyaka, Rajanaka, Ranaka, Samanta* and *Mahasamanta* (Vassal kings), *Mahasandhi-vigrahika* (Foreign minister), *Duta* (Head Ambassador), *Rajasthaniya* (Deputy), *Aggaraksa* (Chief guard), *Sasthadhikrta* (Tax collector), *Chauroddharanika* (Police tax), *Shaulkaka* (Trade tax), *Dashaparadhika* (Collector of penalties), and *Tarika* (Toll collector for river crossings), *Mahaksapatalika* (Accountant), *Jyesthakayastha* (Dealing documents), the *Ksetrapa* (Head of land use division) and *Pramatr* (Head of land measurements), the *Mahadandanayaka* or *Dharmadhikara* (Chief justice), the *Mahapratihara, Dandika, Dandapashika,* and *Dandashakti* (Police forces), *Khola* (Secret service).

Agricultural posts like *Gavadhakshya* (Head of dairy farms), *Chhagadhyakshya* (Head of goat farms), *Meshadyakshya* (Head of sheep farms), *Mahishadyakshya* (Head of Buffalo farms) and many other like *Vogpati, Vishayapati, Shashtadhikruta, Dauhshashadhanika, Nakadhyakshya.*

Pala Literature

The proto-Bangla language was born during the reign of the Palas. The Buddhist texts of the Charyapada were the earliest form of Bangla language. This Proto-Bangla language was used as the official language in Tibet, Myanmar, Java and Sumatra. Books on every aspect of knowledge were compiled during the Pala Rule. On philosophy: *Agaman Shastra* by Gaudapada, *Nyay Kundali* by Sridhar Bhatta, *Karmanushthan Paddhati* by Bhatta Bhavadeva; On Medicine: *Chikitsa Sangraha, Ayurvedidwipika, Bhanumati, Shabdachandrika, Dravya Gunasangraha* by Chakrapani Dutt; *Shabda-Pradip, Vrikkhayurveda, Lohpaddhati* by Sureshwar; *Chikitsa Sarsangraha* by Vangasena; *Sushrata* by Gadadha Vaidya; *Daybhaga, Byabohar-Matrika, Kalvivek* by Jimutvahan etc. Atisha compiled more than 200 books. The great epic Ramacharitam written by Sandhyakar Nandi the court poet of Madanpala was another masterpiece of the Pala literature. The Pala copperplate inscriptions were of excellent literary value. This distinctive inscriptions were called *Gaudiya Style.*

Pala Art and Architecture

The most brilliant side of the Pala Empire was the excellence of its art and sculptures. Palas created a distinctive form of Buddhist art known as the "Pala School of Sculptural Art." The gigantic structures of Vikramshila Vihar, Odantpuri Vihar, and Jagaddal Vihar were masterpieces of the Palas. These mammoth structures were mistaken by the forces of Bakhtiar Khilji as fortified castles and were demolished. The Somapura Mahaviharaa, a creation of Dharmapala, at Paharpur, Bangladesh, is the largest Buddhist Vihara in the Indian subcontinent, and has been described as a "pleasure to the eyes of the world." UNESCO made it World Heritage Site in 1985. Sompur Bihara, also built by Dharmapala, is a monastery with 21 acre (85,000 m^2) complex has 177 cells, numerous stupas, temples and a number of other ancillary buildings. In 1985, the UN included the Sompur Bihara site in the world Cultural Heritage list.

The Pala architectural style was followed throughout south-eastern Asia, China, Japan and Tibet. Bengal rightfully earned the name "Mistress of the East". Dr. Stella Kramrisch says: "The art of Bihar and Bengal exercised a lasting influence on that of Nepal, Burma, Ceylon and Java". Dhiman and Vittpala were two celebrated Pala sculptors. About Sompura Mahavihara, Mr. J.C. French says with grief: "For the research of the Pyramids of Egypt we spend millions of dollars every year. But had we spent only one percent of that money for the excavation of Sompura Mahavihara, who knows what extraordinary discoveries could have been made." – "The Art of the Pala Empire of Bengal".

Pala Foreign Relations

Palas came in contact with distant lands through their conquests and trades. The Sailendra Empire of Java, Sumatra and Malaya was a colony of the Palas. Devapala granted five villages at the request of the Sailendra king Balputradeva of Java for the upkeeping of the matha established at Nalanda for the scholars of that country. The Prime minister of the Balputradeva Kumar Ghosha was from Gauda. Dharmapala who extended his empire to the boundary of the Abbasid Empire and had diplomatic relations with the caliph Harun Al-Rashid. Coins of Harun-al-Rashid have been found in Mahasthangarh. Palas maintained diplomatic and religious relation with Tibet. During the military expeditions of the Pala kings the Pala generals would establish kingdoms of their own in Punjab and Afghanistan. Recent discoveries in the Punjab hills showed the influence of the Pala Dynasty.

There is a strong and continuous tradition that the ruling families in certain states are descended from the "Rajas of Gaur in Bengal". These states are Suket, Keonthal, Kashtwar and Mandi. In the ancient Rajput states tradition has immense force and accuracy. Of Kashtwar it is related that Kahan Pal – the founder of the state – with a small band of followers arrived in the hills in order to conquer a kingdom for himself. He is said to have come from Gaur, the ancient capital of Bengal and to have been a cadet of the ruling family of the place. The demise of the Turkshahi rule in Gandhar and the rise of the Hindushahi dynasty in that region might have connection to the invasion of the Palas in that region.

Pala Armed Forces

The Palas of Bengal in comparison with other contemporary empires such as the Rashtrakutas of Deccan and the Pratiharas of Malwa in the focal point of "Kanauj Triangle."

Palas had fourfold army consisting of: infantry, cavalry, elephants and chariots. In the copperplates of Vatsaraja Dharmapala had been mentioned as the owner of unlimited number of horses, elephants and chariots. It is amazing that when the use of chariots had been backdated in India and other parts of the world the kings of Bengal still depended on four-horsed heavy chariots. Being a riverine land and swarthy climate Bengal was not good enough for breeding quality war-horses.

So the Palas had to depend upon their vassal kings for war horses. Pala copperplate inscriptions reveal that mercenary forces were recruited from the Kamboja, Khasa, Huna, Malwa, Gujarat, and Karnata. The Kamboja cavalry were the cream of the Pala army who would later become as powerful as the Janissary army of the Ottoman Empire. The Kamboja forces maintained smaller confederates (Sanghas) among themselves and were staunch follower of their commander. Palas had the army divided into following posts: Senapati or Mahasenapati (General) controlling foot soldiers, cavalry, soldiers riding elephants and camels, and the navy, and the various army posts like Kottapala (Fort guards) and Prantapala (Border guards). Palas had a huge army and the legend of "Nava Lakkha Shainya" (Nine lac soldiers) were popular during the reigns of Dharmapala and Devapala. According to Hudud al-Alam a Persian text written in 982-983 Dharmapala possessed an army of 300,000 soldiers. According to Sulaiman the Arab traveller Devapala set out for his every military expedition with an army of 50,000 elephants and his army had 10,000-15,000 slaves for the maintenance and caretaking of his armies.

Legacy

Palas legacy gets remembered not much in Bengal but elsewhere in Asia. Tibet's modern culture and religion is heavily influenced by Palas. Palas are credited with spreading Buddhism to Tibet and around the world through missionaries. Atisa, a Palan, is a celebrated figure in the Tibetan Buddhism in tradition and in establishment. Atisa also invented bodhichitta or known as "mind training" that is practiced around the world today. Another important Palan figure in Tibetan Buddhism is Tilopa who founded the Kagyu lineage of Tibetan Buddhism and developed the Mahamudra method, a set of spiritual practices that greatly accelerated the process of attaining bodhi (enlightenment).

Palas literature is widely studied by Buddhist around the world. Pala architectural style was copied throughout south-eastern Asia, China, Japan, and Tibet. Nalanda University and Vikramshila University are two of the greatest Buddhist universities ever recorded in history.

Gurjara-Pratihara

The Gurjara Pratihara Empire, also known as *Gurjar Parihars,* formed an Indian dynasty that ruled much of Northern India from the 6th to the 11th centuries. At its peak of prosperity and power (c. 836–910), it rivaled the Gupta Empire in the extent of its territory.

Origin

According to a legend given in later manuscripts of Prithviraj Raso, the Gurjar Pratiharas were one of the *Agnikula* clans of Rajputs, deriving their origin from a sacrificial fire-pit (agnikunda) at Mount Abu. The myth is apparently absurd. Historians such as Hermann Kulke, Dietmar Rothermund stated that Kannauj was capital of imperial Gurjara Pratiharas.. The Pratihara dynasty is referred to as *Gurjara pratiharanvayah,* i.e., *Pratihara clan of the Gurjaras,* in line 4 of the "Rajor inscription (Alwar)". Vincent Smith believed that the Pratiharas were certainly of Gurjara (or Gujjar) origin, and stated that there is possibility of other Agnikula Rajput clans being of same origin. Dr. K. Jamanadas also states that the Pratihara clan of Rajputs descended from the Gujjars, and this "raises a strong presumption that the other Rajput clans also are the descendants from the Gurjaras or the allied foreign immigrants". D. B. Bhandarkar also believed that Pratiharas were a clan of Gujjars. In his book *The Glory that was Gujardesh* (1943), Gurjar writer K. M. Munshi stated that the Pratiharas and some other Rajput clans were of Gujjar (or Gurjar) origin.

However, H. A. Rose and Denzil Ibbetson stated that there is no conclusive proof that the Agnikula Rajput clans are of Gurjara origin; they believed that there is possibility of the indigenous tribes adopting Gurjara names, when their founders were enfiefed by Gurjara rulers. Dasrath sharma believed that Gurjara was applied for territory and conceded that although some sections of the Pratiharas (eg. the one to which Mathanadeva belonged) were Gujjars by caste, the imperial Pratiharas of Kannauj were not Gujjars. The author Rama Shankar Tripathi asserts that a close perusal of the Rajor inscription confirms the Gurjara origin of the Pratiharas. In line 12 of this inscription, occur words which have been translated as "together with all the neighbouring fields cultivated by the Gurjaras". Here, the cultivators themselves are clearly called Gurjaras and therefore it's reasonable to presume that, in line four too, the term bears a racial signification.

The Rashtrakuta records, as well as the Arab writers like Abu Zaid and Al-Masudi (who allude their fights with the *Juzr or Gurjara* of the north) indicate the Gurjara origin of the Pratiharas. The Kanarese poet Pampa expressly calls Mahipala *Ghurjararaja.* This ephithet could hardly be applied to him, if the term *Ghurjararaja* bore a geographical sense denoting what after all was only a small portion of Mahipala's vast territories. Tripathi believes that all these evidences point to the Gurjara ancestry of the Pratiharas.

Rulers

Gurjar pratihar rulers (650-1036 AD)	
Dadda I-II-III	(650-750)
Nagabhata I	(750-780)
Vatsaraja	(780-800)
Nagabhata II	(800-833)
Ramabhadra	(833-836)
Mihir Bhoja the Great	(836-890)
Mahendrapala I	(890-910)
Bhoj II	(910-913)
Mahipala I	(913-944)
Mahendrapala II	(944-948)
Devpala	(948-954)
Vinaykpala	(954-955)
Mahipala II	(955-956)
Vijaypala II	(956-960)
Rajapala	(960-1018)
Trilochanpala	(1018-1027)
Jasapala (Yashpala)	(1024-1036)
Court Poet	Rajasekhara

Harichandra is said to have laid the foundation of this dynasty in the 6th century. The Harichandra line of Pratihar Gurjar established the state of Marwar, based at Mandore near modern Jodhpur, which grew to dominate Rajasthan. The Pratihara kings of Marwar also built the temple-city of Osian.

Nagabhata I (730-756) extended his control east and south from Mandor, conquering Malwa as far as Gwalior and the port of Bharuch in Gujarat. He established his capital at Avanti in Malwa, and checked the expansion of the Arabs, who had established themselves in Sind. In this Battle of Rajasthan (738 CE) Nagabhata led a confedracy of Gurjars to defeat the Muslim Arabs who had till then been pressing on victorious through West Asia and Iran. Nagabhata I was followed by two weak successors, who were in turn succeeded by Vatsraja (775-805).

Vatsraj sought to capture Kannauj, which had been the capital of the seventh-century empire of Harsha. His ambitions brought the Pratiharas into conflict with the Pala dynasty of Bengal and the Rashtrakutas of the northern Deccan, with whom they would contest for primacy in northern India for the next two centuries. Vatsraja unsuccessfully challenged the Pala ruler Dharmapala (c. 775-810) for control of Kannauj. In about 786 the Rashtrakuta ruler Dhruva (c. 780-793) crossed the Narmada River into Malwa, and from there tried to capture Kannauj. Vatsraja was defeated by Dhruva around 800, and died in 805.

Vatsraj was succeeded by Nagabhata II (805-833). Nagabhata II was initially defeated by the Rashtrakuta king Govinda III (793-814), but later recovered Malwa from the Rashtrakutas, conquered Kannauj and the Ganges plain as far as Bihar from the Palas, and again checked the Muslims in the west. He rebuilt the great Shiva temple at Somnath in Gujarat, which had been demolished in an Arab raid from Sind. Kannauj became the center of the Gurjar Pratihara state, which covered much of northern India during the peak of their power, c. 836-910.

Rambhadra (833-c. 836) briefly succeeded Nagabhata II. Bhoja I or Mihir Bhoja (c. 836-886) suffered some initial defeats by the Pala king Devapala (810-850), but recovered to expand the Gurjar dominions west to the border of Sind, east to Magadha, and south to the Narmada. His son Mahenderpal 1 (890-910) expanded further eastwards in Magadha, Bengal, and Assam. Junaid, the successor of Qasim, finally subdued the Hindu resistance within Sindh. Taking advantage of the conditions in Western India, which at that time was covered with several small states, Junaid led a large army into the region in early 738 CE. Dividing this force into two he plundered several cities in southern Rajasthan, western Malwa, and Gujarat. The Arab chroniclers claim that he acquired immense wealth, slaughtered large numbers of infidels. Bhoja II (910-912) was overthrown by Mahipal 1 (912-914). Several feudatories of the empire took advantage of the temporary weakness of the Gurjar Pratiharas to declare their independence, notably the Paramaras of Malwa, the Chandelas of Bundelkhand, and the Kalachuris of Mahakoshal. The Rashtrakuta king Indra III (c.914-928) briefly captured Kannauj in 916, and although the Pratiharas regained the city, their position continued to weaken in the 10th century, partly as a result of the drain of simultaneously fighting off Turkic attacks from the west and the Pala advances in the east. The Gurjar-Pratiharas lost control of Rajasthan to other Rajput clans, and the Chandelas captured the strategic fortress of Gwalior in central India, c. 950. By the end of the tenth century the Gurjar Pratihara domains had dwindled to a small kingdom centered on Kannauj. Mahmud of Ghazni sacked Kannauj in 1018, and the Pratihara king Rajapala fled. The Chandela ruler Gauda captured and killed Rajapala, placing Rajapala's son Trilochanpala on the throne as a proxy. Jasapala, the last Gurjar king of Kanauj, died in 1036.

The Pariharas of Mandore, Marwar lost control of the region in the 13th century to the Rathor clan of Rajputs. In 1395, Chundaji Rathore married a Parihar princess named Mohil. The Parihar Raja Dhara Singh established the state of Nagod in 1344, and his descendants ruled there until 1950. It can be understood from many Arabic sources that armies of the Muslim invaders greatly feared the might of the Gurjar Pratiharas. The Persian traveller Ahmad ibn Rustah praised the Gujara-Pratihara ruler Mihir Bhoja I in his *Kitâb al-A'lâk an-Nafîsa* thus: "In Hind there is a Malik (king) who is called Al-juzar (Gujar). Such is awdl (justice) in his kingdom, if the gold is dropped in the way, there is no danger of its being picked up and stolen away by any body. His empire is very vast. Arab traders go to him, he makes ahsan (favour) to them, purchases merchandise from them; the purchase and sale are carried in gold coin called tatri. When the Arabs request him to provide a body guard, he says, there is no thief in my empire. If there is any incident or loss to your goods, merchandise and money I stand surety. Come to me, I will pay the compensation."

Bibliography

Adikaram, E. W.: *Early History of Buddhism in Ceylon*, D. S. Puswella, Migoda, 1946.

Agrawala, V. S.: *Shiva Mahadeva: The Great God*, Veda Academy, Varanasi, 1966.

Ahmad, Imtiaz: *State and Foreign Policy: India's Role in South Asia*, Vikas, New Delhi, 1993.

Ahmad, Jamil-ud-din: *Some Recent Speeches and Writings of Mr. Jinnah*, Lahore, Ashraf, 1952.

Aiyar, R. Krishnaswami: *Outlines of Vedaanta*, Chetana, Bombay, 1978.

Archer, W. G.: *The Kama Sutra*, Unwin Hyman, London, 1990.

Ashton, S.R. : *British Policy Towards the Indian States, 1905-1939*, London, Curzon, 1982.

Aurobindo, Sri: *Vyasa and Valmiki*, Acharya Press, Pondicherry, 1956.

Avalon, Arthur and Ellen: *Hymns to the Goddess*, Ganesh and Co., Madras, 1964.

Aziz, Ashraf: *Light of the Universe: Essays on Hindustani Film Music*, Three Essays Collective, New Delhi, 2003.

Bagchi, P. C.: *Studies in Dharmashastra*, University of Calcutta Press, Calcutta, 1939.

Bahadur, K.P.: *The Wisdom of Vedaanta*, Sterling Publishers Private Limited, New Delhi, 1996.

Banerjea, J. N.: *Pauranic and Vedanta Religion*, University of Calcutta, Calcutta, 1996.

Bankimchandra, C.: *Essentials of Dharma*, Sanskrit Book Depot, Calcutta 1979.

Basu, Manoranjan: *Dharmashastra: A General Study*, Shrimati Mira Basu, Calcutta, 1976.

Beaumont, Roger : *Sword of the Raj: The British Army in India, 1747-1947*, Indianapolis, Bobbs-Merrill, 1977.

Benjamin, Joseph : *Scheduled Castes in Inaian Politics and Society*, New Delhi, Ess Ess Publications, 1989.

Bhattacharyya, B.: *Nispannayogavali of Mahapandita Abhyakara Gupta*, Oriental Institute, Baroda, 1949.

Borchert, Bruno: *Mysticism: Its History and Challenge*, Samuel Wiser, York Beach, 1994.

Bose, D. N.: *Dharmashastra: Their Philosophy and Occult Secrets*, Kali Press, Calcutta, 1965.

Bowle, John: *The Imperial Achievement: The Rise and Transformation of the British Empire*, Little, Brown, 1974.

Brockington, J. L.: *Righteous Rama: The Evolution of an Epic*, Oxford, London, 1984.

Bromley, D.: *Krishna Consciousness in the West*, Bucknell University Press, Lewisburg, 1989.

Brooks, E.: *The Original Analects: Sayings of Confucius and His Successors*. Columbia University Press, New York, 1988.

Bruhn, Klaus: *The Jina-Images of Deogarh*, MacMillan, Leiden, 1969.

Burke, Mary Louise: *Swami Vivekananda in America: New Discoveries*, Advaita Ashrama, Calcutta, 1966.

Chaudhary, M.: *Partition and the Curse of Rehabilitation*, Calcutta, Bengal Rehabilitation Organization, 1964.

Chaudhuri, Nirad: *Thy Hand, Great Anarch! India: 1921-1952*, London, Chatto & Windus, 1987.

Coomeraswamy, Ananda K.: *Buddha and the Gospel of Buddhism*, MacMillan, London, 1928.

Crawford, Cromwell S.: *Ram Mohan Roy: His Era and Ethics*, Acharya Press, New Delhi, 1984.

Dalton, Dennis : *Gandhi's Power : Nonviolence in Action*, New Delhi, OUP, 2001.

Danielou, Alain: *The Complete Kama Sutra*, Park Street Press, Rochester, 2000.

Dasgupta, Shahana: *Rani Lakshmibai: The Indian Heroine*, Rupa & Company, Calcutta, 2002.

Datta, V.N.: *Sati: Widow Burning in India*, Manohar, New Delhi, 1990.

David, M. D.: *John Wilson and his Institutions*, Mumbai, 1957.

De Bary: *Self and Society in Ming Thought*, Columbia University Press, New York, 1970.

De, Sushil Kumar: *Ancient Indian Erotics and Erotic Literature*, Firma K. L. Mukhopadhyay, Calcutta, 1959.

Deak, Istvan: *The Lawful Revolution: Louis Kossuth and the Hungarians 1848-1849*, Columbia University Press, 1979.

Dhar, Niranjan: *Vedanta and Bengal Renaissance*, Minerva Associates, Calcutta, 1977.

Dikshit, D.P. *Political History of the Chalukyas of Badami*. New Delhi: Abhinav, 1980.

Donat, K.: *Meditate the Tantric Yoga Way*, George Allen and Unwin, London, 1973.

Doniger, W.: *The Rig Veda: An Anthology*, Penguin, New York, 1981.

Duboi, Abbe: *Hindu Manners, Customs and Ceremonies*, Fifth Indian Impression, CUP, 1985.

Dwivedi, M.: *The Principal Upanishads*, Adyar Library, Madras, 1931.

Eaton, Richard M.: *Sufis of Bijapur, 1300-1700: Social Roles of Sufis in Medieval India*, Princeton University Press, Princeton, 1978.

Edwardes, Michael: *Battles of the Indian Mutiny*, London; B. T. Batsford Ltd., 1963.

Erickson, Erik H.: *Gandhi's Truth: On the Origins of Militant Nonviolence*, Norton, New York, 1970.

Farquhar, J.N.: *Modern Religious Movements in India*, Munshiram, New Delhi, 1967.

Fay, Peter Ward: *The Opium War, 1840-42*, University of North Carolina Press, 1975.

Fisher, Michael H.: *The Politics of British Annexation of India - 1757-1857*, Oxford, 1996.

Frauwallner, E..: *History of Indian Philosophy*, Motilal, Delhi, 1973.

Gambhirananda, S.: *Brahma Sutra Shamkar Bhasya*, Adavita Ashrama, Calcutta, 1977.

Gambhirananda, Swami: *Brahma Sutra Shamkar Bhasya*, Adavita Ashrama, Calcutta, 1977.

Gandhi, M. K.: *The Story of My Experiment With Trust*, Washington, Public Affairs Press, 1948.

Garbe, R.: *The Philosophy of Ancient India*, Chicago University Press, Chicago, 1899.

Goradia, Nayana: *Lord Curzon: The Last of the British Moghuls*, New Delhi, Oxford University Press, 1993.

Goudriaan, T.: *Ritual and Speculation in Early Tantrism*, State University of New York Press, New York, 1992.

Gough, A.E.: *The Philosophy of the Upanisads and Ancient Indian Metaphysics*, MacMillan, London, 1882.

Grant, G. P.: *Philosophy in the Mass Age*, Copp Clark, Toronto, 1959.

Grisenold, H.D.: *Insights into Modern Hinduism*, Oxford, New York, 1934.

Growse, F. S.: *The Ramayana of Tulasidasa*, Motilal Banarsidass, Delhi, 1995.

Gurumurthy, S. : *Hindu Heritage, Assimilative, Not Divisive*, Vigil, Madras 1993.

Haich, E.: *Sexual Energy and Yoga*, Aurora Press, New York, 1982.

Hasan, Murhirul: *Legacy of a Divided Nation: India's Muslims Since Independence*, New Delhi, Oxford, 1997.

Hasan, Mushirul: *India's Partition: Process, Strategy and Mobilization*, New Delhi, Oxford UP, 1993.

Heifetz, Hank: *The Origin of the Young God: Kalidasa's Kumara-sambhava*, University of California Press, Berkeley, 1985.

Heimann, Betty: *Facets of Indian Thought*, Geroge Allen & Unwin, London, 1964.

Heinsath, Charles: *Indian Nationalism and Hindu Social Reform*, Princeton University Press, Princeton, 1964.

Heschel, J.: *God in Search of Man: A Philosophy of Judaism*, Noonday Press, New York, 1997.

Hirschman, Edwin: *White Mutiny: The Ilbert Bill Crisis in India and the Genesis of the Indian National Congress*, New Delhi, Heritage, 1980.

Hixon, L.: *Mother of the Universe: Visions of the Goddess, Tantric Hymns of Enlightenment*, Quest Books, Wheaton, 1994.

Hopkins, J.: *Kalachakra Tantra Rite of Initiation*, Wisdom Publications, Boston, 1982.

Hopkirk, Peter: *The Great Game: The Struggle for Empire in Central Asia*, Kodansha, 1992.

Hume, R.E.: *The Thirteen Principle Upanishads*, Oxford University Press, London, 1971.

Hutchins, Francis: *Spontaneous Revolution: The Quit India Movement*, New Delhi, Manohar, 1971.

Irene, S.: *Vedic Heritage Teaching Program*. Arsha Vidya Gurukulam, Coimbatore, 1994.

Iyar, K.: *Vedanta: The Science of Reality*, Ganesh and Co., Mardas, 1930.

Iyengar, B.K.S.: *Light on the Yoga Sutras of Patanjali*, Aquarian Press, London 1993.

Jacob, K.: *Religion and Ethics in Advaita*, C.M.S. Press, Kottayam, 1982.

Jafar, Malik Muhammad: *Jinnah as a Parliamentarian*, Lahore, Afzar Publications, 1977.

Jain, Kailash Chand, *Lord Mahavira and His Times*, Saraswati Press, Delhi, 1974.

James, Lawrence: *The Rise and Fall of the British Empire*, St. Martin's, 1997.

James, Robert Rhodes: *The British Revolution, 1880-1939*, New York, Knopf, 1976.

Jean, M.: *Tantrik Yoga*, The Aquarian Press, Wellingborough, 1970.

John, B.: *Mantras: Sacred Words of Power*, George Allen and Unwin, London, 1977.

John, Elsner: *Pilgrimage: Past and Present in the World Religions*, Harvard University Press, Cambridge, 1995.

John, K.: *The Origin and Development of the State Cult of Confucius*, Paragon Book, New York, 1966.

Karmarkar, D.: *Sankara's Advaita*, Karnatak University, Dharwar, 1976.

Kaushik, Asha : *Globalization, Democracy and Culture : Situating Gandhian Alternatives*, Jaipur, Pointer, 2002.

Kaviraj, G.: *Aspects of Indian Thought*, University of Burdwan, Calcutta, 1966.

Kavlekar, K.K. : *Non-Brahmin Movement in Southern India, 1873-1949*, Kolhapur, Shivaji University, 19790

Keith, A.B. : *Rigveda Brahmanas*, Harvard University Press, Cambridge, 1920.

Keith, Arthur Berriedale: *The Religion and Philosophy of the Veda and Upanishads*, MacMillan, Delhi, 1925.

Kishwar, Madhu : *Religion at the Service of Nationalism, and Other Essays*, OUP, Delhi, 1998.

Klaus, K.: *A Survey of Hinduism*, State University of New York Press, Albany, 1989.

Knipe, M.: *Hinduism: Experiments in the Sacred*, Harper, San Francisco, 1991.

Knott, K.: *Hinduism, A Very Short Introduction*, Oxford University Press, New York, 1998.

Kosambi, D. D. : *The Culture and Civilisation of Ancient India in Historical Outline*, London, Routledge and Kegan Paul, 1956.

Kottackal, Jacob: *Religion and Ethics in Advaita*, C.M.S. Press, Kottayam, 1982.

Kuiper, F.B.J. : *Aryans in the Rigveda*, Rodopi, Amsterdam, 1991.

Kuppuswamy, Sastri S.: *Compromises in the History of Advaitic Thought*, Kalyani Press, Madras, 1940.

Louis, Fischer: *Essential Gandhi: An Anthology of His Writings*, Vintage, New York, 1983.

Low, D. A. and Brasted, Howard: *Freedom, Trauma, Continuities: Northern India and Independence*, New Delhi, Sage Publications, 1998.

Maheshwari, Shriram: *Rural Development in India: A Public Policy Approach*, New Delhi, Sage, 1995.

Makhan, L.: *The Ramayana of Valmiki*, Munshiram Manoharlal, New Delhi, 1978.

Mathew, Arnold: *Culture and Anarchy*, The University Press, Cambridge, 1935.

Mayer, A. : *Caste in an Indian Village: Change and Continuity 1954-1992*, Delhi, OUP, 1996.

Mazumder, Sukhendu : *Politico-Economic Ideas of Mahatma Gandhi: Their Relevance in the Present Day*, New Delhi, Concept Pub., 2004.

Mearns, David J.: *Shiva's Other Children: Religion and Social Identity amongst Overseas Indians*, Sage, Walnut Creek, 1995.

Mearns, J.: *Shiva's Other Children: Religion and Social Identity amongst Overseas Indians*, Sage, Walnut Creek, 1995.

Mehra, Parshotam: *A Dictionary of Modern Indian History, 1707-1947*, New Delhi, Oxford University Press, 1985.

Metcalf, Thomas R.: *The Aftermath of the Revolt: India, 1857-1870*, Princeton, Princeton University, 1964.

Mohan, K.: *The Mahabharata*, Munshiram Manoharlal, Delhi 1997.

Mookerjee, Ajit: *Kali The Feminine Force*, Thames and Hudson, London, 1988.

Mookerji, Satkari: *Modern Polity and Vedanta*, Sanskrit College, Calcutta, 1972.

Moon, Penderel: *The British Conquest and Dominion of India*, London, Duckworth, 1989.

Morris-Jones, W.H.: *The Government and Politics of India*, London, Hutchinson, 1971.

Nanda, B. R. : *Gandhi and His Critics*, Oxford University Press, Delhi, 1993.

Neale, Walter C.: *Economic Change in Rural India: Land Tenure and Reform in the United Provinces, 1800-1955*, New Haven, 1962.

Nevile, P.: *Lahore: A Sentimental Journey*, New Delhi, Penguin, 1993.

Oddie, G.A. : *Hindu and Christian in South-East India*, London, Curzon Press, 1991.

Pathak, Dr S.P.: *Jhansi during the British Rule*, Ramanand Vidya Bhawan, Delhi, 1987.

Preston, Diana: *The Boxer Rebellion*, Berkley Books, 2000.

Raimundo Panikkar: *The Vedic Experience: Mantramanjari*, Longman Todd, London, 1977.

Raja, C. Kunhan : *The Taittiriya Sarvanukramani of Yaska*, Madras, 1931.

Ramamurti, A.: *Advaitic Mysticism of Sankara*, Visvabharati, Santiniketan, 1974.

Ranajit Guha: *A Construction of Humanism in Colonial India*, CASA, Amsterdam, 1993.

Renou, Louis: *The Nature of Dharmashastra*, Walker and Co., New York, 1997.

Robson, Brian: *Sir Hugh Rose and the Central India Campaign*, Sutton Publishing Ltd for the Army Records Society, UK, 2000.

Satyapal Verma: *Role of Reason in Sankara Vedanta*, Parimal Publication, Delhi, 1992.

Savarkar, Vinayak Damodar : *The Indian War of Independence* 1857 Rajdhani Granthagar, Delhi, 1988.

Scheftelowitz, Isidor : *Die Kasmirische Rezension von Katyayanas Sarvanukramani,* Zeitschrift fur Indologie und Iranistik, 1922.

Shukla, D. N.: *Vastu-Shastra,* Motilal Banarsidass, Delhi, 1966.

Singh, Birendra Kumar: *Early Chalukyas of Vatapi, circa A.D. 500 to 757*, Delhi, Eastern Book Linkers, 1991.

Smith, Col. J. T. : *Silver and the India Exchanges,* Effingham Wilson, London, 1876.

Strauss, L.: *Political Philosophy,* The Bobbs Merrill Co., New York, 1975.

Swami Vishnu Tirtha: *Devatma Shakti,* Swami Shivom Tirth, Rishikesh, 1962.

Talageri, Shrikant : *Aryan Invasion Theory and Indian Nationalism,* Voice of India, Delhi, 1993.

Tejomayananda, Swami: *Hindu Culture: An Introduction,* Chinmaya Publications, Piercy, 1993.

Thapar, Romila : *Ashoka and the Decline of the Mauryas,* London, Oxford University Press, 1961.

Thompson, Edward: *The Making of the Indian Princes,* Oxford University Press, London, 1943.

Trautmann, Thomas R.: *Kautilya and the Arthasastra: A Statistical Study,* Leiden, Brill, 1971.

Trimingham, J.: *Sufi Orders in Islam,* Oxford University Press, New York, 1998.

Utpat, V.N.: *Riddles of Buddha and Ambedkar,* Itihas Patrika Prakashan, Thane 1988.

Vable, D.: *The Arya Samaj. Hindu without Hinduism.* Vikas Publ., Delhi, 1983.

Vedalankar, Pandit Nardev : *Basic Teachings of Hinduism,* Veda Niketan, Durban, 1978.

Visvantha, K.: *Essentials of Hinduism,* Narosa Pub. House, New Delhi, 1989.

Wendy Doniger: *Siva: The Erotic Ascetic,* Oxford University Press, Delhi, 1998.

Zaidi, A. Moin: *Evolution of Muslim political Thought in India,* New Delhi: S. Chand, 1975.

Index

L

M

N

O

P

R

S

□□□